VARIATIONS

The Architecture Photographs of Jenny Okun

VARIATIONS
The Architecture Photographs of Jenny Okun

preface by **THOM MAYNE**

with essays by **HENRY T. HOPKINS** and **MICHAEL WEBB**

fiveTIES

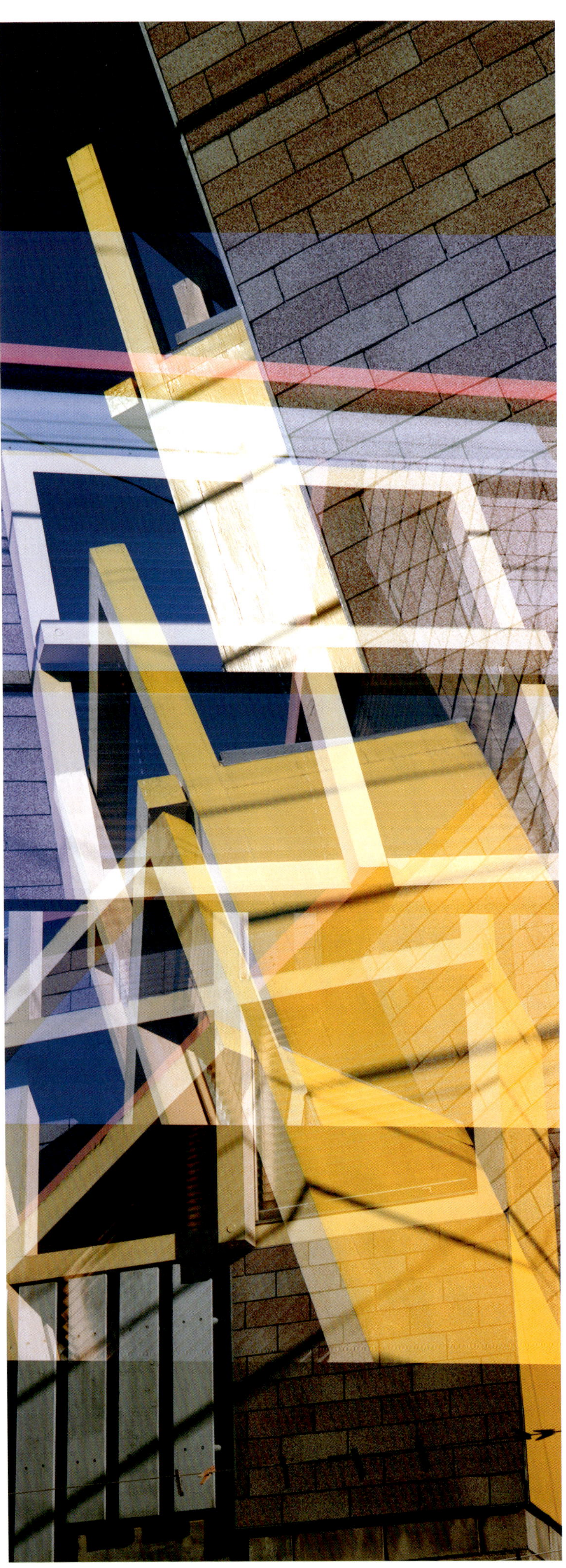

SOME YEARS AGO Jenny Okun showed me her photograph of Morphosis's 2-4-6-8 House that contained within it elements revealing a clear kinship with our conceptual interests. At the level of a working methodology, there was a parallel interest in the overlaying or obfuscation of the differences between plan, section, and elevation that sought to reveal the essence of the project through simultaneous exposure of normally discrete perspectives. Okun's work seeks to illuminate the essential, dynamic, and visceral qualities of the architecture, and in so doing she challenges the conventions of photographic representation.

Okun uses photography as her tool to simultaneously deconstruct and reconstruct the original, layering the fragments, as in Cubist painting, to create a new compositional whole. In discussing the influence of Cubism on early modernist architecture, theorist Robin Evans explores this dual reading by explaining that "when the totality of the simultaneously presented image is emphasized, Cubism appears to strive for wholeness; yet when the inherent dislocation of parts is emphasized, Cubism reveals fragmentation."

The images Okun creates bring to mind another body of photographs influenced by Cubist ideas. As in David Hockney's Polaroid collages, her fragmented photos seek to bring the viewer closer to the physiological act of seeing—to create an experience akin to the phenomenon of sight itself. The human eye is incessantly darting, focusing and immediately re-focusing as it changes its perspectival position. As in Hockney's work, there is a layering, not only of fragments, but also of time. One is made aware of the distance between segments as registered through shadow and through shifts in the camera's perspective. Comprehension of architecture requires scanning while moving in order to absorb multiple perspectives over time that will crystallize into a cohesive mental map of the space. In stark contrast to the representation of architecture provided by normative photographic techniques, Okun's work captures the space that can normally be understood only through movement. Hers is a multivalent, contemporary conception of space, one that challenges the timelessness rooted in the nineteenth-century notion of reality such as that of an Ansel Adams. Casting aside the singular perspectival composition, which would require multiple photographs to allow for an understanding of space, Okun chooses instead to use movement and complex layerings to develop the narrative within a single image.

As an architect uses bricks and mortar, Okun uses the finished architecture as her raw material. The resulting images are *her* artistic work yet they retain the fundamental DNA of the architect's project, brilliantly elucidating the character and essence of the three-dimensional work via carefully orchestrated perceptual fragments. Her process is recursive, using nested applications of parallel idea structures in photography and in architecture—whereby one medium builds up a new coherency in another—while it clearly navigates a territory completely separate and wholly its own.

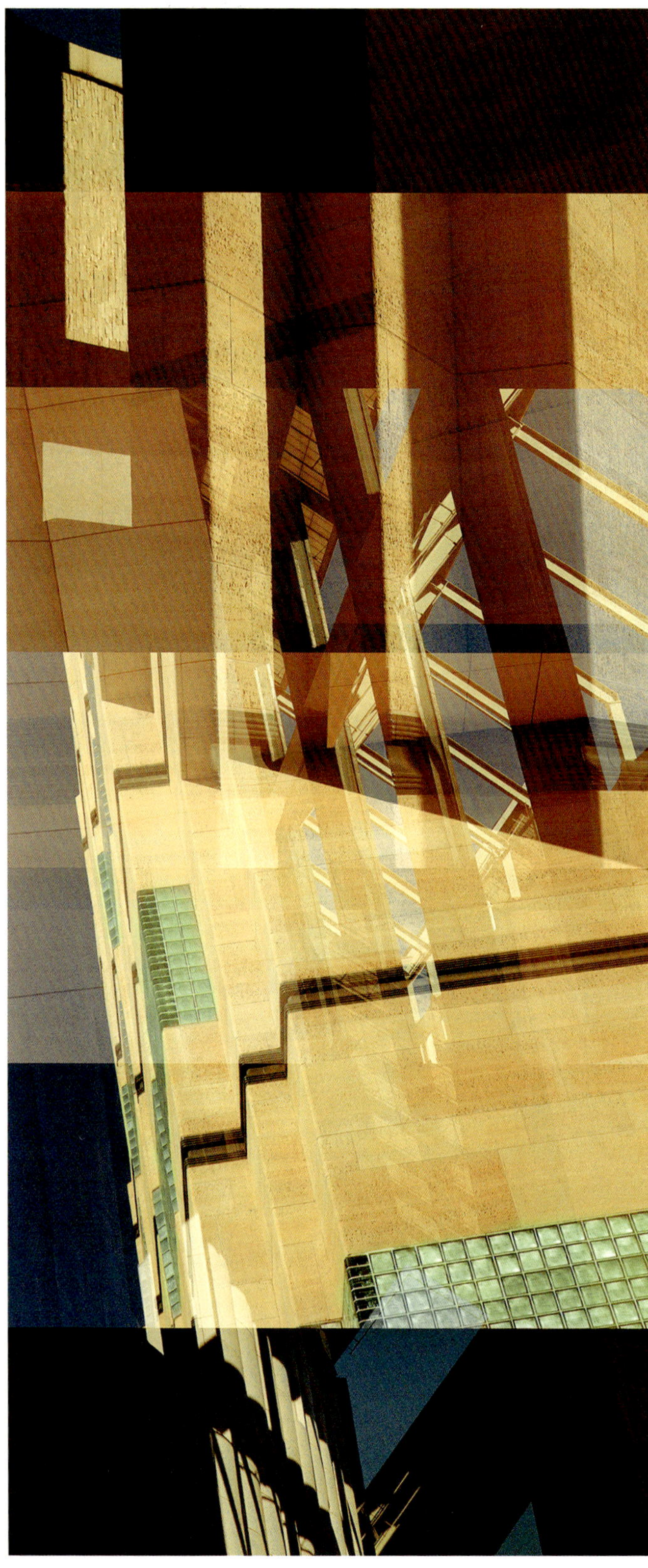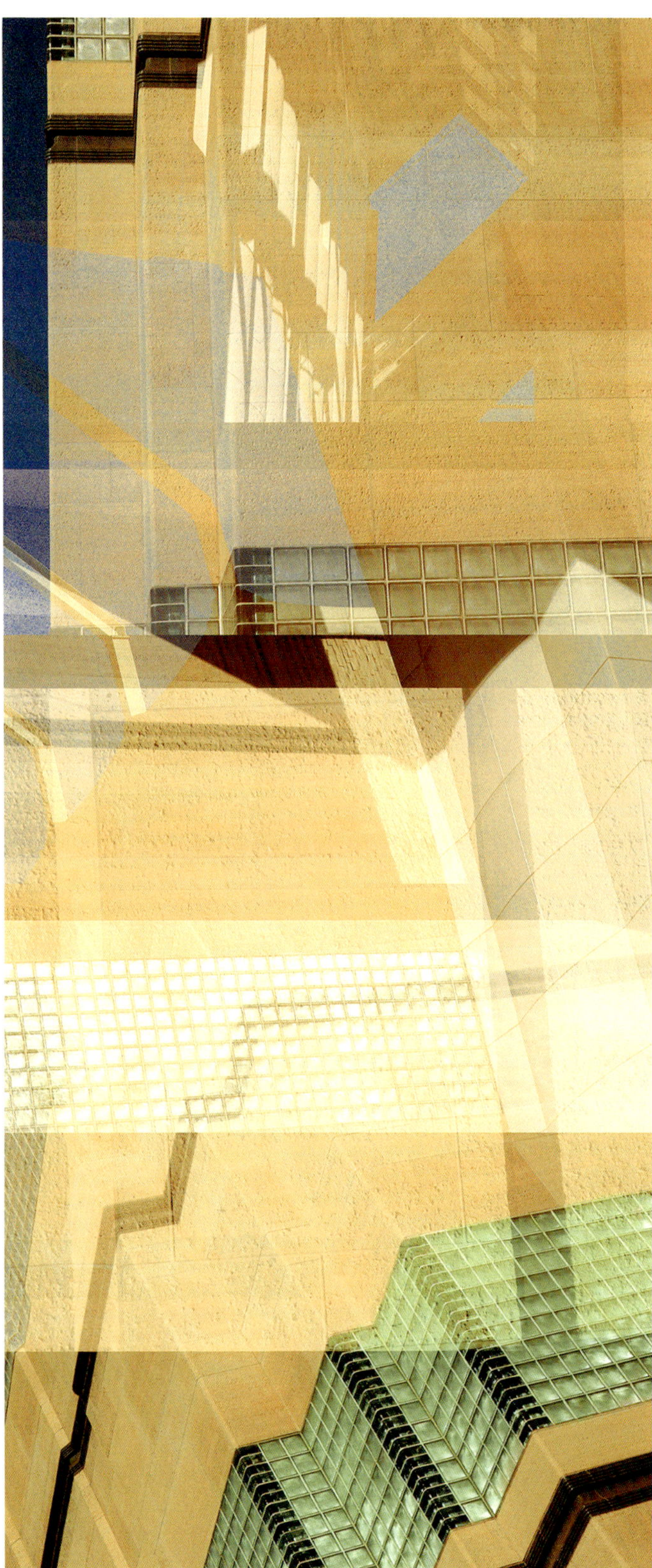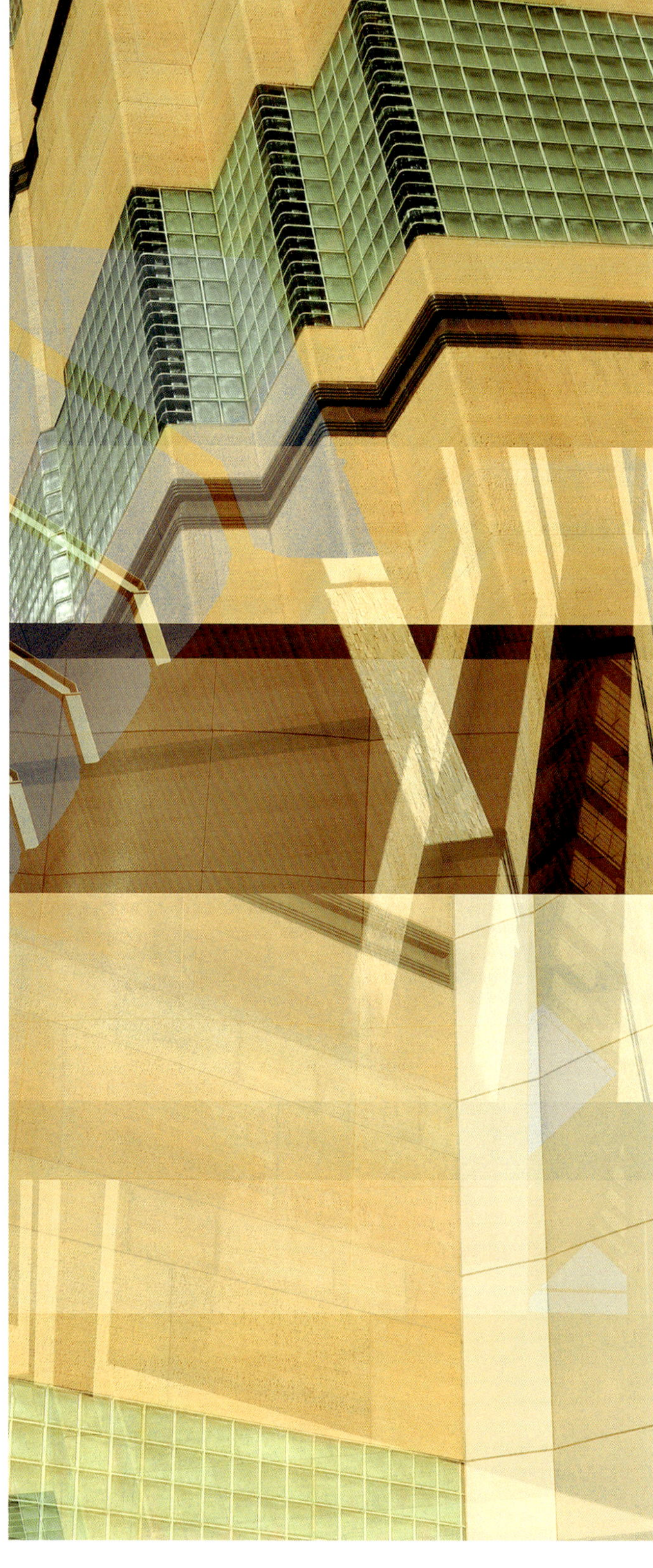

Los Angeles County Museum Triptych   Los Angeles, California, 1988   ARCHITECT: Hardy Holzman Pfeiffer

IN EVERY SUCCESSFUL LIFE there is a defining moment when all of the time spent in intensive labor, love, and creative input hits a high note. For Jenny Okun it was a moment during a recent reception in Italy when one of the guests, after looking at her portfolio, asked if he could borrow an image, which he then took over to the piano and used as a musical score. It was a John Cage moment that combined every aspect of the creative process—an epiphany, a certification, and a moment of pure joy.

Jenny Okun was born on October 3, 1953, in New Jersey, which hardly counts, since within a year she was taken to Greenwich Village, and then ten years later to a suburb of Manhattan. She is the progeny of a music-producer father and an artist-writer mother who early on instilled a love of art and music into their daughter through endless museum visits and concert attendances.

Okun considers her early public school education to be marginal, undoubtedly impacted by the fact that she was found to be dyslexic, a not uncommon malady for many who are drawn to the visual arts. She suffered through extensive "memory" training, which helped her manage her dyslexia and left her with a deep respect for rigorous mental exercise that she feels has had an ongoing influence on her work. During her high school years she became adept at landscape mural painting, and earned enough money to buy her first camera by decorating the walls of friends' houses and painting stage scenery for local theater groups. The camera was a 35mm Konica.

In 1971, at the age of eighteen, the time came to further her education in the arts. She chose to go to British schools that didn't impose academic courses as a degree requirement and where she could spend as much time as possible in the studio. She began at the Wimbledon School of Art, where she studied painting, photography, and filmmaking. She then transferred to the Chelsea School of Art, where she received her degree in painting, and finished in 1978 at the Slade School of Art as a postgraduate student in experimental media.

Okun's achievement was recognized through offers of teaching jobs in painting, photography, and filmmaking at the Central School of Art and Design and, later, at the Chelsea School of Art. During this same period she was co-director of the London Film-makers' Co-operative and co-selected entries for "Film London," an international avant-garde festival. In reflection she has stated, "For many years I have had one foot in America and one foot in England with studios in both countries. I have the 'get up and go, let's try anything' attitude of an American and the 'let's sit back and analyze every detail before we start' attitude of the British."

From the outset Okun's use of the camera has been experimental. She began by making sequential images by shooting the entire film and then rolling the film back to the start and superimposing a second set of shots on top. The results were not satisfactory, and she now refers to the process as being too "hit and miss." To gain more control over her medium she next experimented with projecting images onto the wall. By using multiple projectors she was able to superimpose one image over another until she achieved the desired "collage" effect. The results were not permanent so she used a Lindhoff plate camera to record the transient projected image onto film. The results were satisfactory but the process was cumbersome. This method did lead however to some early commissions from companies needing visuals for annual reports and helped to supplement her teaching income. The company would send her multiple transparencies, which she then projected and superimposed to create desirable commercial results.

Okun liked the square format of the projected images, so her next camera purchase was a two-and-a-quarter-inch square format Yashica that she found at a London police auction. This new format worked well, and she has used it ever since. In her own words,

"This format allowed me to make successful sequences by exposing the film as I advanced it through the camera in small increments, producing what appeared to be overlapping superimposed images that had enough control and enough experimental surprise. This method also led to another surprise when, in London, I took my film to a local chemist for processing. The film was then sent off to Kodak where it would be returned with a pleasant note saying that there must be something wrong with my camera. In my return package they also included a free role of film. I survived on these replacement rolls throughout my early career until I started using a professional lab."

Okun's early photographic interests were related to landscape and to a stunning, panoramic vista looking from the shores of England across the Irish Sea. This early image embodies all of the elements mentioned above, and still hangs on Okun's studio wall. Soon, however, the fates stepped in, and a new latent passion that is the subject of this book grabbed her attention. The first signs of this passion are revealed in a statement about her work: "As a teenager I spent one summer in a rented house opposite the building site for Charles Gwathmey's studio that he created for his father in Amagansett. My cousin, Richard Bender, who was also an architect and a friend of Gwathmey's, took me around the building. It was the beginning of my love for the shapes and ideas in architecture. I was particularly entranced by a long, thin window near the ceiling that was placed there for watching the moon at night. I also loved the conical staircase and the brilliant yellow I-beams that supported the structure. Years later I returned to photograph the studio, and it still had the quality of a perfect piece of architectural jewelry.

"Another turning point in my evolution occurred when I was commissioned by Peter Palumbo in London to photograph his Mies van der Rohe Farnsworth House in Illinois. The house was more than anyone could describe. I photographed the structure, and then went on to the Aspen Design Conference where I met and listened to the architects Piers Gough, James Stirling, and Norman Foster. After that I was hooked, and I set out on my lifelong ambition to photograph great architecture."

Since that time Okun has photographed the life force of hundreds of buildings and sites, most of them twentieth century in origin and classic. But scattered among the prints are those of older cathedrals and lesser structures that have also captured her imagination. She thinks of herself as a daylight photographer primarily so she can play with the atmospheric conditions that affect the building. And yet this body of work does include some night shots that deal more with the environment than with any specific structure.

When we look at or pass through architecture, most of us see it as a series of spaces created to function well and to enhance the lives of the people who use it. And, when most people think of architectural photography, they think of images that make these attributes visible. If this is true, then Jenny Okun is not an architectural photographer. She is an artist who uses the camera as a compositional and scanning device to capture the poetic essence of a structure without regard for its function. Her interest is not in the architecture itself but rather in the innovative and formal elements from which it is composed. It is this quality that makes her images unique and memorable. Instead of looking at the whole, Okun becomes absorbed in the details: the planes, the angles, the transparencies that serve the building as overhanging eaves, windows, or entryways. The process of invention is to interpret how these elements interact to create a multifaceted organism.

Certainly her early encounter with Cubism at the Museum of Modern Art holds a key. It is not surprising that her favorite artists are not Pablo Picasso or George Braque but rather Juan Gris, the most intellectual of the group, and Fernand Léger, the most

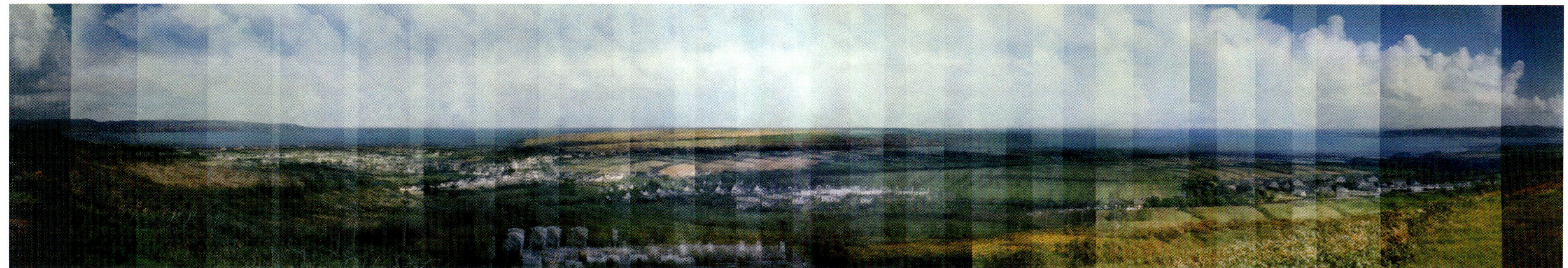

architectonic. On a recent visit to Okun's studio I was confronted with a monumental image of Frank Gehry's Walt Disney Concert Hall, in Los Angeles, with its glorious synthesis of cool blues and grays. I couldn't help but think of Charles Sheeler, the great American "Precisionist" who used the camera as a prop to create double-exposure images that he then turned into paintings of the American industrial landscape.

It should be remembered that Sheeler was painting his Cubist masterpieces during the Great Depression when most American art was dealing with issues of social unrest, as in the cases of Ben Shahn and Jack Levine; or with the glorification of the nation's rural lifescape, as in the cases of the "Regionalists" Grant Wood and Thomas Hart Benton. In his own mind Sheeler was a positivist who believed in picturing the advance of industry as an aid to soothing a limping economy. In this context, Okun is a Sheeler clone, which a recent quote makes clear: "This aspect of my work is an homage to the enjoyment of ideas embodied in the work of those lucky architects who were able to realize their dreams in concrete, glass, and steel. When I go to a construction site I feel that everything is well with the world. I am elated that someone has been able to move from theory to practice to produce something grand. This gives me great hope for the human race. For me, architecture is a celebration of life, and I am appalled when a building is destroyed by a developer or by a force of nature. This is the only time that I become depressed."

Even her process of collecting data within her camera is reflective of the inner workings of a Cubist painter. "As I work, I move the camera, photographing details, using the edges of the frame as a counterpoint to the subject as well as keeping an overall rhythm to the angles. Also, depending on the sequence, I sometimes have to shoot in reverse with my last shot coming first to make the exposures in the right sequence to read from left to right. Sometimes I draw the sequence in a sketchbook, since it is very difficult to keep them all in my head. Had it not been for my early memory training to correct my dyslexia I probably couldn't do it at all.

"I never use a tripod unless I have to, and I usually hold my camera sideways with my left arm extended. More recently, when I began using a Hasselblad, people would become distressed while watching what I was doing and interrupt my shoot to explain the proper use of the camera. I must look like a lunatic shooting one shot and then advancing the film slightly and then opening the back of the camera to cock the shutter and then replacing the back and repeating the whole process again. I guess you could say that I have an 'Alice in Wonderland' upside-down and backward experience looking through my viewfinder. Many times I will have to reshoot, visiting a site as many as a dozen times. After analyzing the first attempts in my studio I then draw new sequences to try on location, and if they work I am ready to print.

"Now, in my Los Angeles studio, I am working with a Canon digital camera, and I do not need to revisit a location unless I want a different light situation. I am printing my editions digitally with pigmented inks on an Epson 9600. For this I owe a great debt of gratitude to R. Mac Holbert of Nash Editions, who convinced me to stop printing photographically and to start using an Iris Printer on Arches paper. My photographs came alive, and it was as if I had cataracts removed from my eyes. New colors materialized and details became hyper-real. It took me a while to learn to tone down the color and get the correct appearance of grain, but under Holbert's tutelage I became a master printer."

In the early days of photography, after the development of the glass negative and light-sensitive paper, the great breakthrough was that one could produce an endless number of prints of the same image. This had never been possible before. Even the surface of the printmaker's plate or stone eventually wore out. Photography was to become the medium for every day and every man. Now, when merchandizing and the concern of collectors has so much to do with the art world, the issue of editioning has become a factor that has to be taken into account.

As an idealist, Okun would like it if she could hand out prints to anyone who asked, the more the merrier. With her the issue is not about wealth but about maintenance and getting the work out there. Keeping two large studios and the equipment to run them is an increasingly costly venture. She is pleasantly self-effacing but this is not to say that she lacks ambition and ego, which remain absolutely necessary ingredients for any successful practitioner of the arts.

When she began exhibiting her work in 1978, Okun declared an edition to be one hundred identical prints but, unlike a lithographer or etcher, the images were produced only on an as-needed basis. This means that in much of the early work only three or four images of the one hundred have actually been printed. More recently she has reduced her editions to ten. Since her photography has commercial appeal along with artistic merit she is sometimes approached for particular commissions. To insure the integrity of her creative input she produces a series of acceptable prints that she then submits to her clients. From these they may choose without exerting any influence on the image. A case in point is the popular poster she produced for the J. Paul Getty Museum.

The list of galleries that represent Okun's work in the United States and Europe is impressive, and most are not photography galleries as such. It is her feeling that her work is too painterly and too experimental for most collectors of photography, and she feels more at home in galleries that have a broader vision. To say that Okun is in real life much like her work is an absolute. During a three-hour interview I realized that I was dealing with a person who from the day she was old enough to hold a thought has simply piled one on top of another so that today, in her mid-fifties, she embodies every moment of her existence. Perhaps, this too can be traced to her early memory training. The experience is truly Proustian. . . .

Okun talks the way that she sees through her camera's lens: in composites and overlaps, where time disappears. One loses track of when something happened in the past since her memory speaks of it as if it is happening right now. It is really quite remarkable when one recognizes that in this kind of mind nothing is ever old and everything is still in play. To say that she lives and works in the moment is an understatement. Her spacious Los Angeles studio is filled with work. The walls, the tables, and the floor are neatly hung, stacked, and piled with images framed and unframed. Her preferred size is monumental and her preferred compositional layout takes the form of a triptych. When I asked her about this she replied that the large-scale and triptych format was "more painterly and looked less like a photograph." I was also struck by the thought that when installed on the wall they became like windows opening up the space. With its controlled light, the studio is a pleasant and professional working environment. Okun is a prolific producer. The images at hand cover an extended period of time and yet one feels a sense of timelessness. This is particularly true since what may have been a twenty-year-old photographic image is now a brand-new inkjet print.

Among the many photographic images are a large number of handsome charcoal drawings for which the photographs serve as inspiration. The drawings are done in serial fashion and represent the primary forms included in a given photograph. As the series evolves the forms are abstracted and simplified. And, even though the drawings are abstract, the process is not unlike the one used by Henri Matisse to transpose, through a series of drawings, a naturalistic figure into a simplified decorative motif.

As a final thought I would add that even though this volume documents Jenny Okun's deep affection for the elemental creative force behind architecture, one should not be seduced into thinking that this is the only arrow in her quiver. There is much else yet to come.

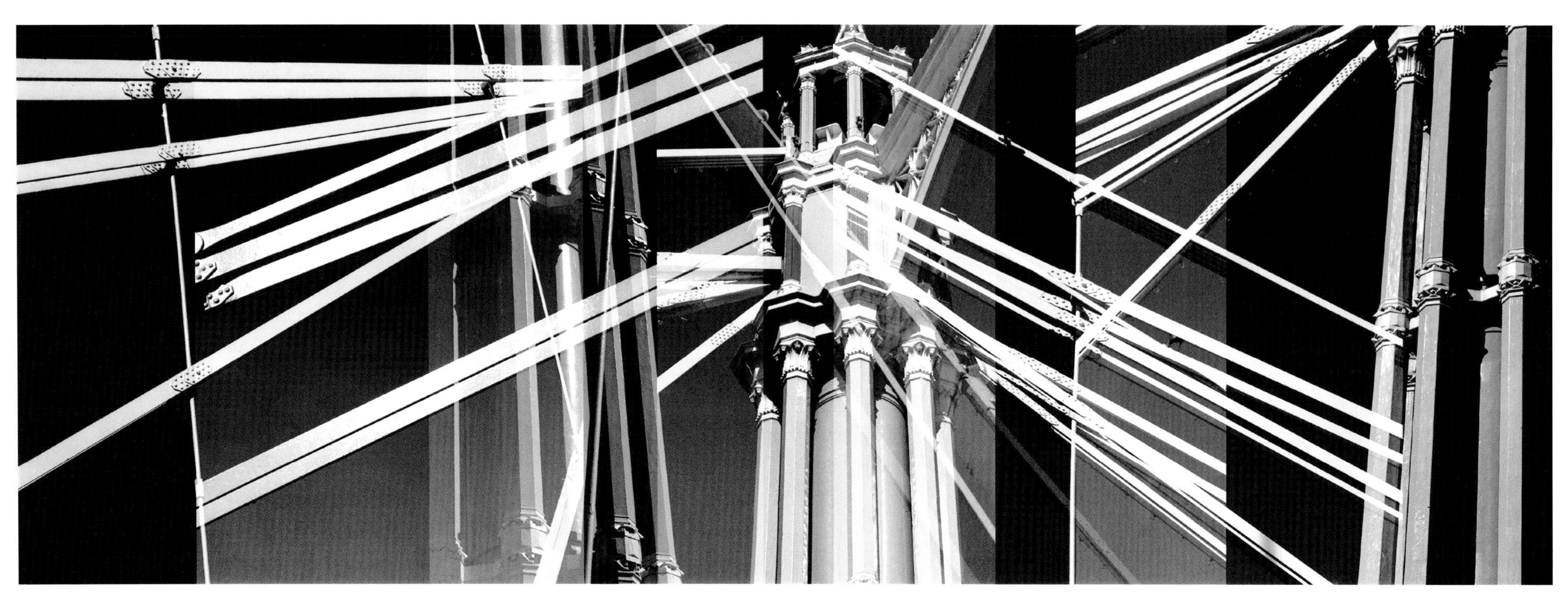

Albert Bridge   London, England, 1985   ARCHITECT: Rowland Ordish   012

I CAN'T SAY I'VE DREAMED of Jenny Okun, but I think about her every morning when I wake, for the first thing I see as I open my eyes is her composite portrait of the Albert Bridge in London hanging on my bedroom wall. In some ways, it's an odd choice. I grew up in London and have fond memories of the elegant suspension bridge that links Chelsea to Battersea across the Thames. However, I'm a committed modernist, and I could easily have chosen a seductive mosaic of a new building I admire by Frank Gehry, Richard Rogers, or Santiago Calatrava—architects who are also among Okun's favorites. Instead, I picked this nineteenth-century gem, both for the geometrical complexity of the composition and for the provocative juxtaposition of the decorative and functional.

The Victorians tolerated nudity in history paintings, but buildings, like human bodies, were covered up. In an age when engineers were pushing cast iron to daring extremes, the proprieties had to be observed. The platforms of London's St. Pancras railway station are canopied by a soaring iron vault that was once the widest in the world. This technological marvel is entirely concealed behind a craggy red-brick Gothic hotel that could have sprung from the imagination of Sir Walter Scott. The Albert Bridge, named for Queen Victoria's consort and built in 1873, clearly reveals its structure. However, unless you are an engineer, your eyes are drawn to the clustered iron columns with their foliated Corinthian capitals, without sparing much attention for the riveted straps that support the roadway. Okun gives equal weight to both and overlays them—to emphasize the contradiction of styles and the abstract beauty of the tracery.

This bridge is framed by the windows of Foster and Partners, located close by on the Battersea waterfront, and it may have inspired the Millau Viaduct that the firm recently completed in central France. Even Okun might have a hard time shooting a structure that extends more than a mile over a gorge that is a thousand feet deep and one in which the engineering admits of no artistic deception. I hope she'll try, because it is a wonder of twenty-first-century engineering, in which the beauty grows directly out of the slender, bifurcated piers and the fanned cables that gleam like celestial harps from afar.

I remember how inspired she was by another visionary project—Richard Rogers's Millennium Dome, down the Thames at Greenwich. It is less a dome than a gently curved membrane, stretched taut by cables radiating from splayed steel trusses, and it promised to be a worthy successor to the Lloyds Building and to Rogers's fledgling collaboration with Renzo Piano on the Pompidou Center in Paris. Okun and I went there together during construction, when the vast interior was still a muddy expanse that made the huge earthmovers look like toys. The project architect took us to the hub of the circle and showed us how, by some trick of perspective, the gently angled ribs around the periphery seemed suddenly to snap into a vertical position.

It was a typical London day—brief downpours alternating with brilliant flashes of sun—and we dodged inside and out, as Okun captured the play of light and shadow on the translucent canopy. Though she was unable to trap the illusion, she did master the scale and the thrilling sweep of open space, bathed in a soft glow from above. We came away walking on air, little knowing that within a year the Dome would be cluttered with tacky exhibits and dismissed as an extravagant folly.

What makes Okun's work so different from conventional architectural photography is its fragmentation, abstraction, and emphasis on a few telling details. She looks harder and longer at buildings than most architectural aficionados do and sees things that escape our attention. Her compositions often defy easy identification, having taken on an identity of their own. Sometimes a single detail is enlarged and repeated and it may not be the one others have singled out as a tool for recognition. I was living in Washington, D.C., when I. M. Pei built the East Building of the National Gallery of Art and spent many happy hours in the lofty atrium, hypnotized by the scarlet Calder mobile that revolved slowly overhead. Okun looked beyond that aerial ballet to focus on the hooks from which the mobile is suspended and on the triangular skylights with serried louvers that block direct sunlight. A single red rod punctuates the sharply angled monochromatic grid. Pei's architecture, which serves as both frame and backdrop for art, is restored to primacy.

Even today, most architectural photography is like Beaux Arts drawing, presenting buildings as idealized objects, detached from their surroundings, with formally composed interiors. The goal is to project an image—of corporate power, institutional dignity, or gracious living—that flatters the egos of the architect and client, while seducing editors and readers. Julius Shulman in Los Angeles, Hedrich Blessing in Chicago, and Ezra Stoller in New York were masters of their craft. They created iconic images that embodied the spirit of an era or a place and helped forge the reputations of Richard Neutra, Mies van der Rohe, Louis Kahn, and other great modern formgivers. Despite moments of high drama, as in Shulman's legendary image of two women in white in a living room that seems to float out over a magic carpet of lights, their priority was to document what they saw. The aesthetic was pictorial, and their static, precisely balanced compositions were achieved with elaborate lighting and tripod-mounted large-format cameras. Their successors may use lightweight digital equipment and rely on natural light, but, except for the switch from black and white to color, the conventions of architectural photography haven't changed much in fifty years.

In contrast, Okun's images are hand-held, asymmetrical, and kinetic. Over the more than twenty-five years she has been photographing buildings, she has gone from using wide-angle to telephoto lenses, notably a 150mm Hasselblad, and has recently switched from film to digital, but her mode of operation hasn't changed significantly. She deconstructs and then reconstructs buildings, animating them in cinematic sequences. "It starts intuitively, looking for pieces that go together," she explains. "I construct the final picture in my head, setting up overlapping images and establishing a rhythm from one shot to the next. I try to discover the essence of the building and make the eye travel around it in the right sequence. The goal is to capture the excitement I felt when I was there."

There is a feeling of restless energy that provides a fresh take on familiar landmarks and makes you want to venture out in search of new work. The images of Christian de Portzamparc's Cité de la Musique in Paris suggest frames from an animated film; it's as though you are hearing music as you look. The Alcoa Building in Pittsburgh resembles a tribal necklace made of high-tech elements. Okun sees Calatrava's Lyon-Satolas TGV train station at the Lyon airport in France as a giant butterfly that has just landed and not yet folded its wings.

Everyone—and ambitious architects in particular—wants to know how Okun chooses her subjects. "I've usually seen the latest work in a magazine and I look for buildings that have great shadows that create sculptural effects," she says. "If they have color, I'm there. Simple buildings with character are best; there are almost too many choices with a Gehry or Rogers design." Antoine Predock's United Blood Services Building in Albuquerque scored on two counts: It's a plain block painted a searing red. And it inspired Okun to interrupt a family expedition to Santa Fe for a few hours, while she bathed in red and discovered unexpected angles.

In the twenty years that she has lived in Beverly Hills, Okun has chronicled the work of L.A.'s most adventurous architects. Frank Gehry has provided her with a steady stream of inspiration, and she has created some of the defining images of two of his masterworks. She was especially successful in capturing the soft, cushiony character of the titanium scales that clad the Bilbao Guggenheim like a shimmering cloak, in contrast to the sleek, sharp, etched-steel sails that wrap the Walt Disney Concert Hall. The dizzying ascent of Morphosis is traced from the tiny 2-4-6-8 House in Venice to the bristling fortress of the Caltrans headquarters downtown.

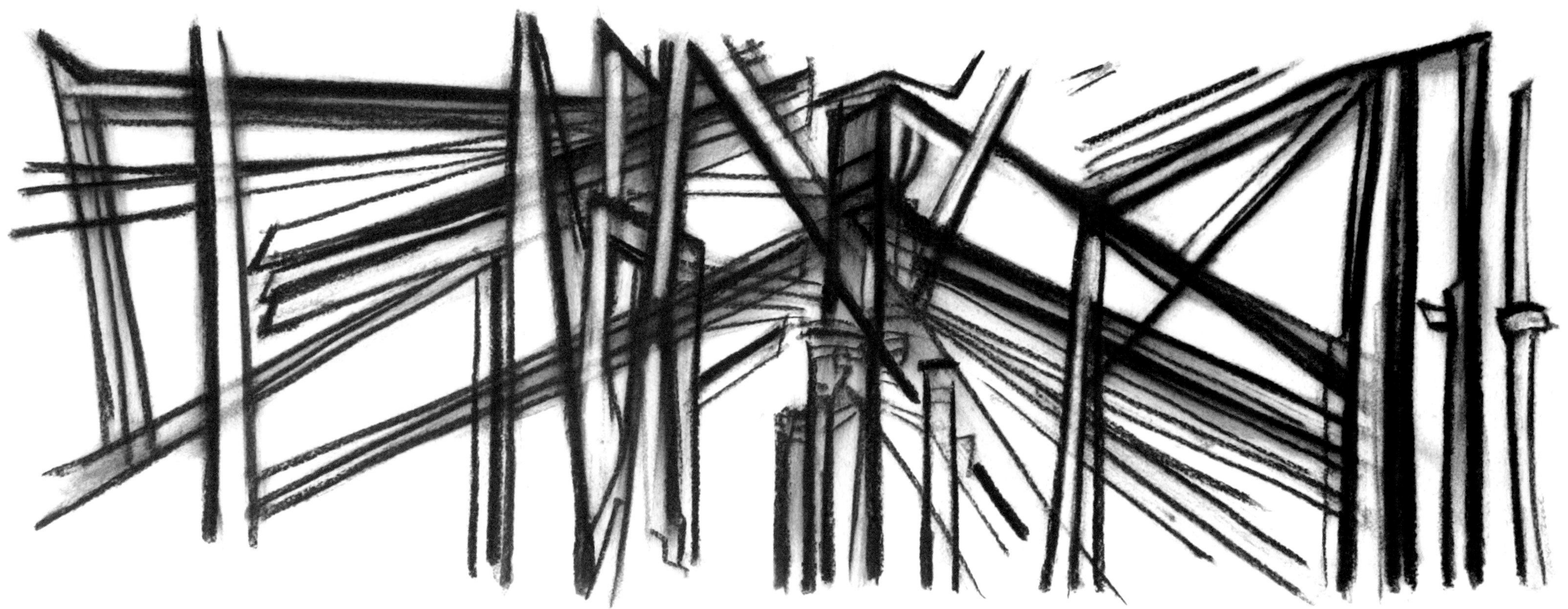

Even mundane buildings can yield beautiful images through the process of transmutation. Architects in London were incensed that Okun chose a spec office building as a subject and exhibited images of it in their hallowed galleries, but she insisted it was beautiful in the way it reflected the clouds. Another daring choice was the public lavatory in west London, designed by maverick architect Piers Gough as a local landmark in green tile with a signature clock, which becomes a magical labyrinth in Okun's photograph.

For all the madcap improvisation of Okun's life and the spontaneity of her work, the images are meticulously finished. Foliage and people have no place in her compositions. She carefully painted out the pigeons that alight on the coiled parapet of the Guggenheim Museum in New York—a laborious task in the years before Photoshop. But she chose to leave in the penguins waddling up the intertwined ramps of Berthold Lubetkin's Penguin Pool at the London Zoo, as a gesture of thanks to Peter Palumbo, who paid for the restoration of this modernist masterpiece.

"With traditional buildings you spend a lot of time trying to look past the details," Okun explains. "Some buildings, like Gaudí's Sagrada Familia in Barcelona, are too rich and don't work for me. With Florence Cathedral, I eliminated color to make the building appear stark and gritty." Often, she uses color in an expressive way, turning the white cube of the Robert Graham–designed Doumani house on Venice beach in Los Angeles into a jagged tracery in tones of blue. Strategies of this kind compel the viewer to re-examine the buildings she's transformed and give them renewed appreciation.

Over the years, Okun has built up a roster of close and creative friends, and they provide her with a constant stream of suggestions. She returned several times to the tough, raw house that Aviva Carmy, an Israeli-born architect who apprenticed to Morphosis, built for herself above Beverly Hills and rented out for movie shoots. And she drove into the desert beyond Los Angeles to find Josh Schweitzer's The

Monument—a playfully inflated name for a vacation house comprised of three colored stucco cubes perched among the rocks near Joshua Tree National Monument. Sometimes, she discovers wonderful subjects by chance, such as a factory turned house in Lecce, a baroque town in the southern tip of Italy that was hosting an exhibition of her work.

Some jobs come as commissions. The J. Paul Getty Museum wanted a poster, and Okun created a bestseller. The Tate Modern in London requested an image they could use on a variety of merchandise, from folding umbrellas to T-shirts. An Indianapolis law firm commissioned images of all their clients' buildings. Six months pregnant and eager to get to London for the birth, Okun gave herself six days to shoot eighteen buildings and was able to net fifteen in a frantic dash around the city.

Still more breathless was a last-minute request over lunch for an image of the Whitney Museum of American Art in New York, to be used as the cover of a catalogue that was about to go to press. She was still recovering from a four-year ordeal with trigeminal neuralgia, which affected her jaw and made it painful to speak. She scribbled a note of acceptance, and raced downtown to retrieve her camera and buy film in order to take the shots before her plane left for London that evening. Arriving at the museum, she discovered that the only place from which she could get a tight shot of the signature window of Marcel Breuer's building was from the center of traffic-thronged Madison Avenue. That required a kind of Russian roulette—dashing into the street whenever the light turned red, focusing, shooting, and dashing back when the light turned green to a chorus of horns and curses. She had the film processed in a couple of hours, bought a new Apple laptop to manipulate the imagery, and flew to London, where she spent twenty hours straight to finish the job and Fed Ex the composite to New York.

There's a streak of madness in every good artist, but these adventures are atypical. "There are way too many buildings to choose from and it takes a long time to finish, so I only complete fifteen works in a year," Okun says. "I do it by city when I travel, shooting a lot more buildings than I end up using. I prefer making repeated visits and taking a long time to explore buildings in order to find their power and presence. With some buildings, the impact is very emotional. I work with lines and shadows to recreate the feeling I had when I first saw them. However, if I'm unlikely to get back, I try to do everything at once."

Okun's night shots have a special beauty. A triptych of Christmas lights on Wilshire Boulevard in Beverly Hills—a scene that sadly lacks allure when seen close-up, except, perhaps, to an impressionable six year old—becomes as mysterious as a Hubble Space Telescope photo of a distant galaxy with its trails and gauzy clouds of luminous gas. The fountains of the Bellagio Hotel in Las Vegas suggest an alternative universe of fiery hoops. The towers of Harrods department store in west London, outlined in tiny lights, become the stuff of fairytale, a castle for Sleeping Beauty.

I have a special fondness for the luminous tracery of the Flamingo on the Las Vegas Strip. Tom Wolfe noted that, in the early years, the signs upstaged the hotels. "They revolve, they oscillate, they soar—in shapes before which the existing vocabulary of art history is helpless," he gushed. In the early 1980s, I went to Vegas to complete a book on neon, spending patient hours in the darkness, taking time exposures of this and other vintage signs. Most have been demolished, swept away in favor of prosaic billboards and the Pharaonic towers that replaced the original road houses. Okun's images celebrate the unabashed exuberance of a vanished era.

Indeed, to the extent that much of the world's architecture survives only as imagery, Okun's pictures do double duty as art and record. First signage, then buildings will be swept away by the relentless quest for larger, newer, more profitable structures, and not just in Las Vegas. Neglect, shifts of taste, and changes in ownership will take their toll. These images, assembled and refined over hours and days, are the product of microseconds, a fleeting glimpse of reality filtered through an artist's eyes and enriched by her vision.

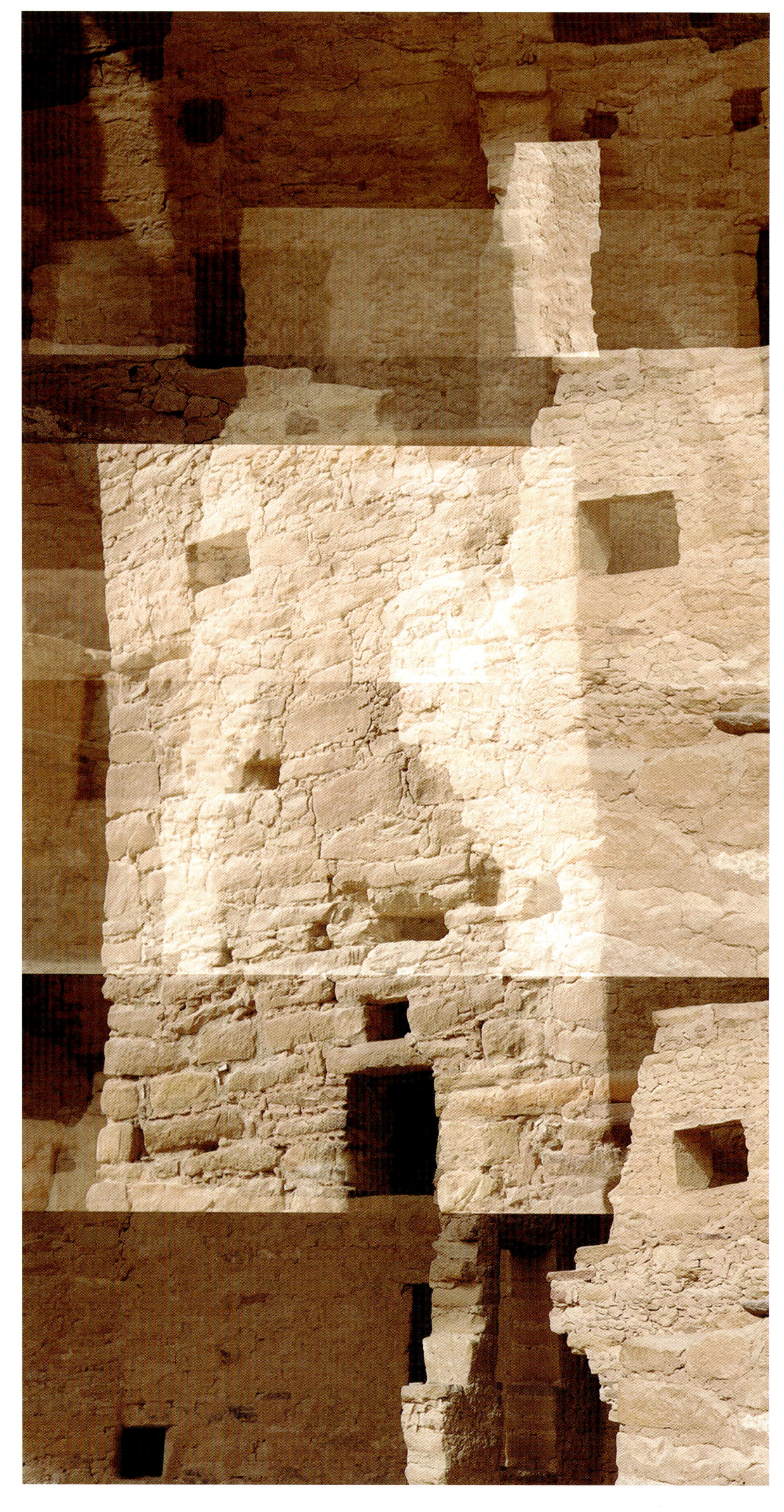

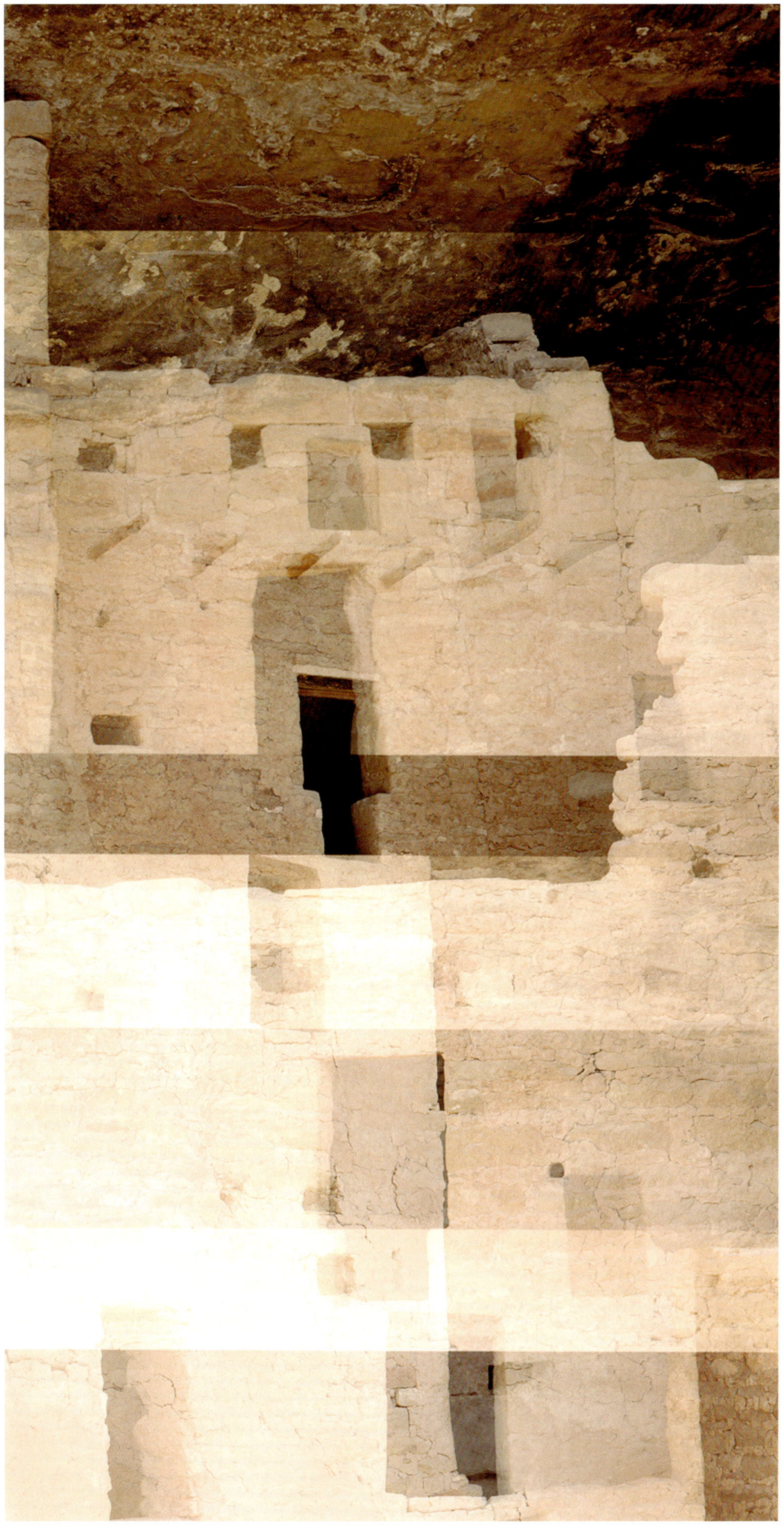

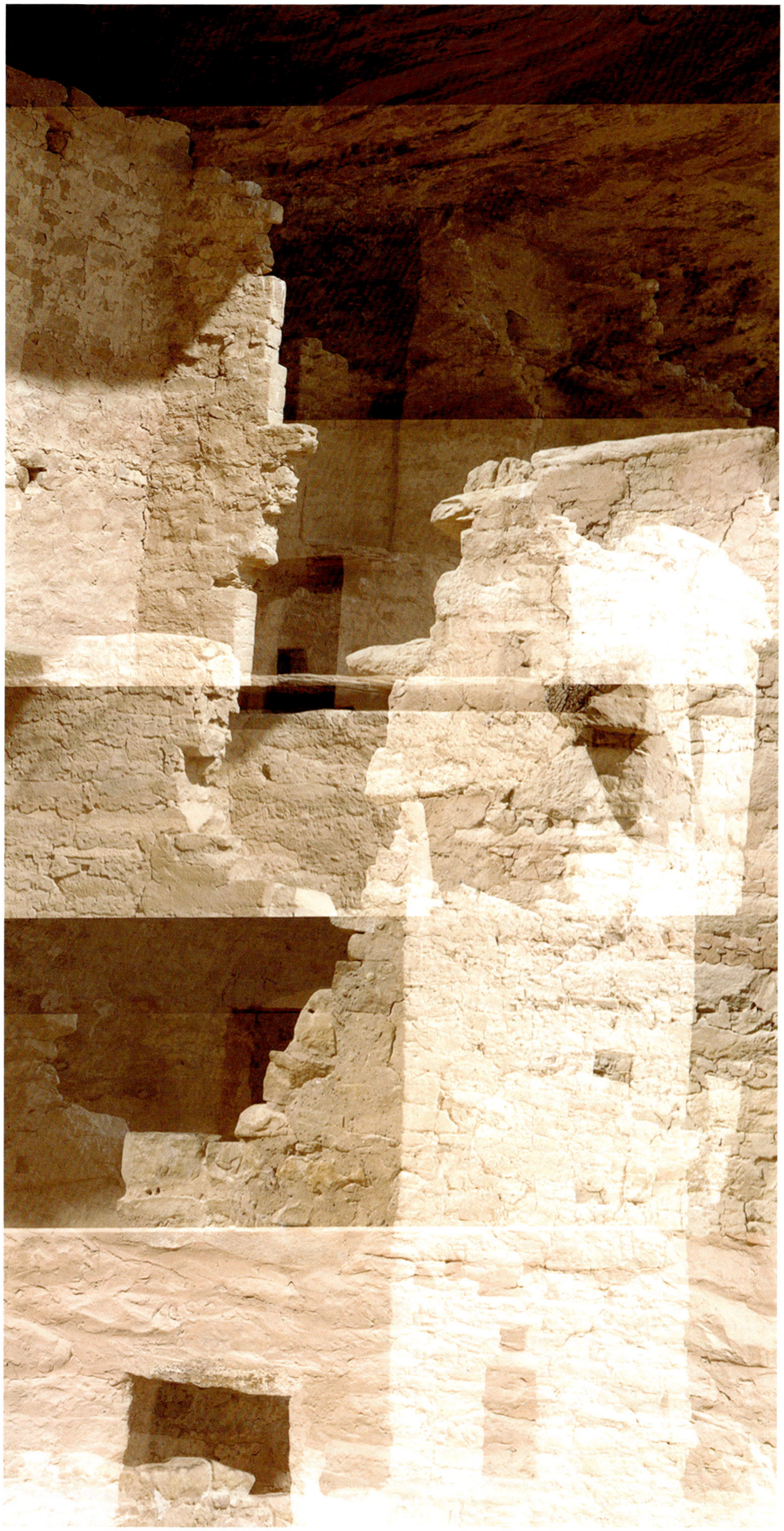

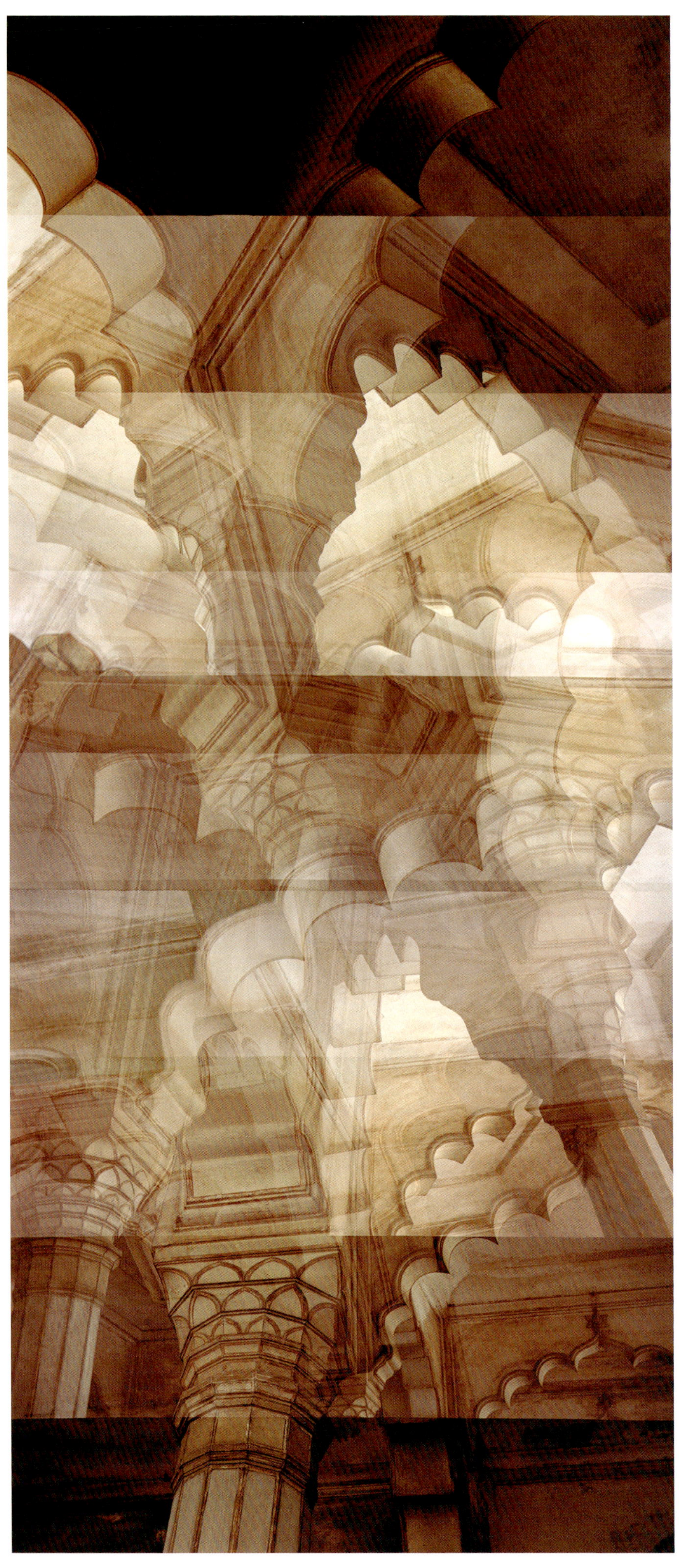

India Pillars   Agra, India, 1988

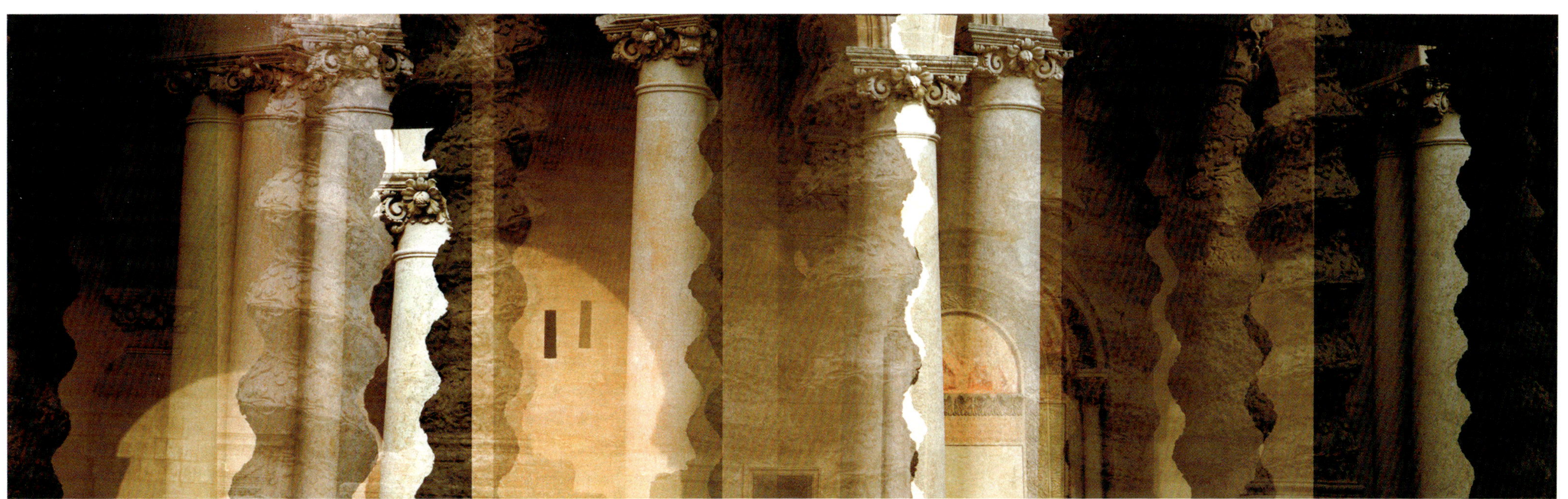

Lecce Pillars II   Lecce, Italy, 1999

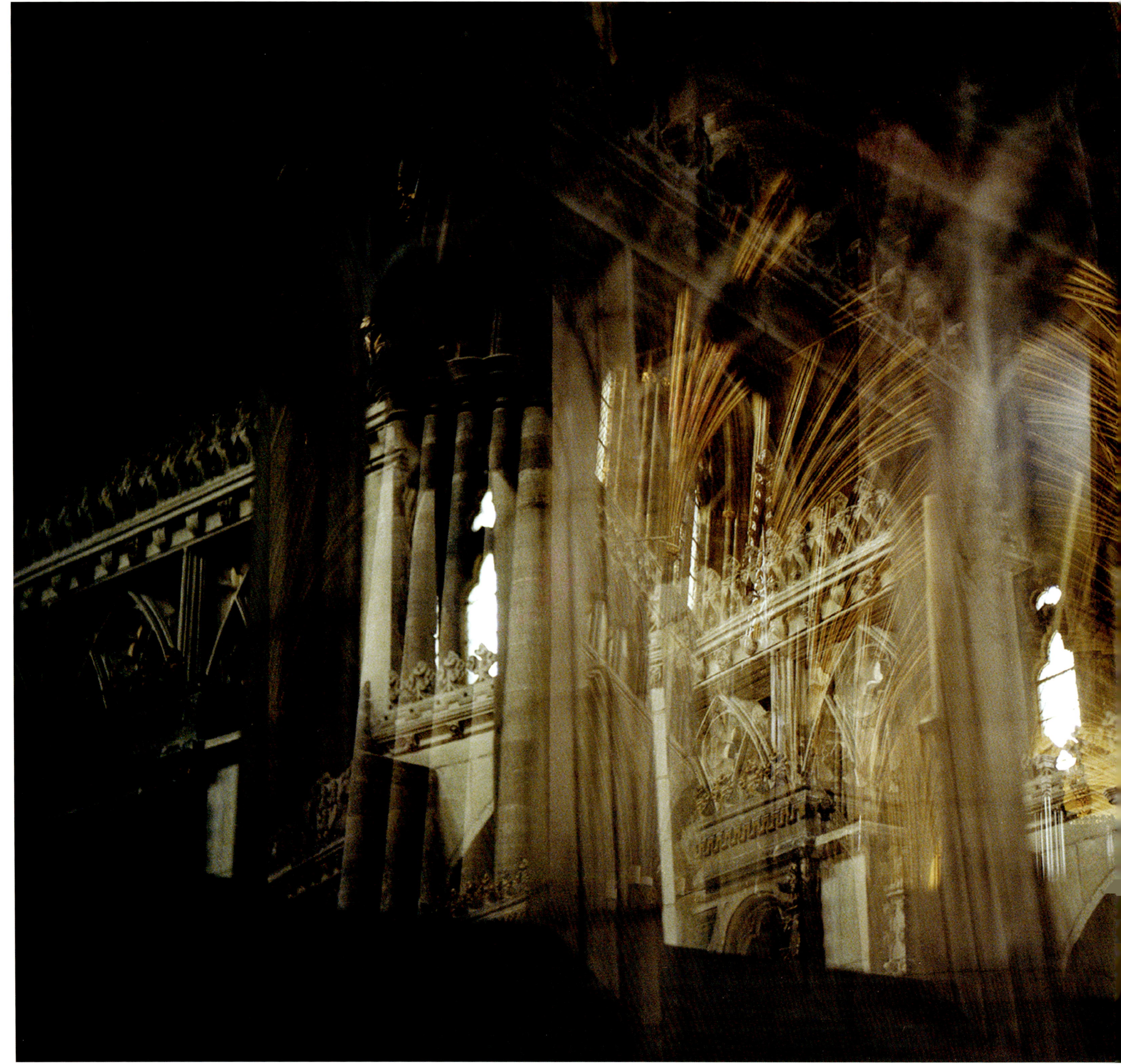

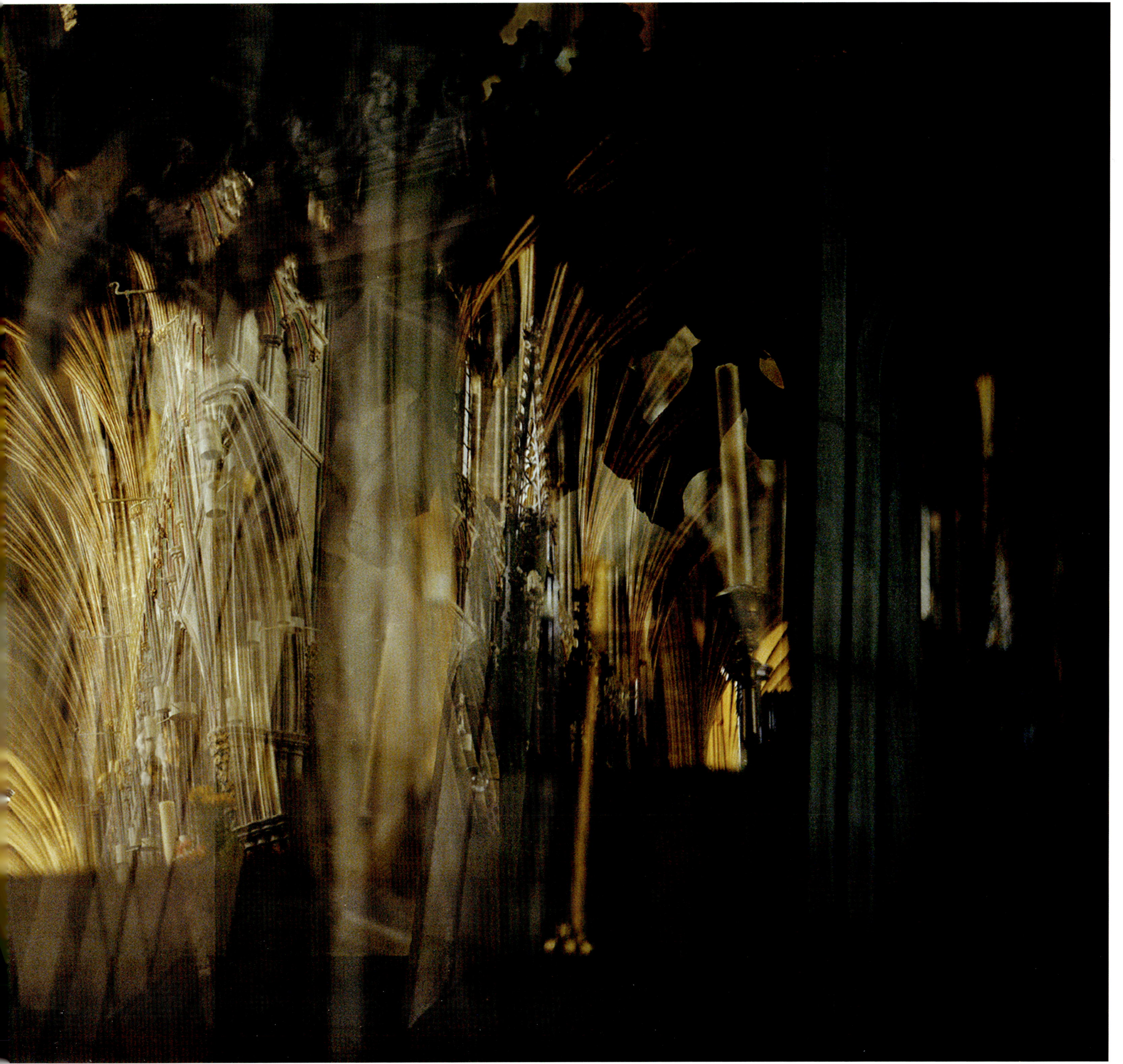

Exeter Cathedral   Exeter, England, 1979

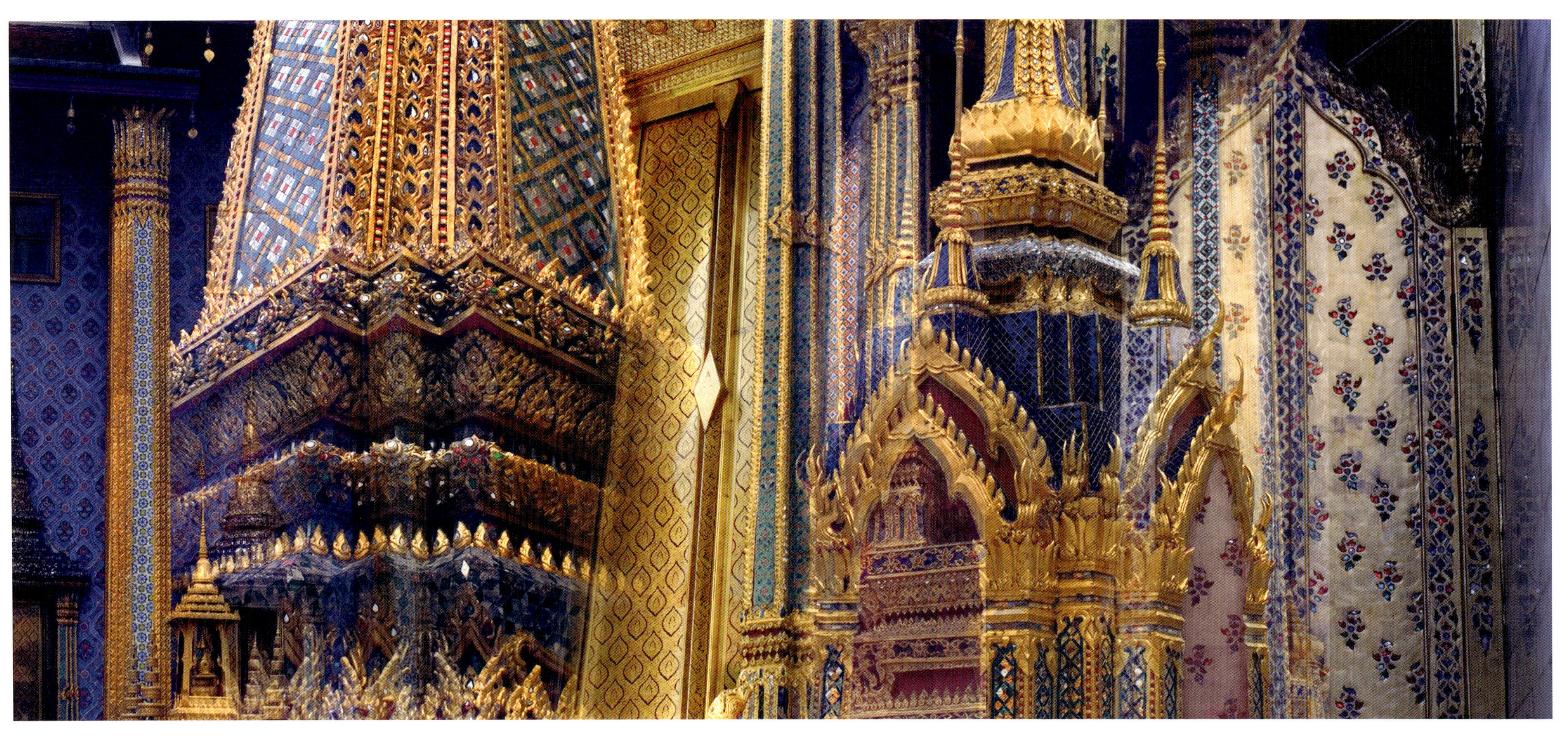

Thai Temple Purple   Bangkok, Thailand, 2004

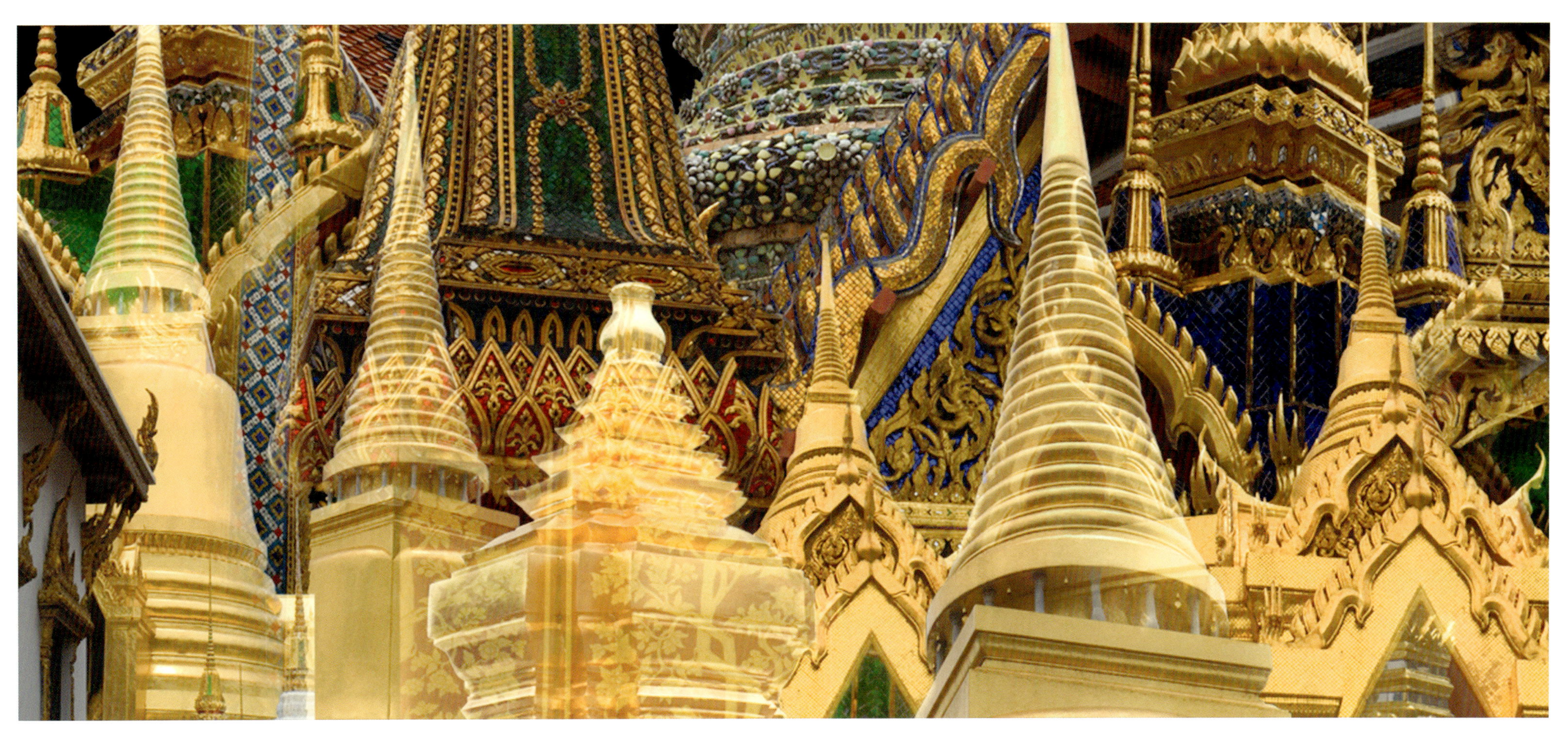

Thai Temple Gold   Bangkok, Thailand, 2004

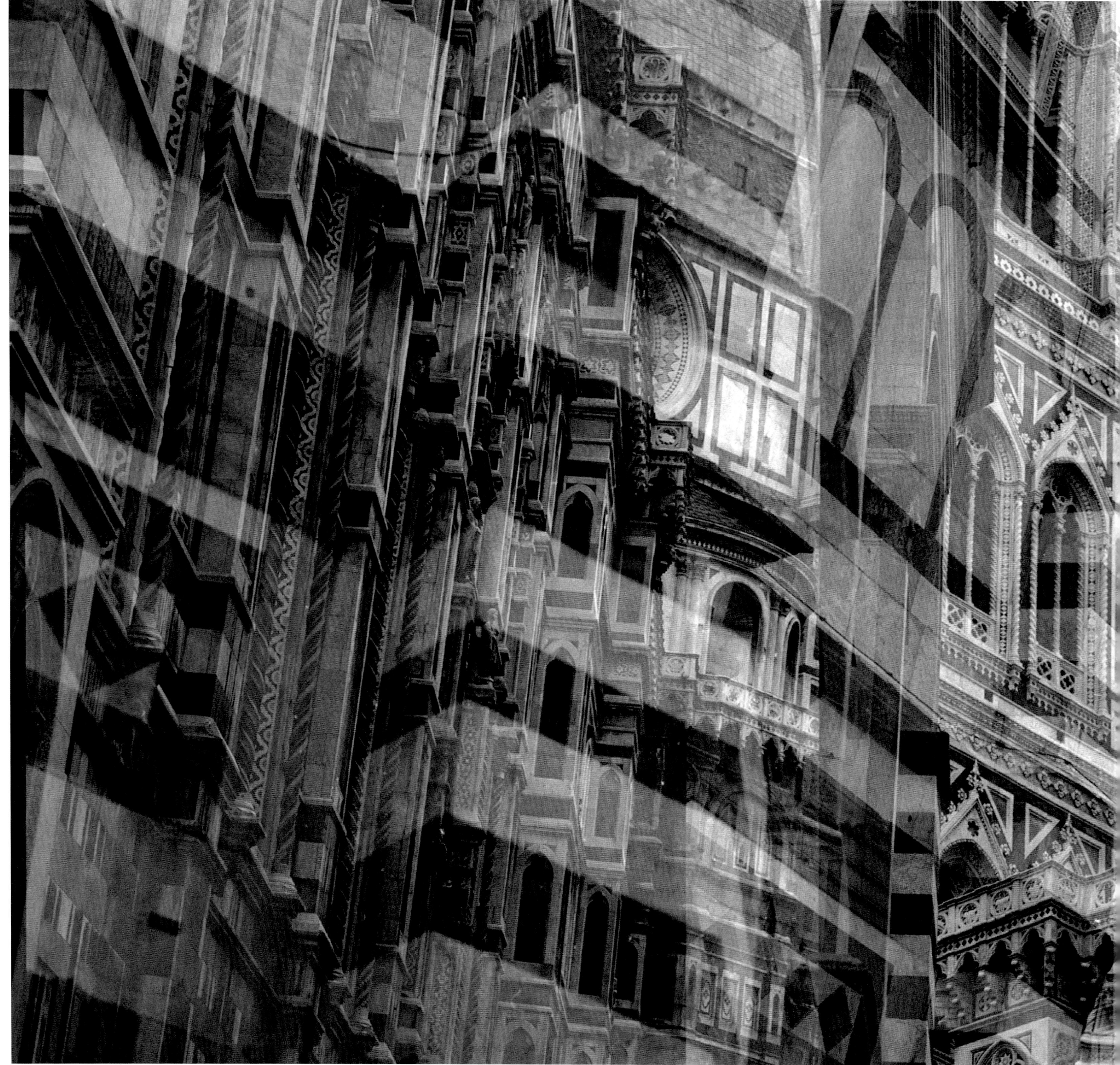

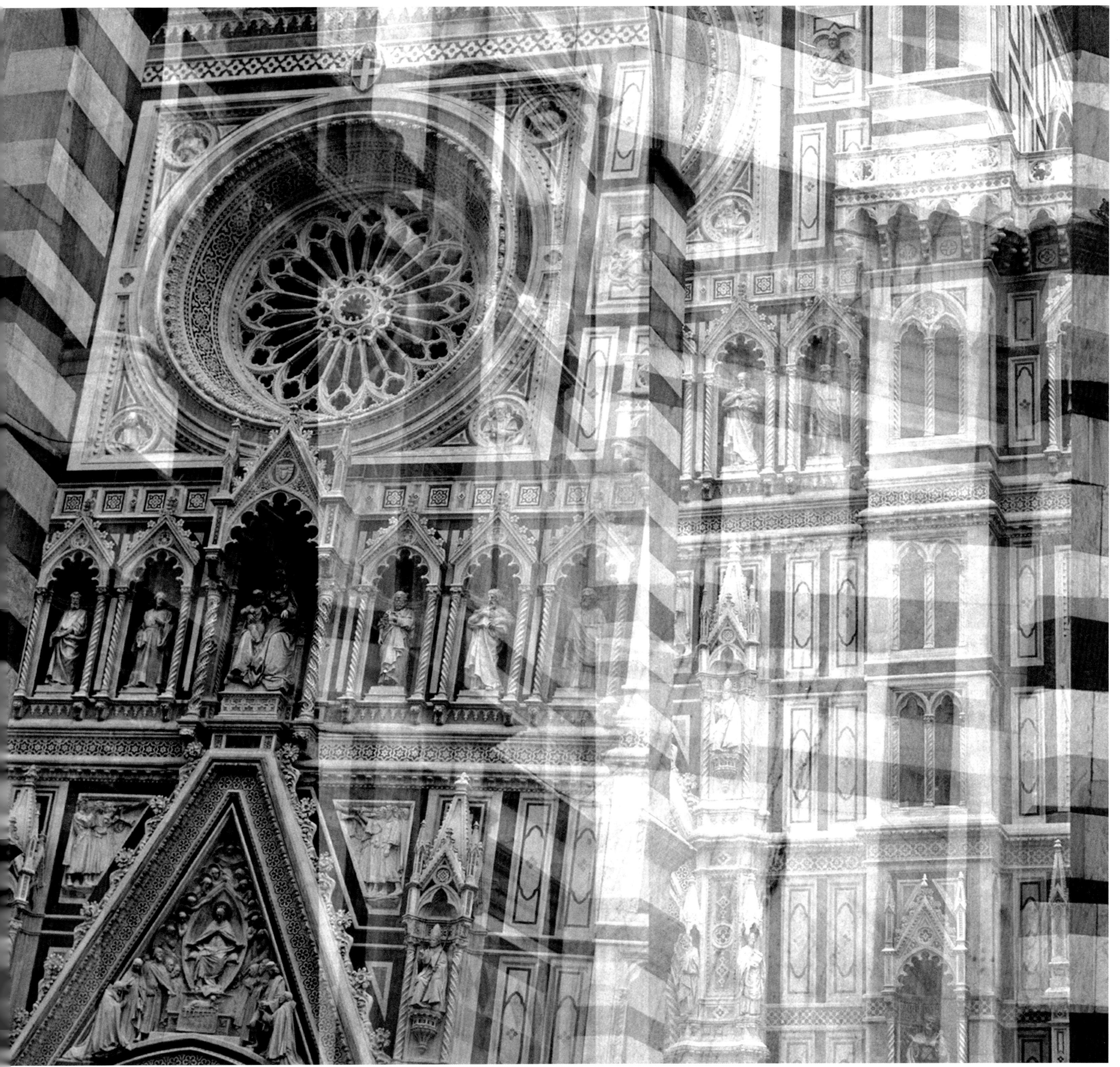

Florence Duomo   Florence, Italy, 1999

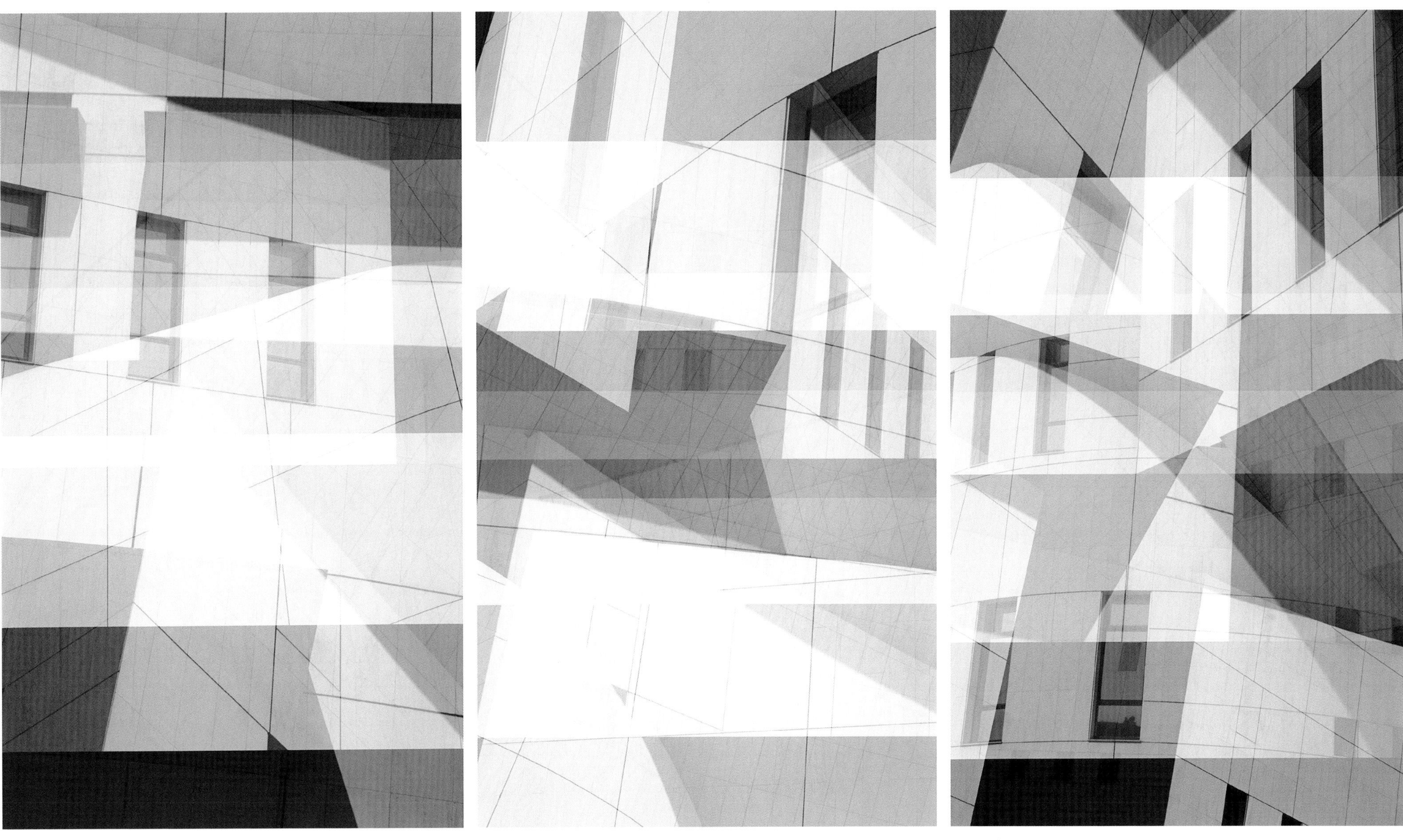

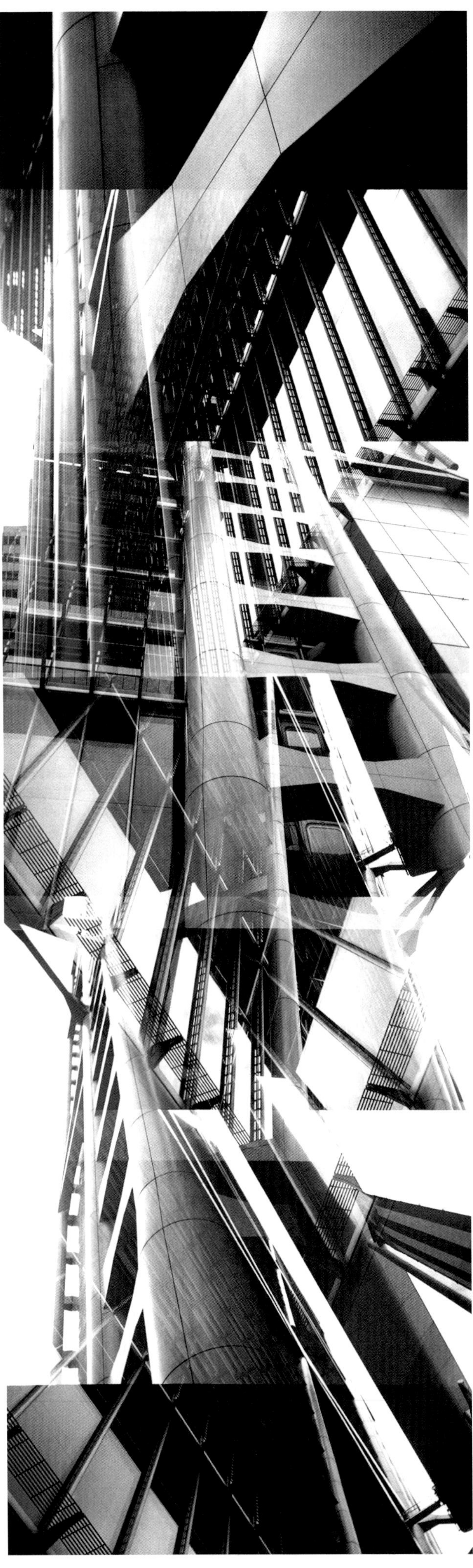

Hong Kong & Shanghai Bank   Hong Kong, 1988   ARCHITECT: Norman Foster

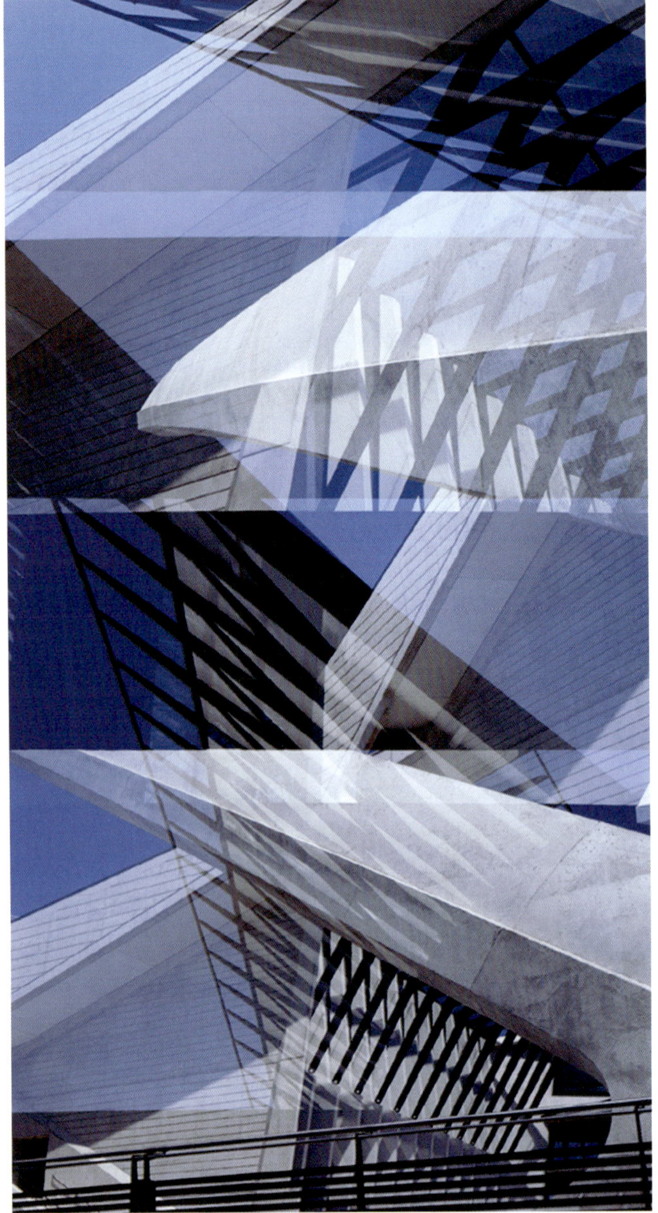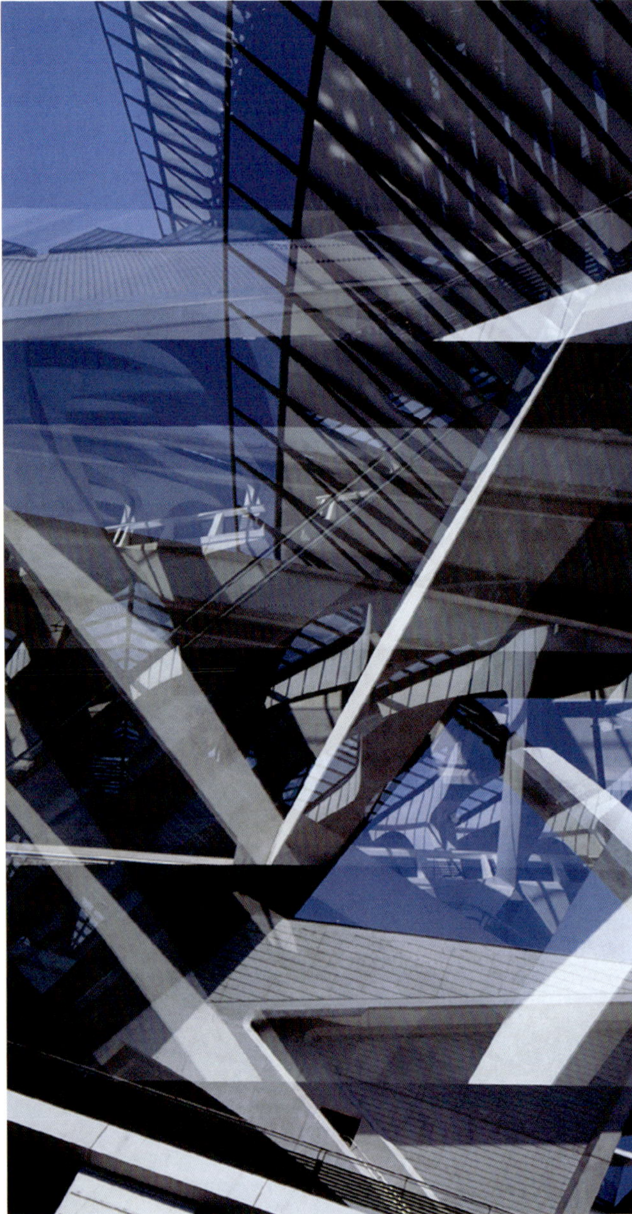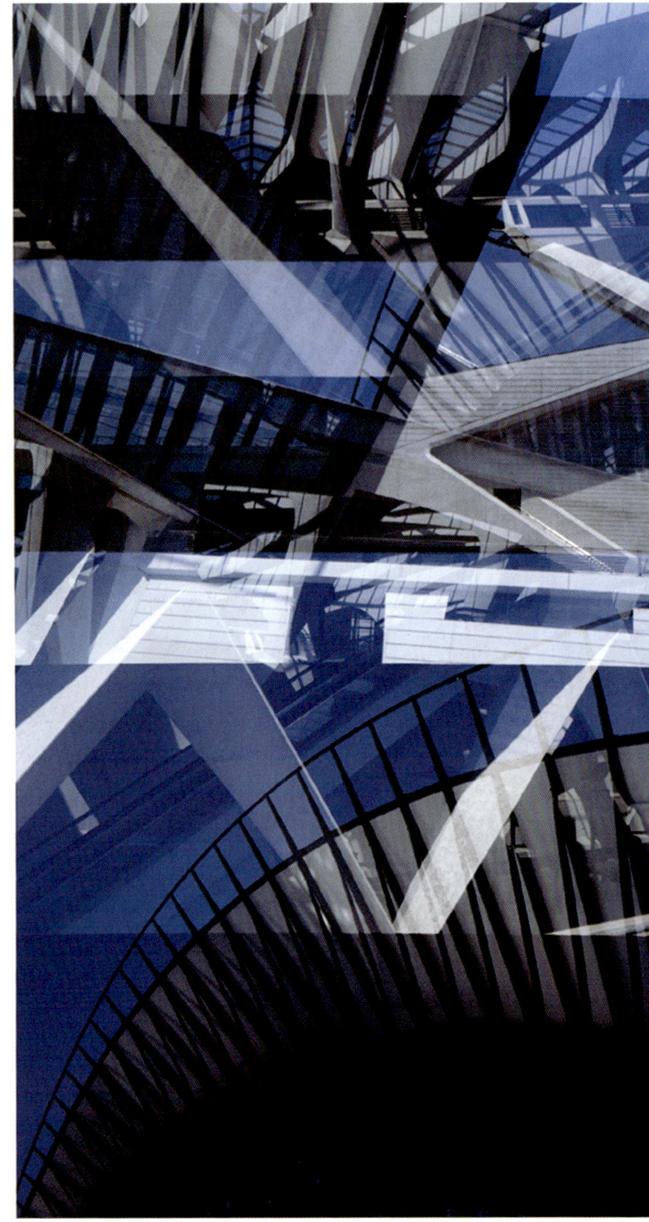

Lyon Train Station Pentaptych   Lyon, France, 1998   ARCHITECT: Santiago Calatrava

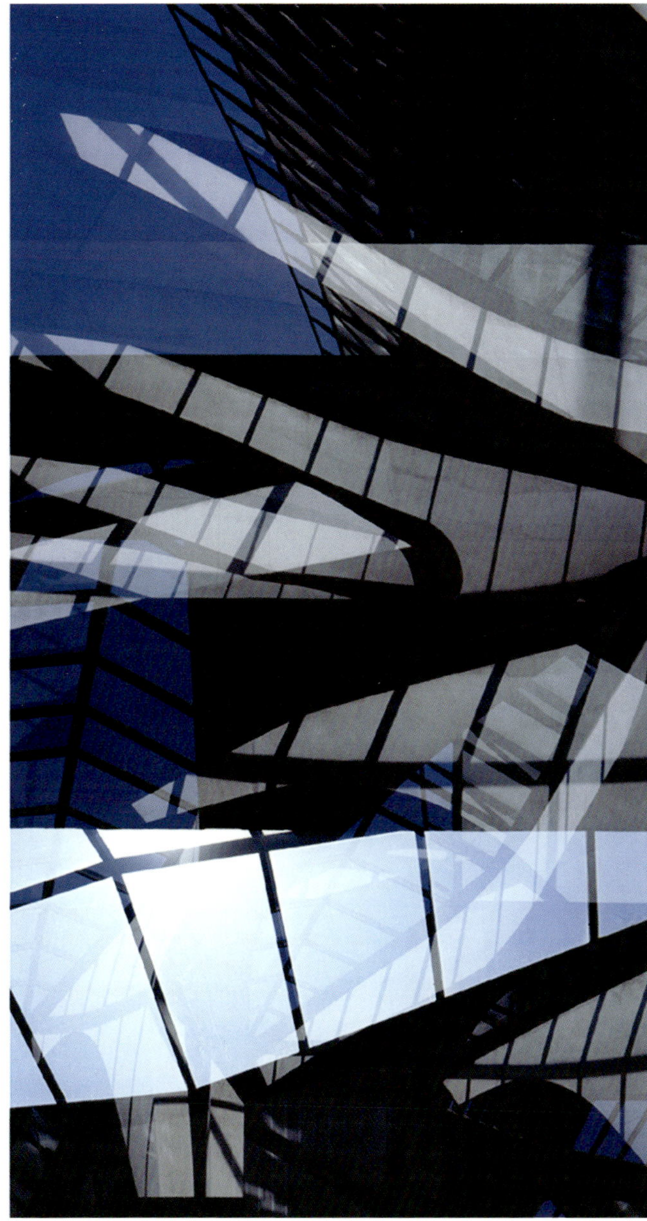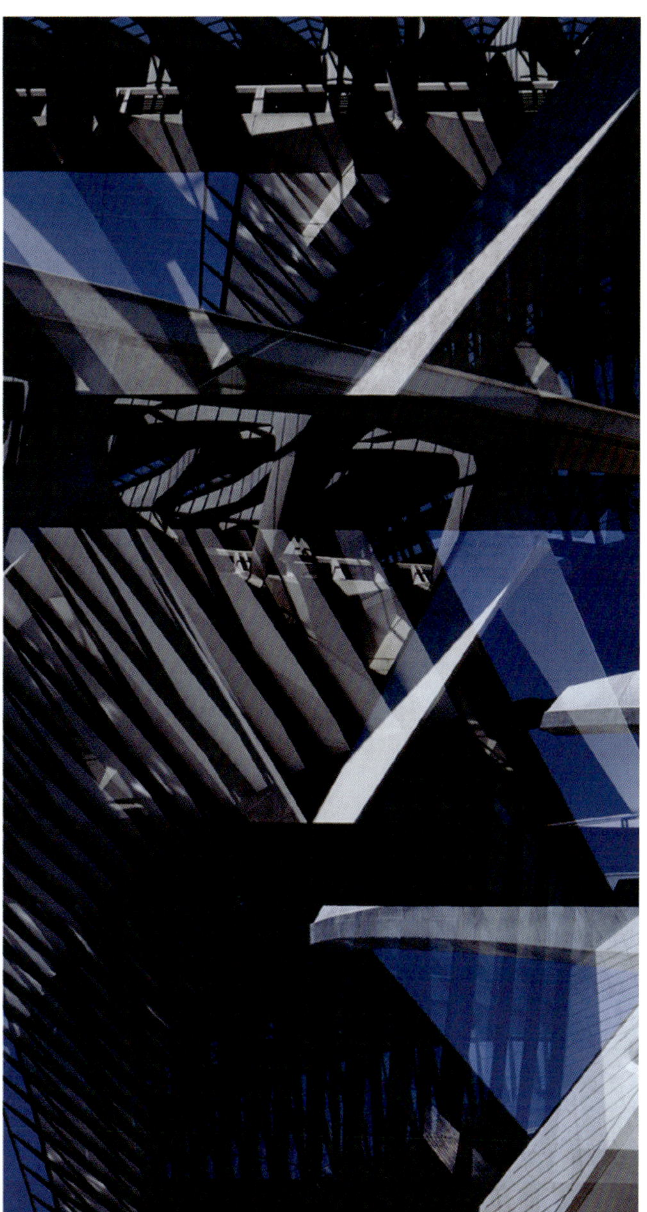

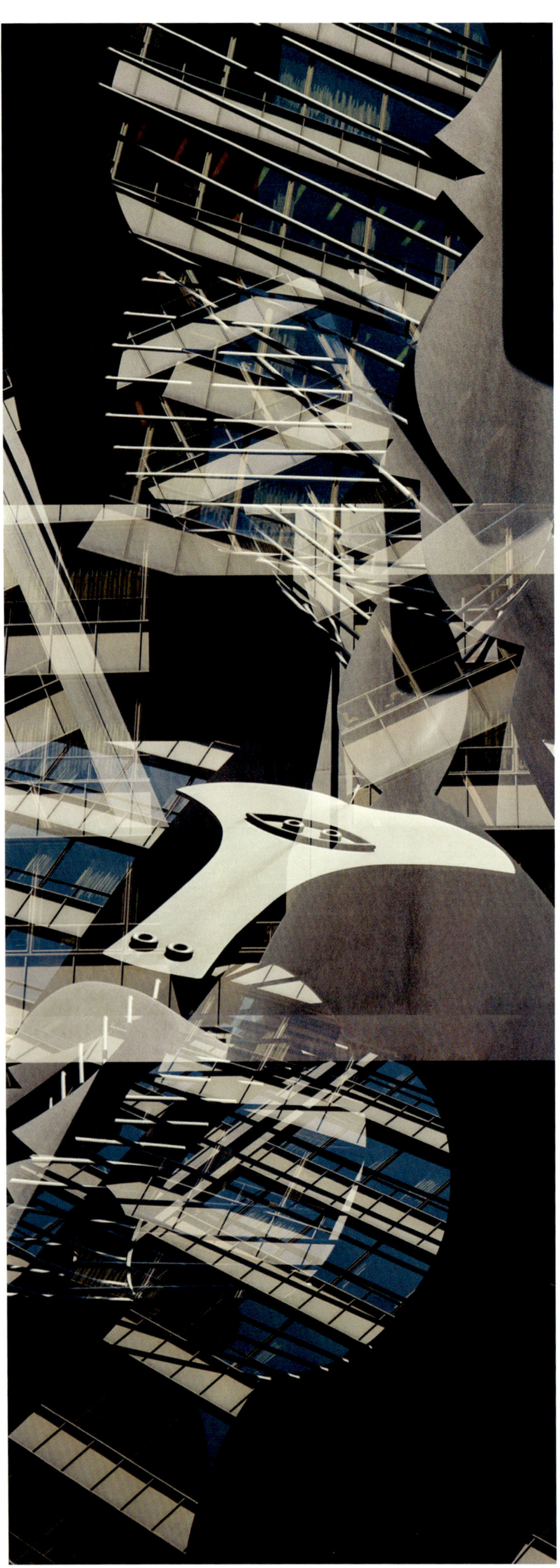

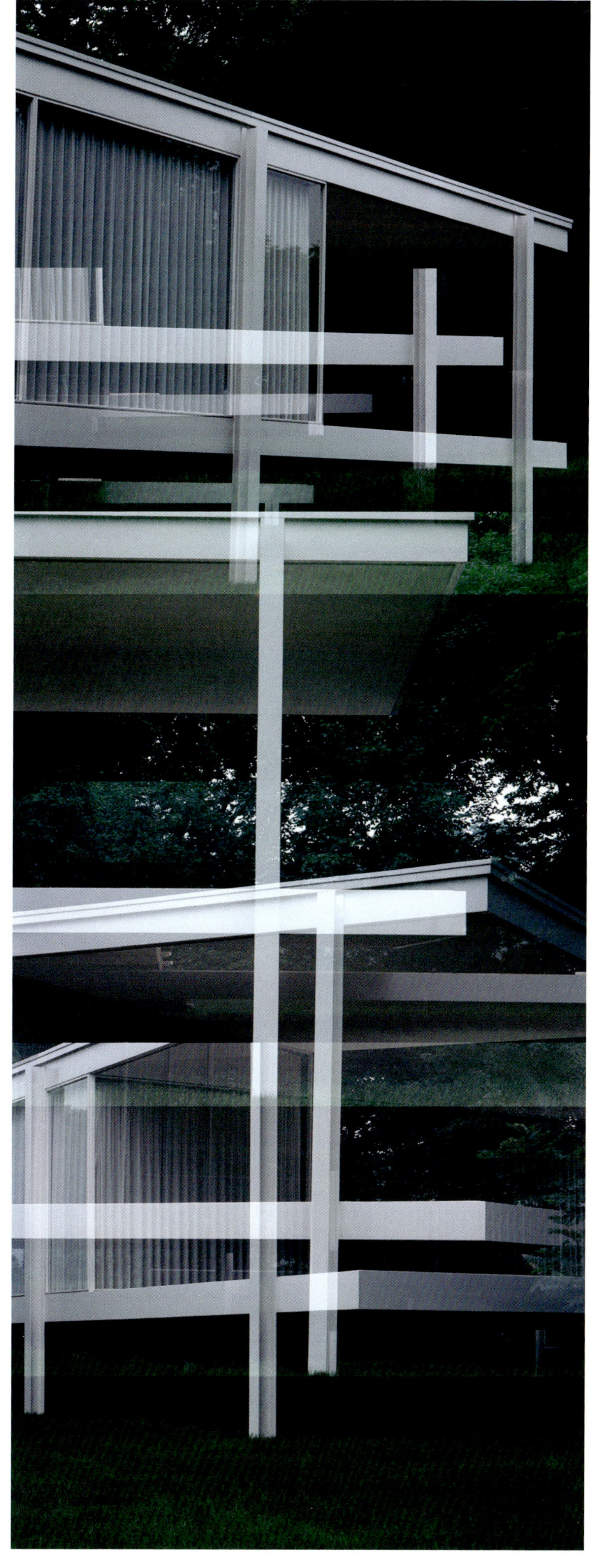

Farnsworth House   Plano, Illinois, 1986   ARCHITECT: Mies van der Rohe

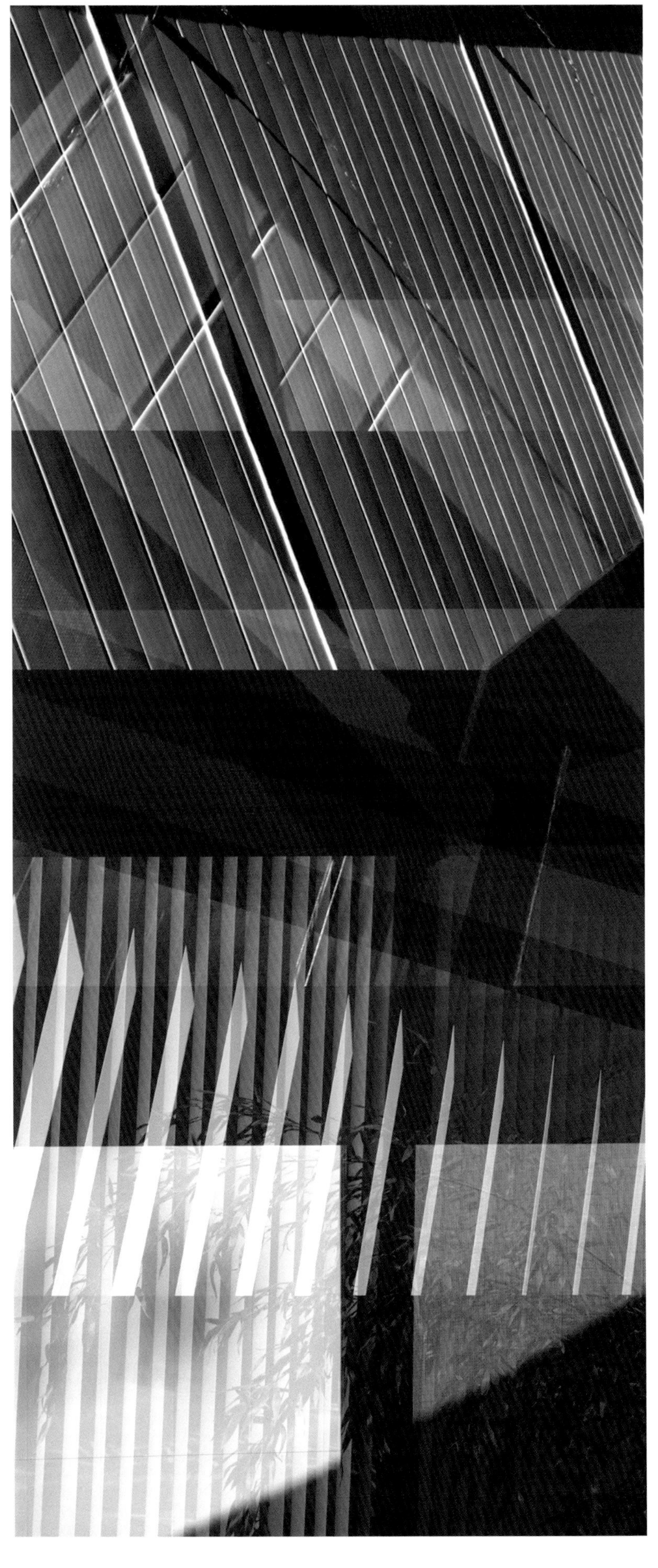

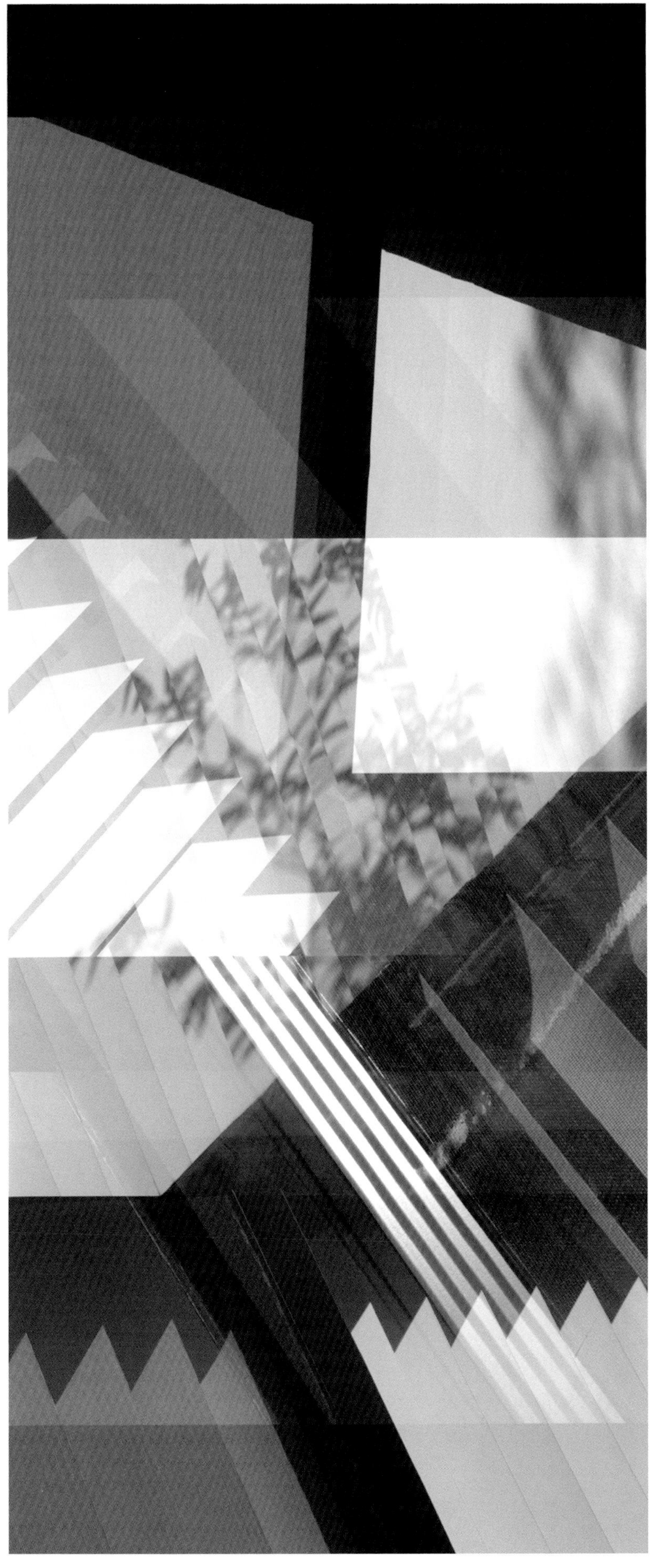
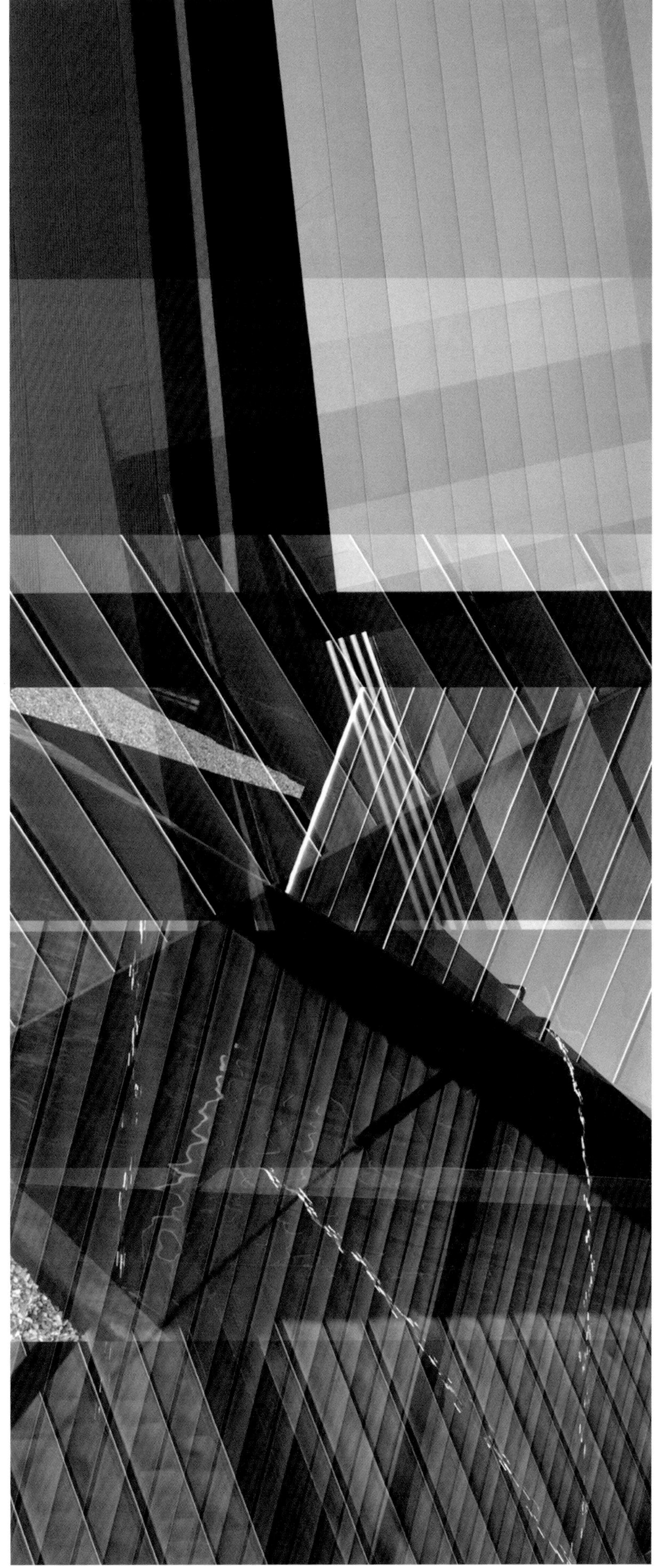

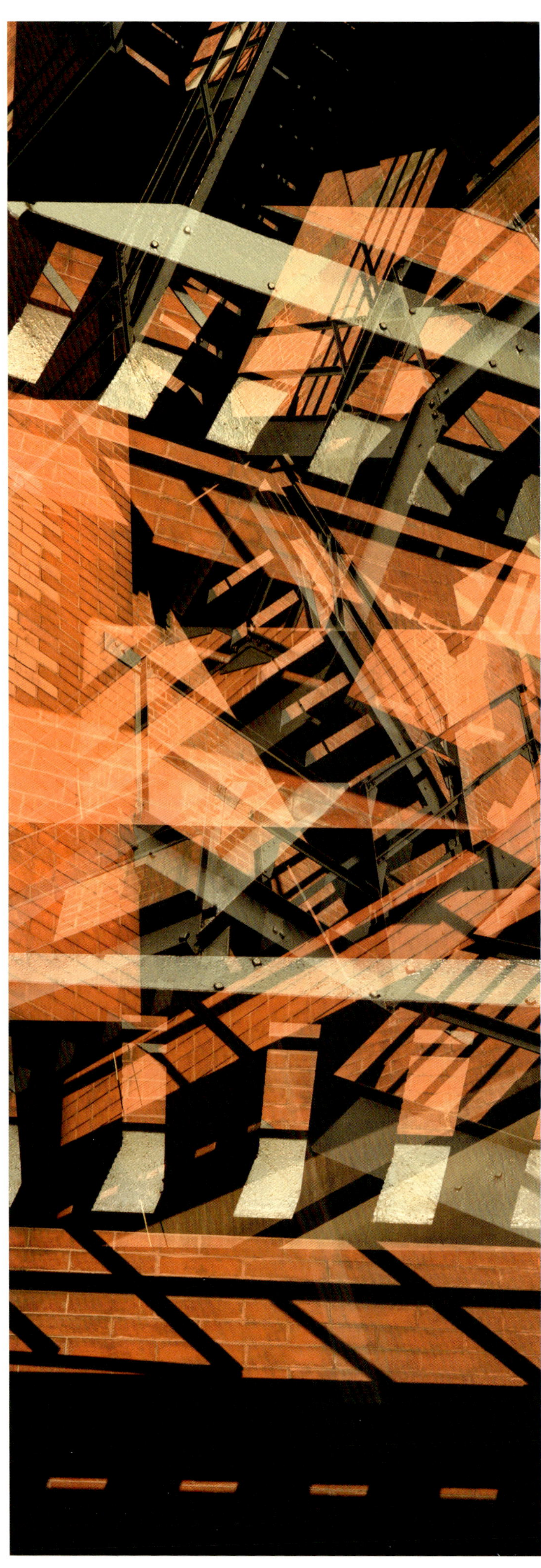

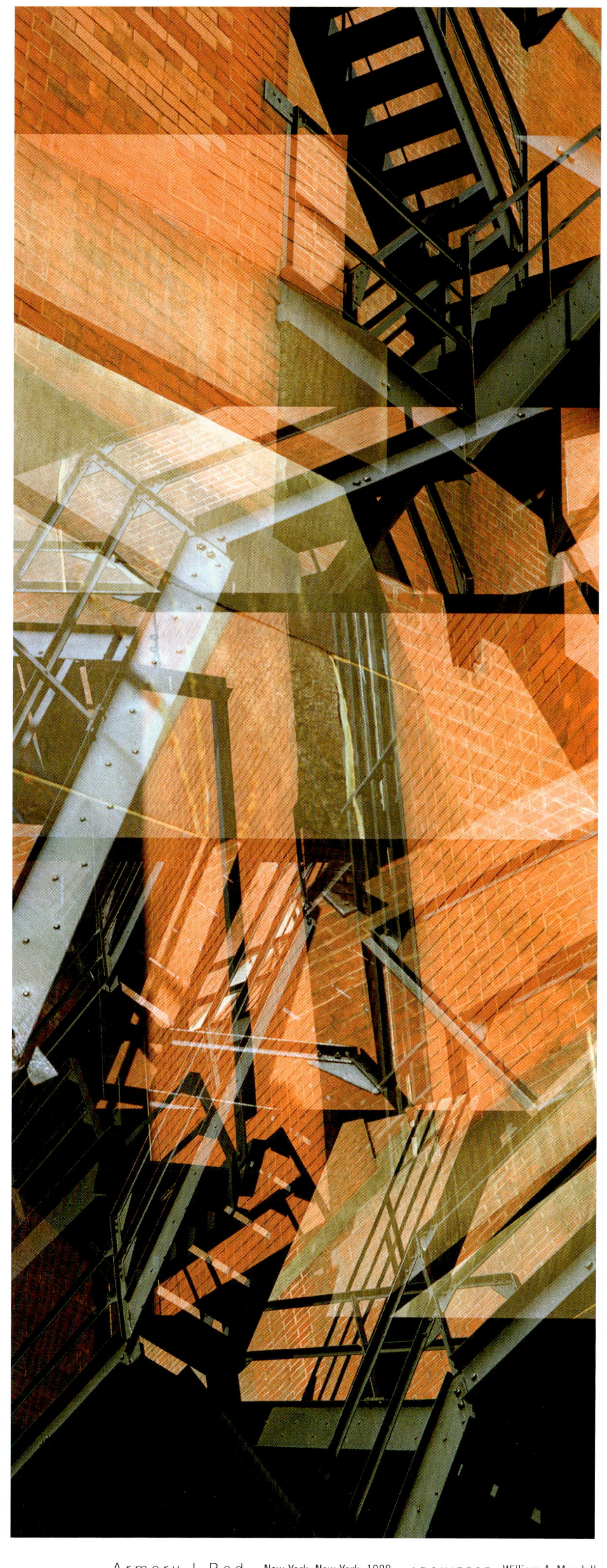

Armory I Red   New York, New York, 1988   ARCHITECT: William A. Mundell

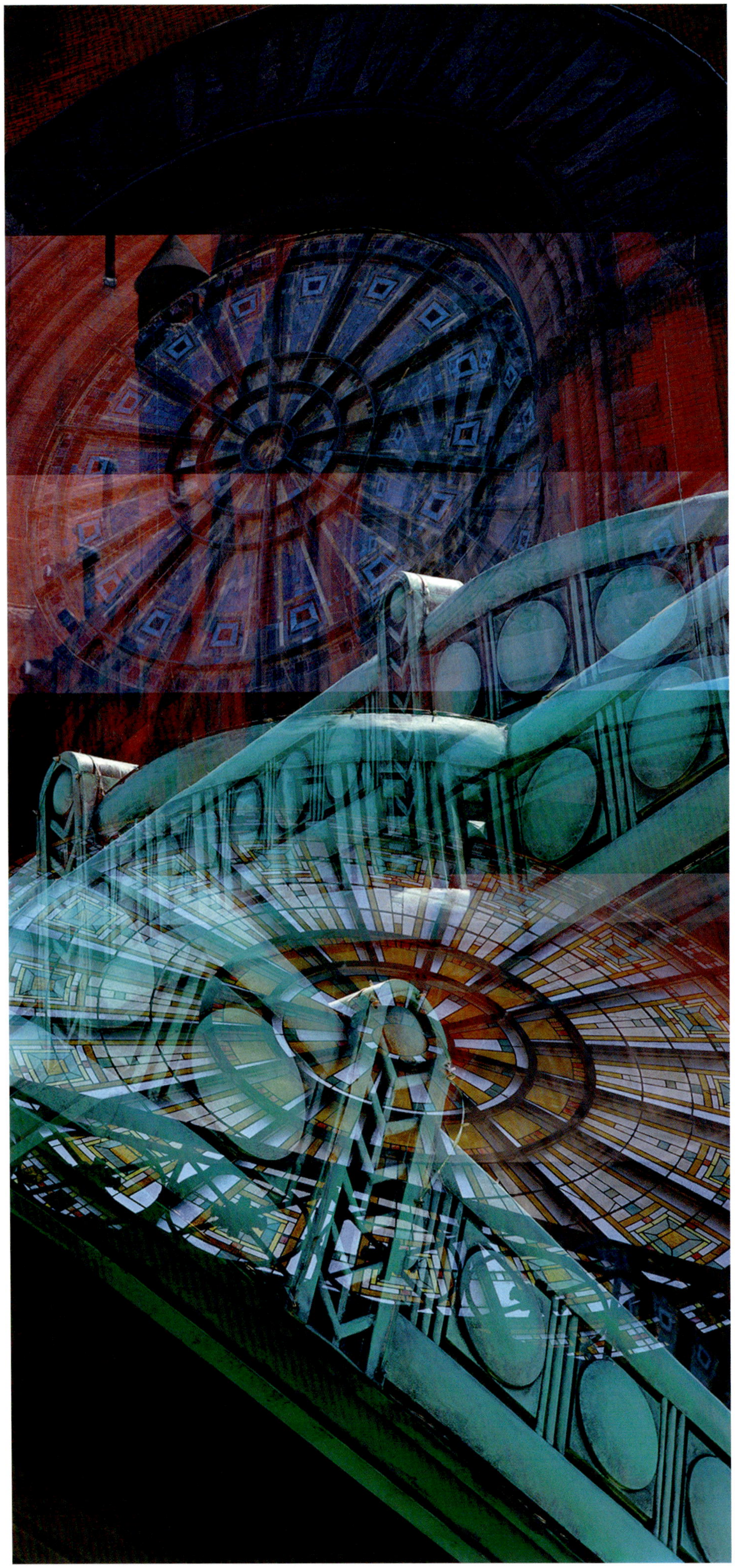

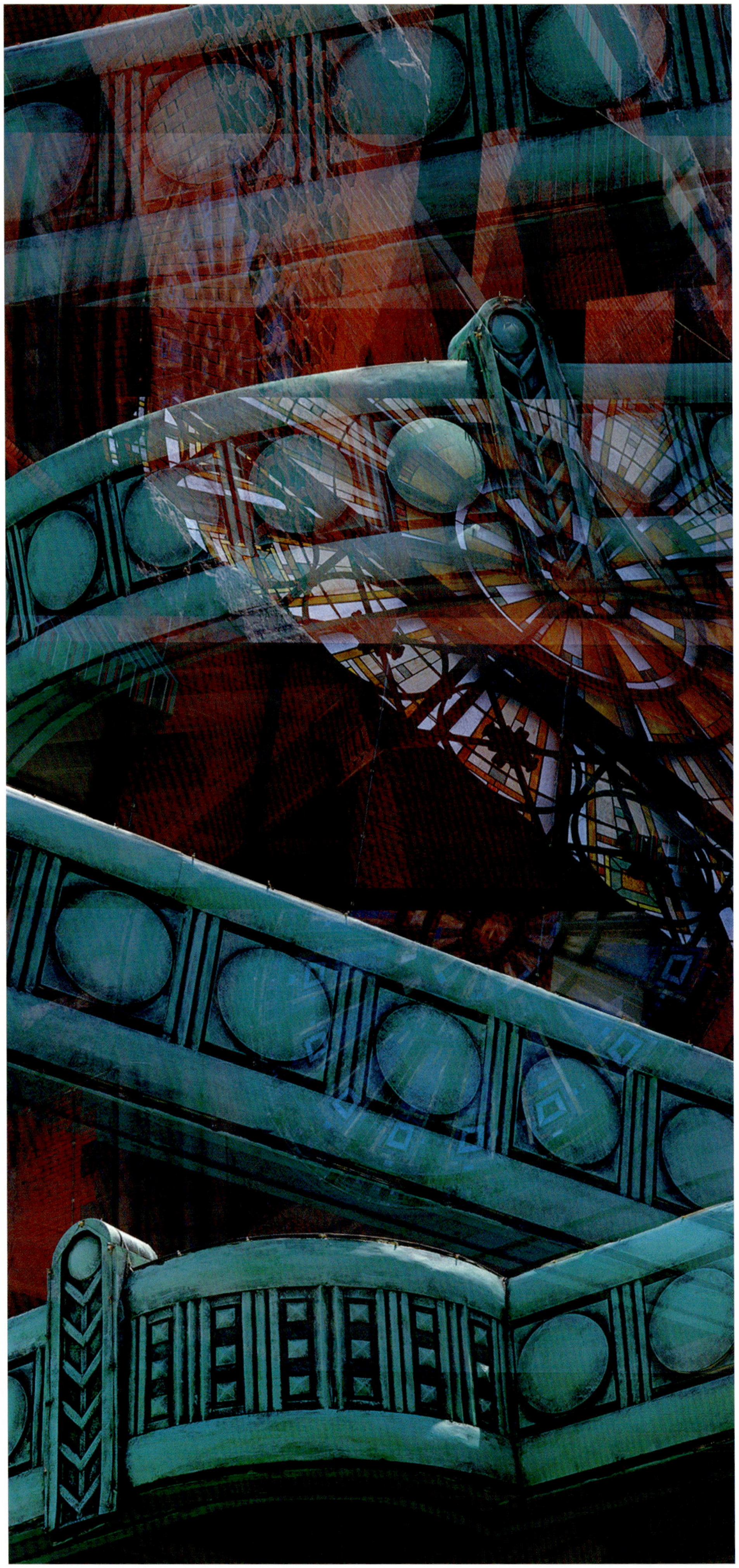

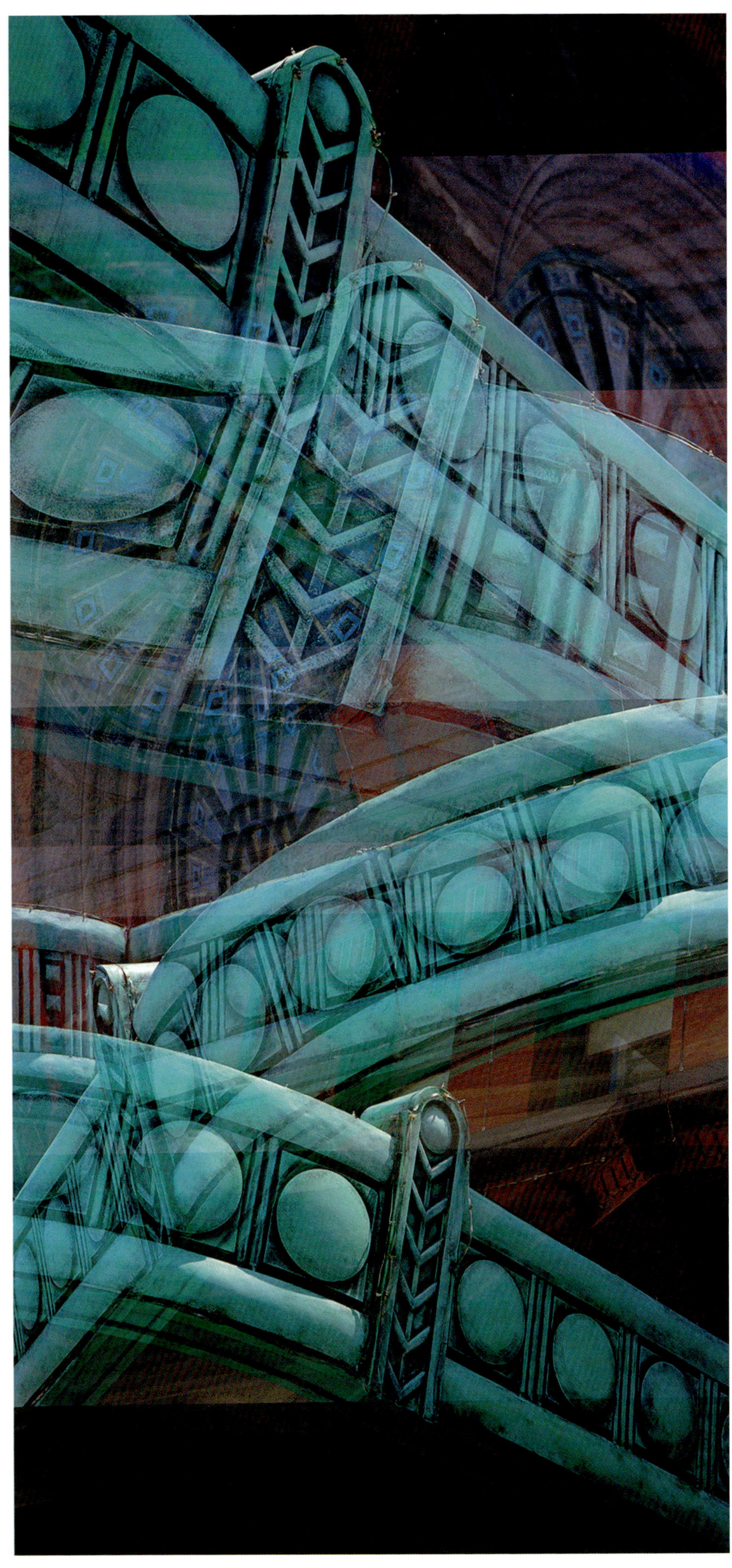

Indianapolis Union Station Triptych   Indianapolis, Indiana, 1989   ARCHITECT: Thomas Rodd

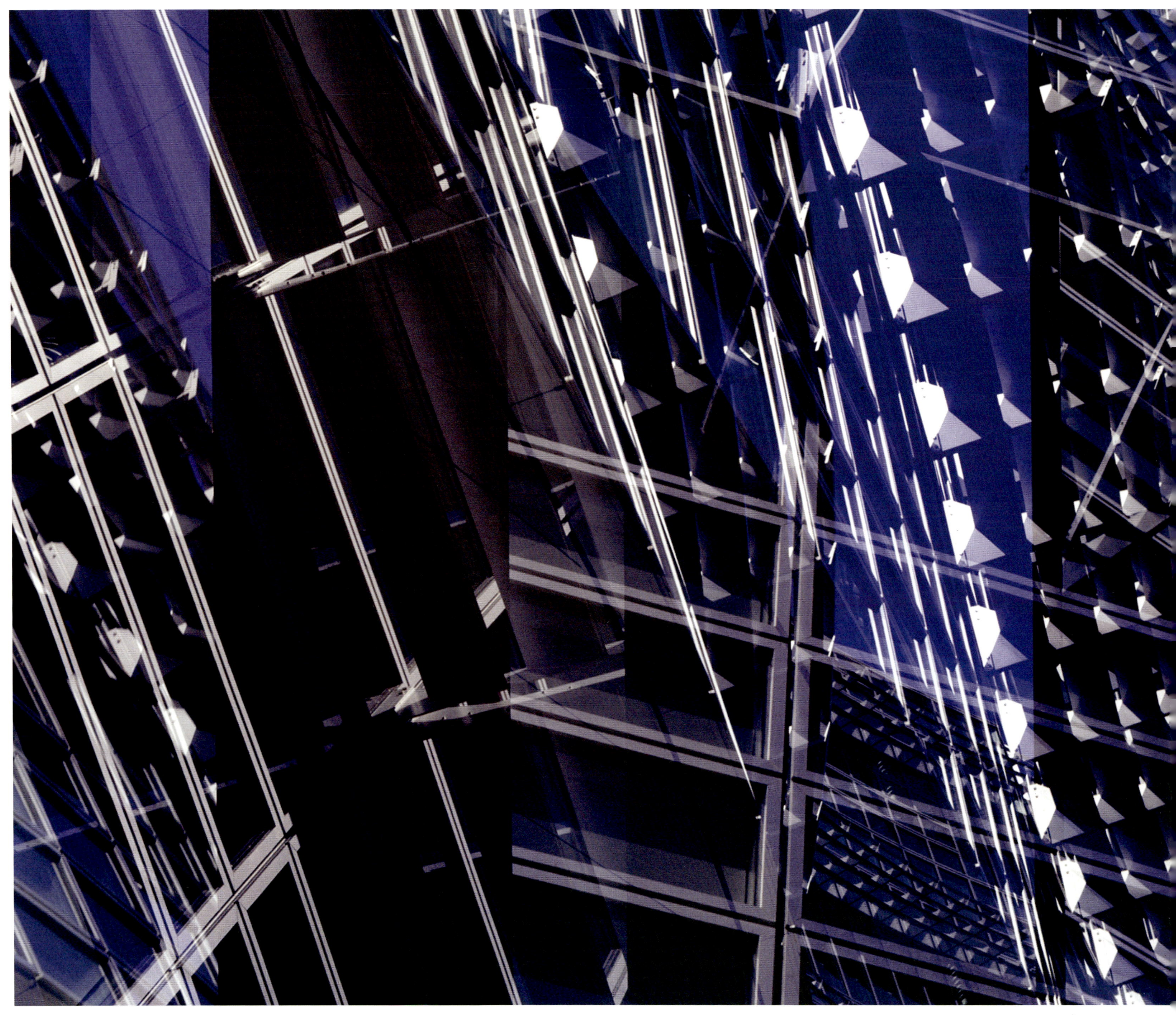

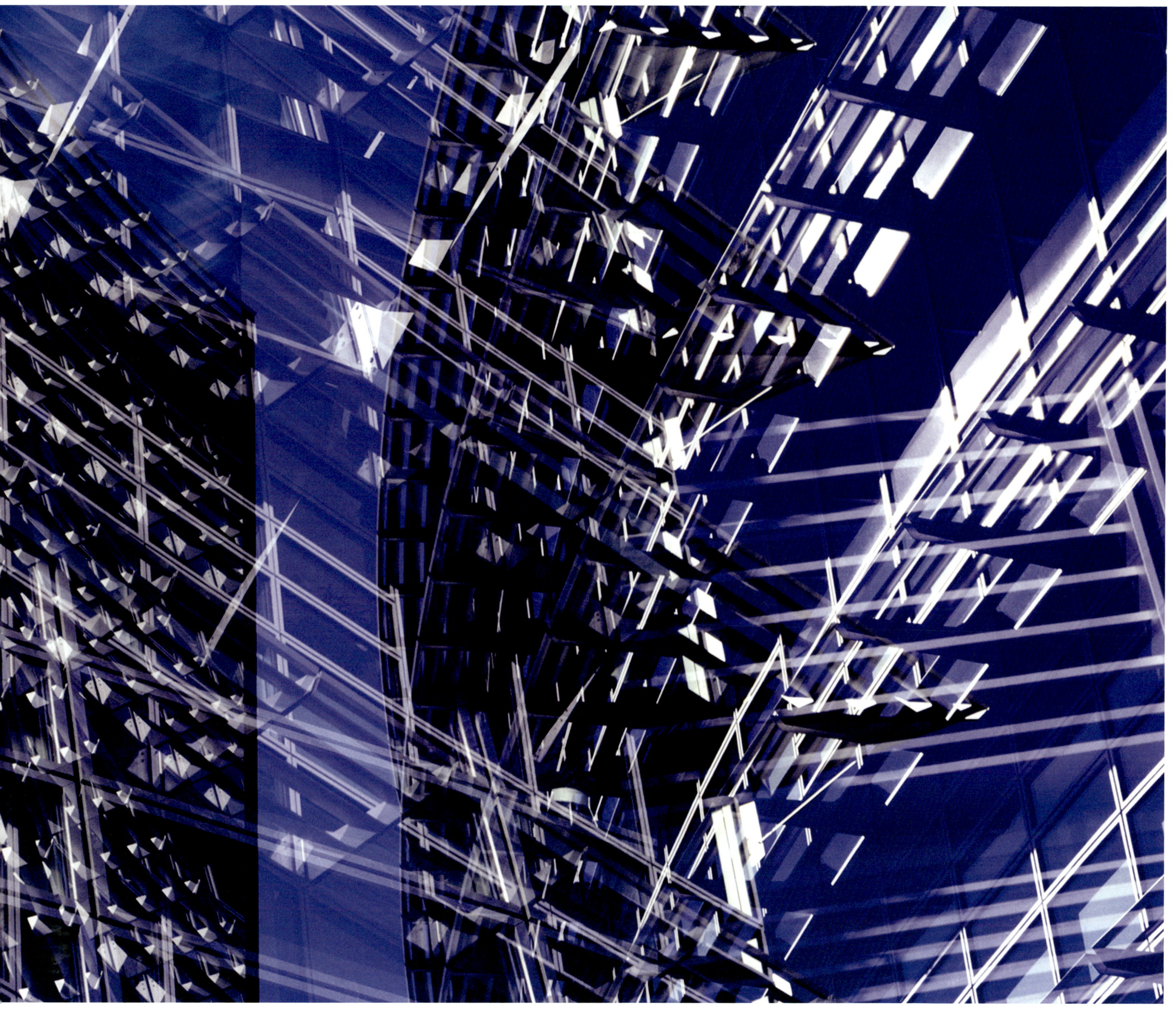

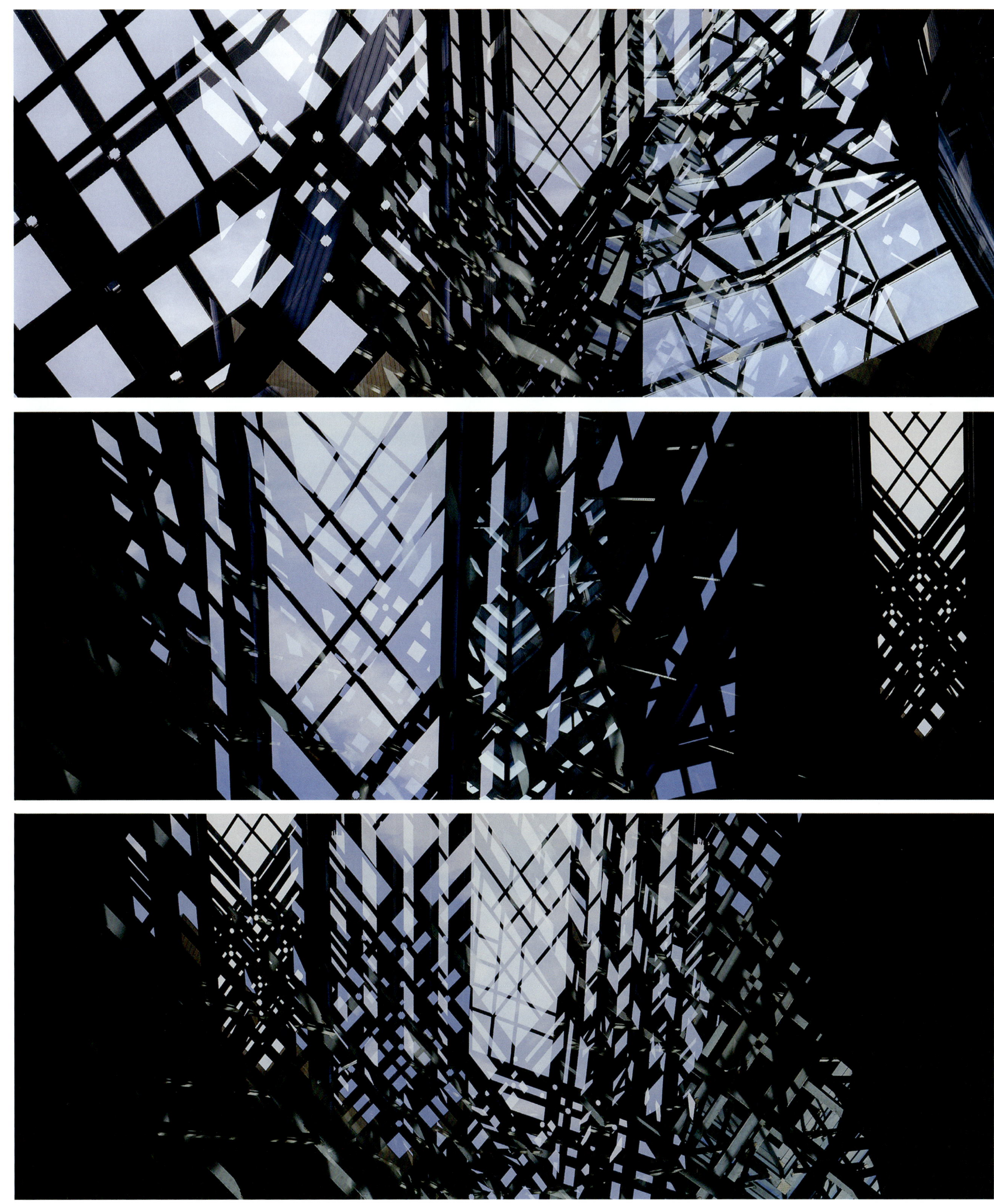

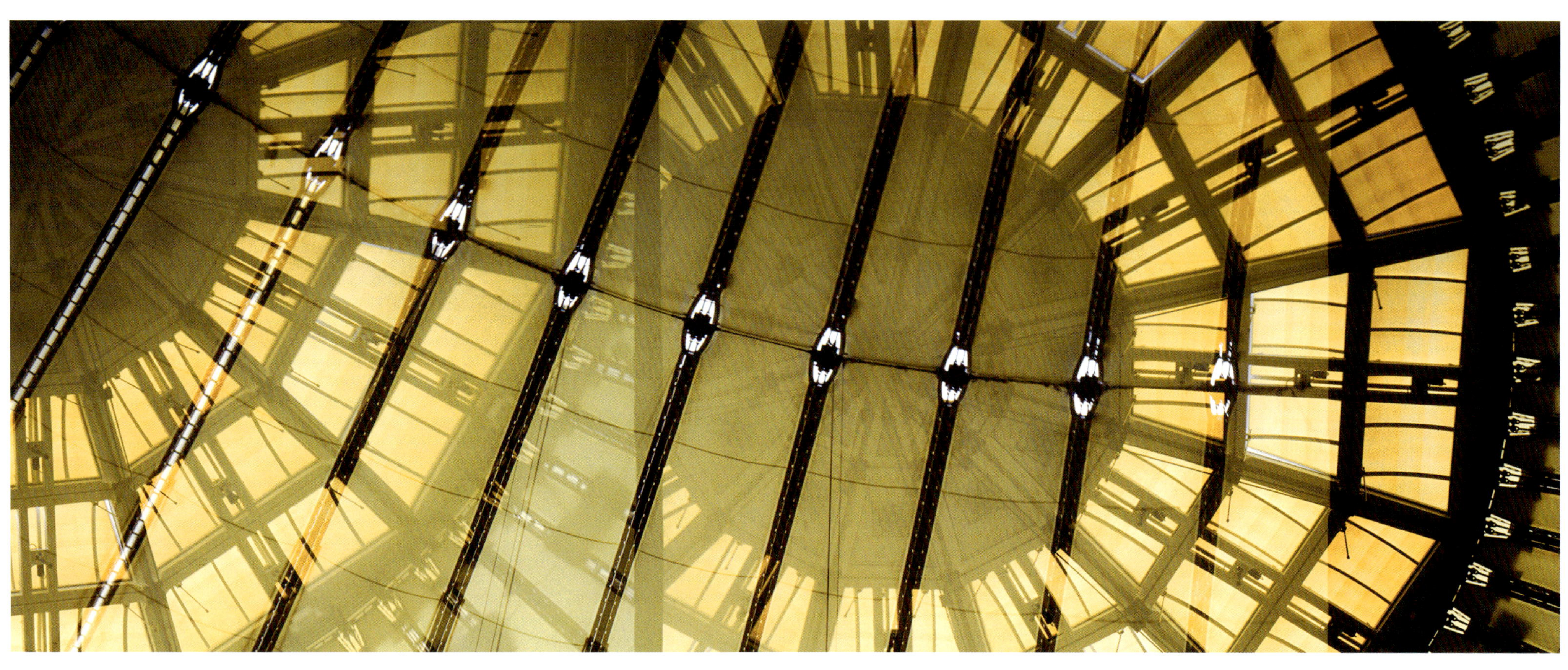

Millennium Dome Gold   London, England, 1999   ARCHITECT: Richard Rogers Partnership

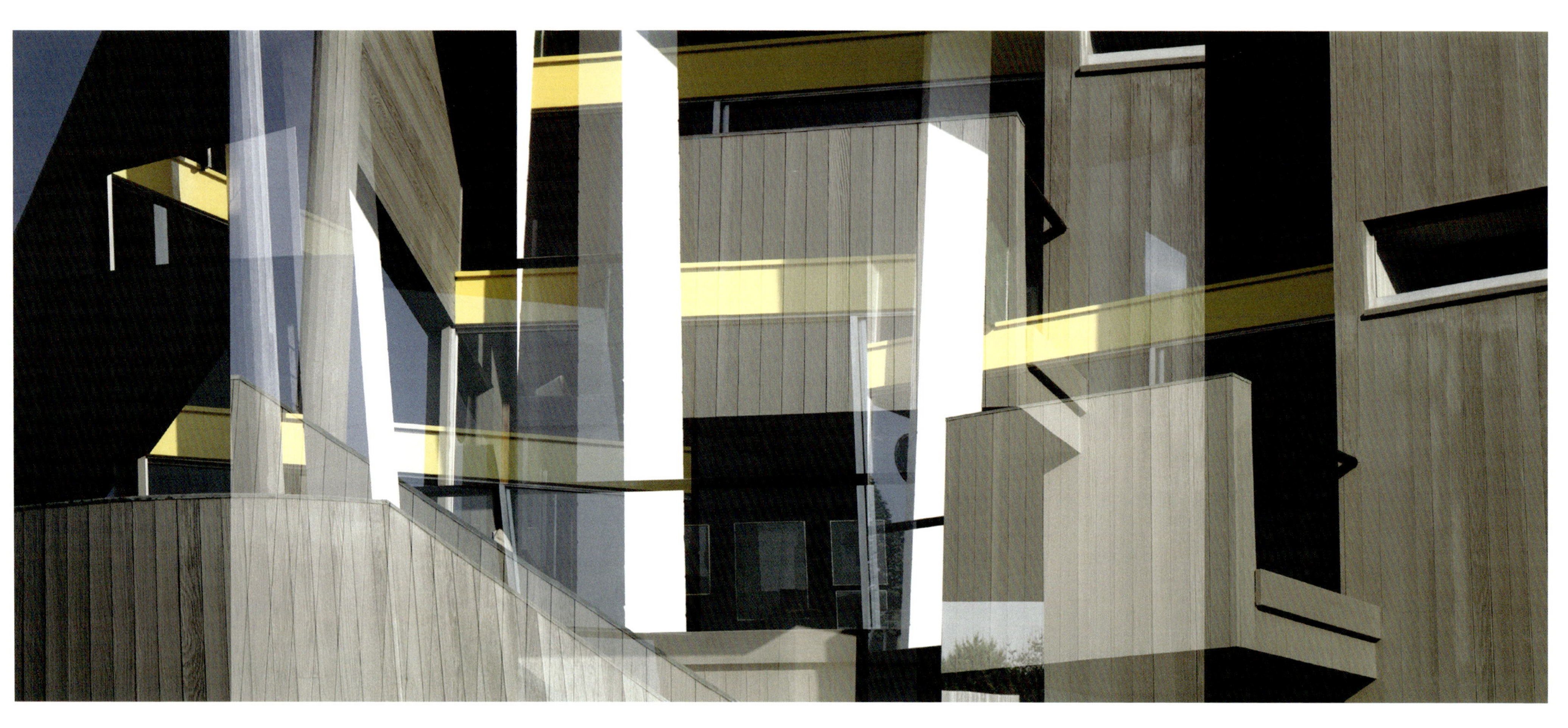

Gwathmey House   Amagansett, New York, 1986   ARCHITECT: Charles Gwathmey

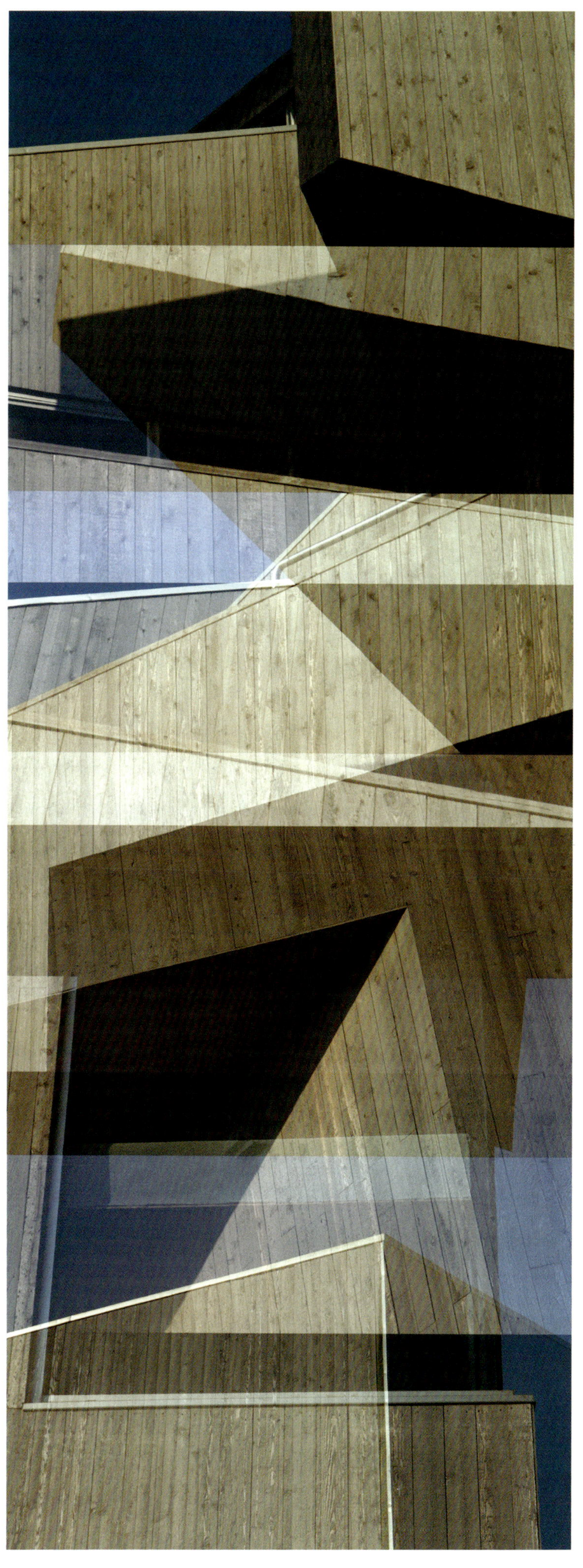

Amagansett Beach House I   Amagansett, New York, 1985.   ARCHITECT: Charles Gwathmey

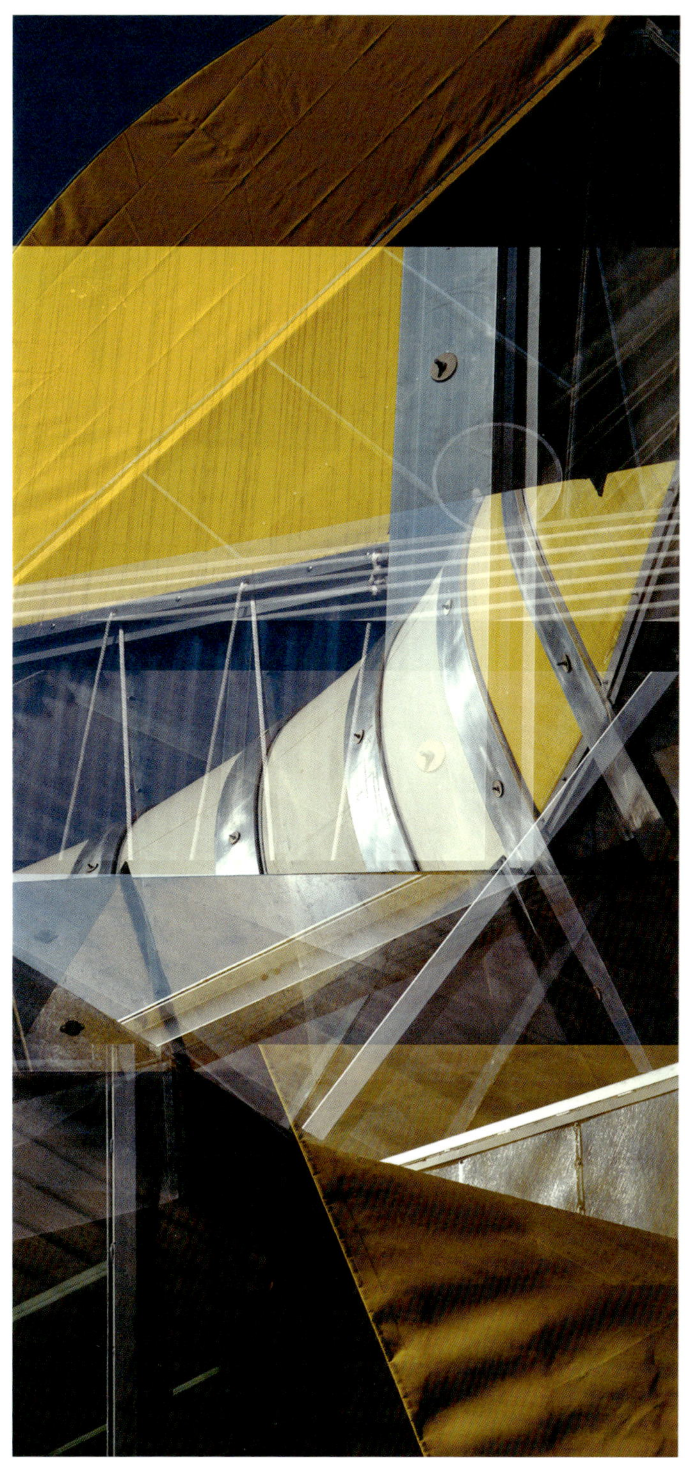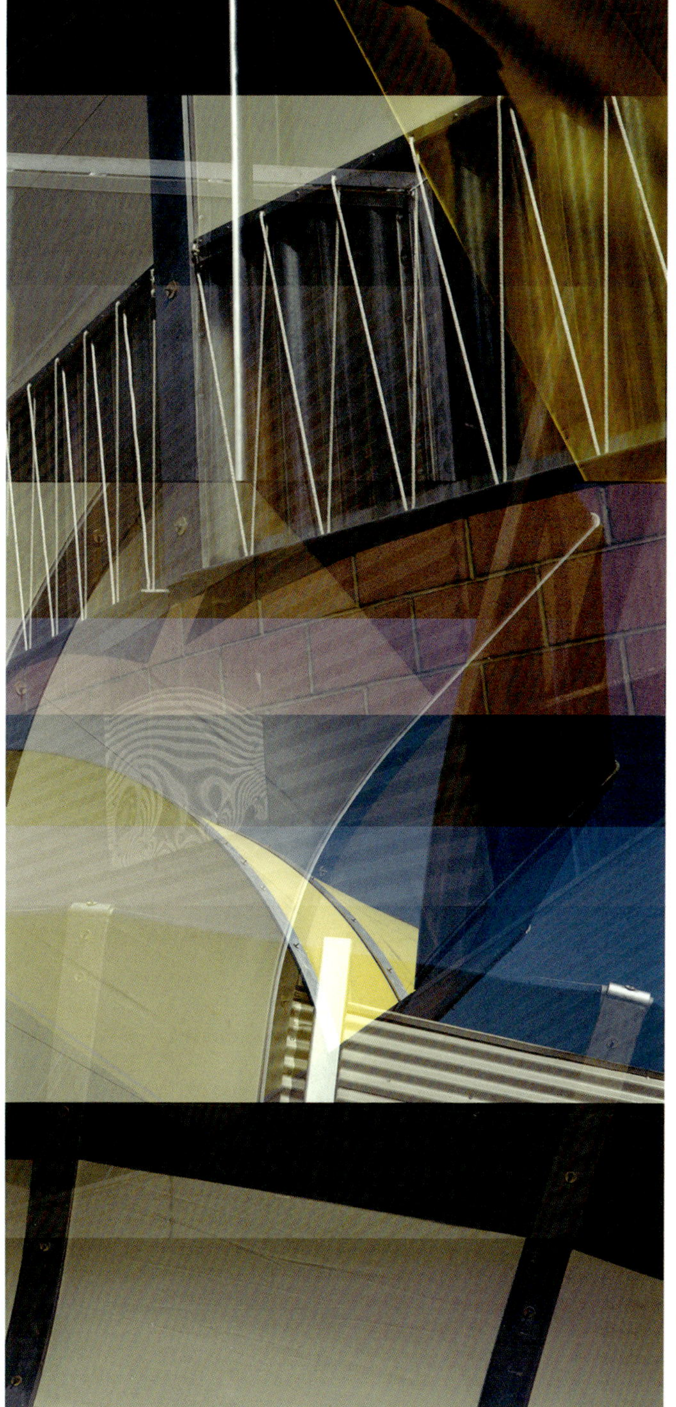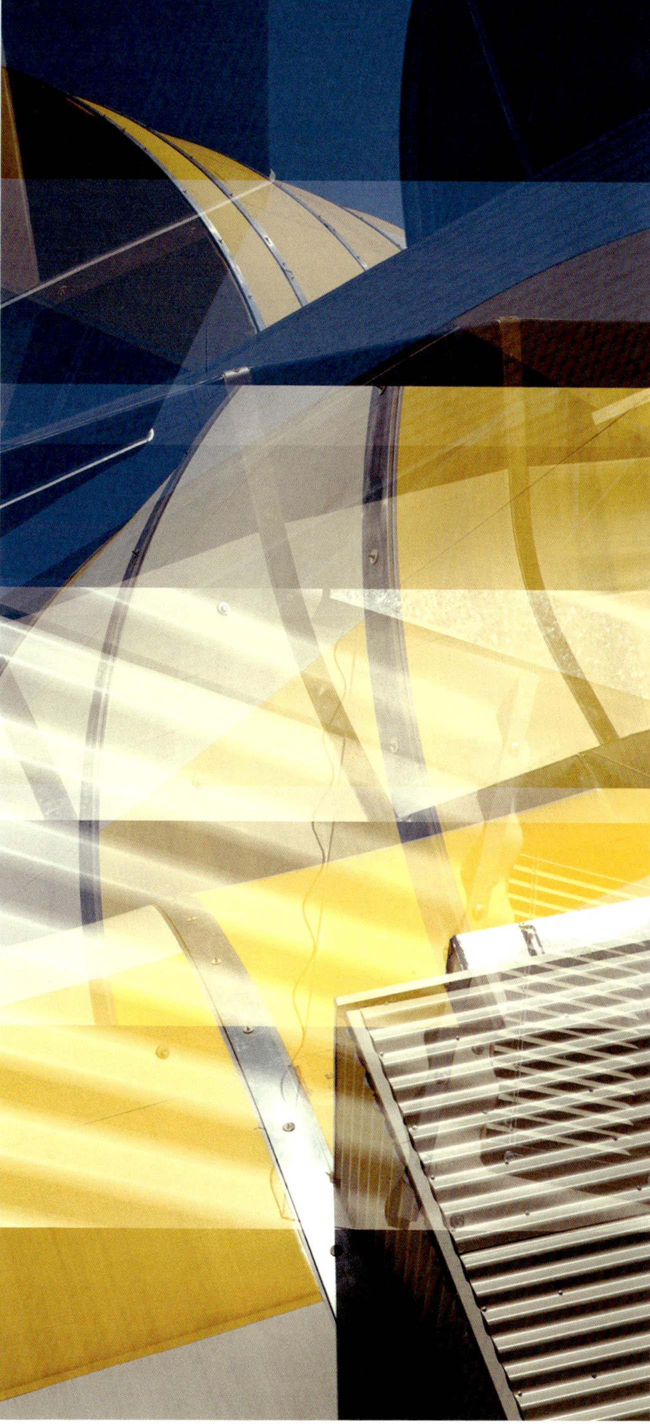

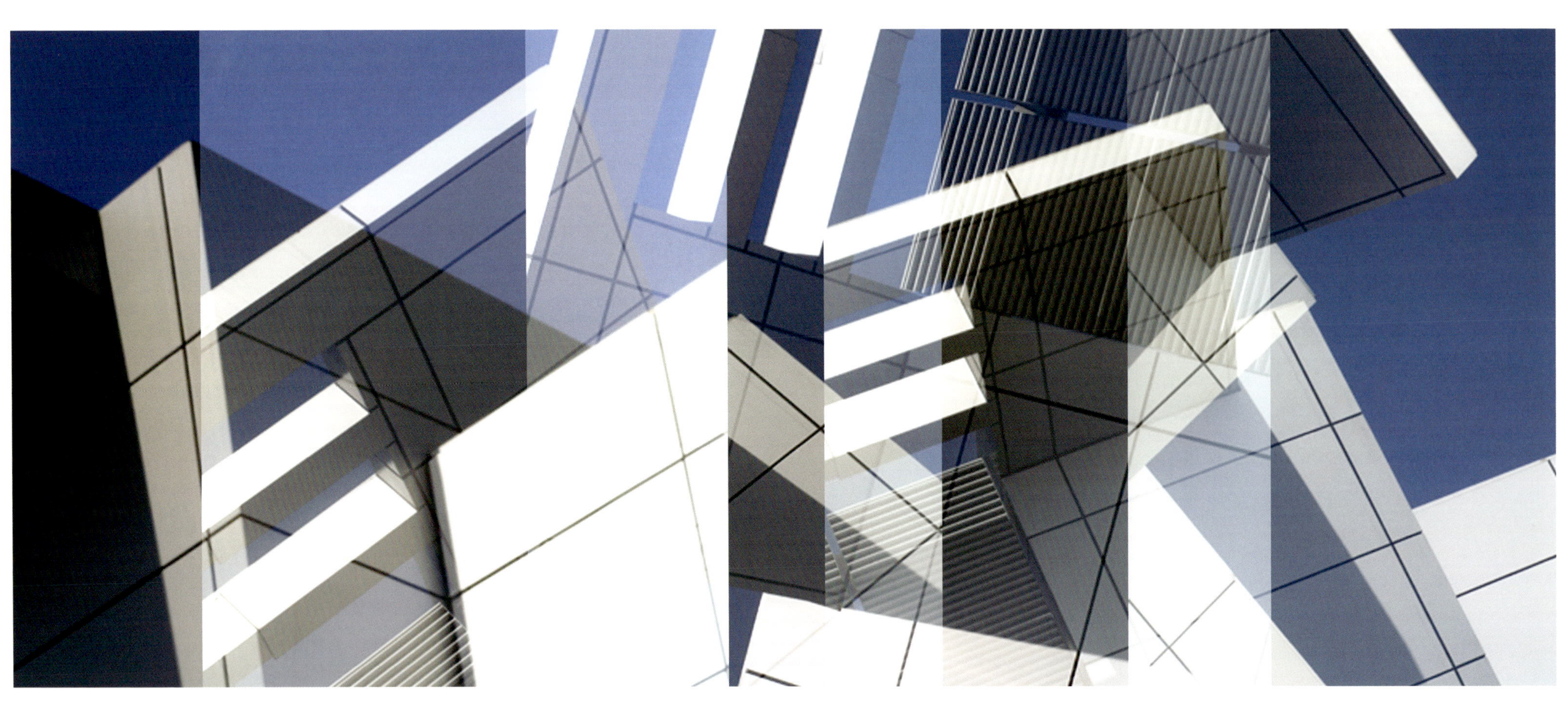

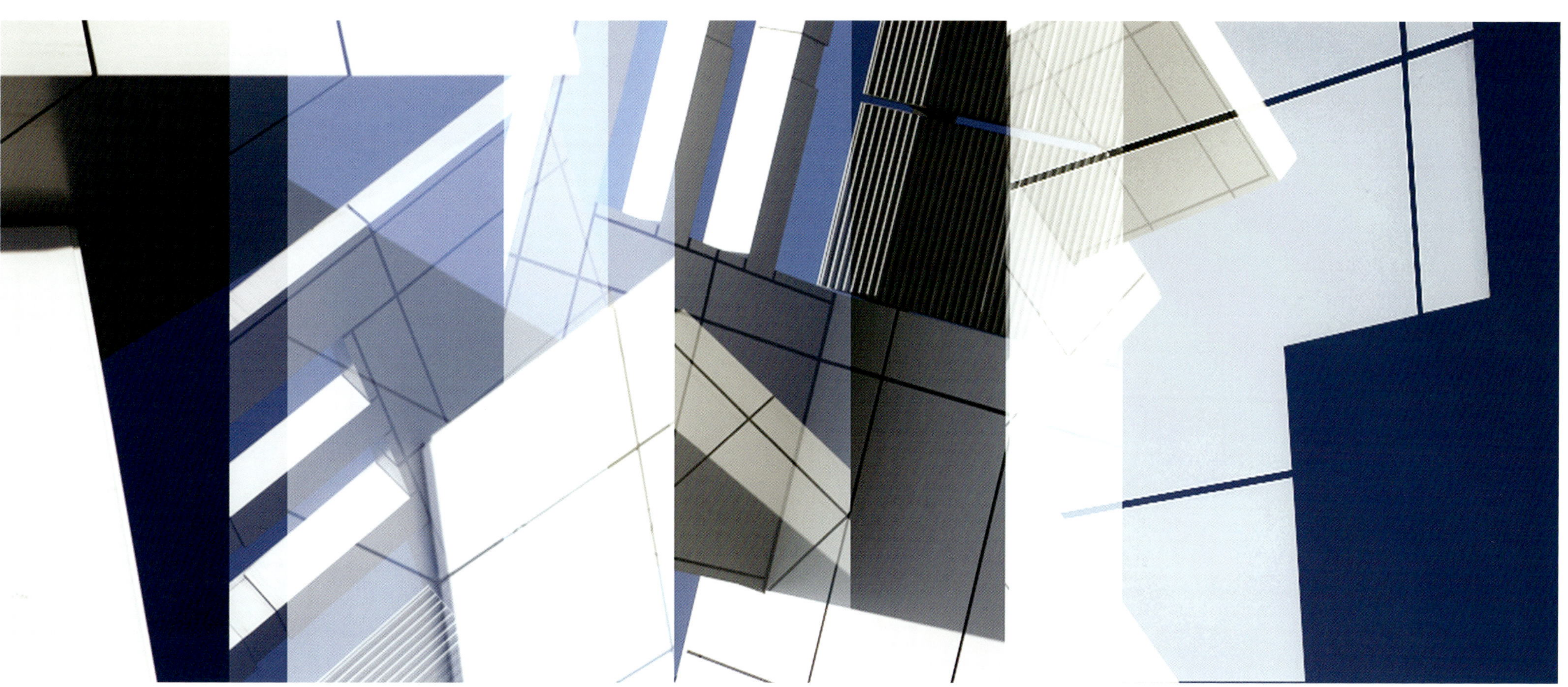

Binder 3   Orthopaedic Hospital Medical Center, Los Angeles, California, 2004   ARCHITECT: Rebecca Binder

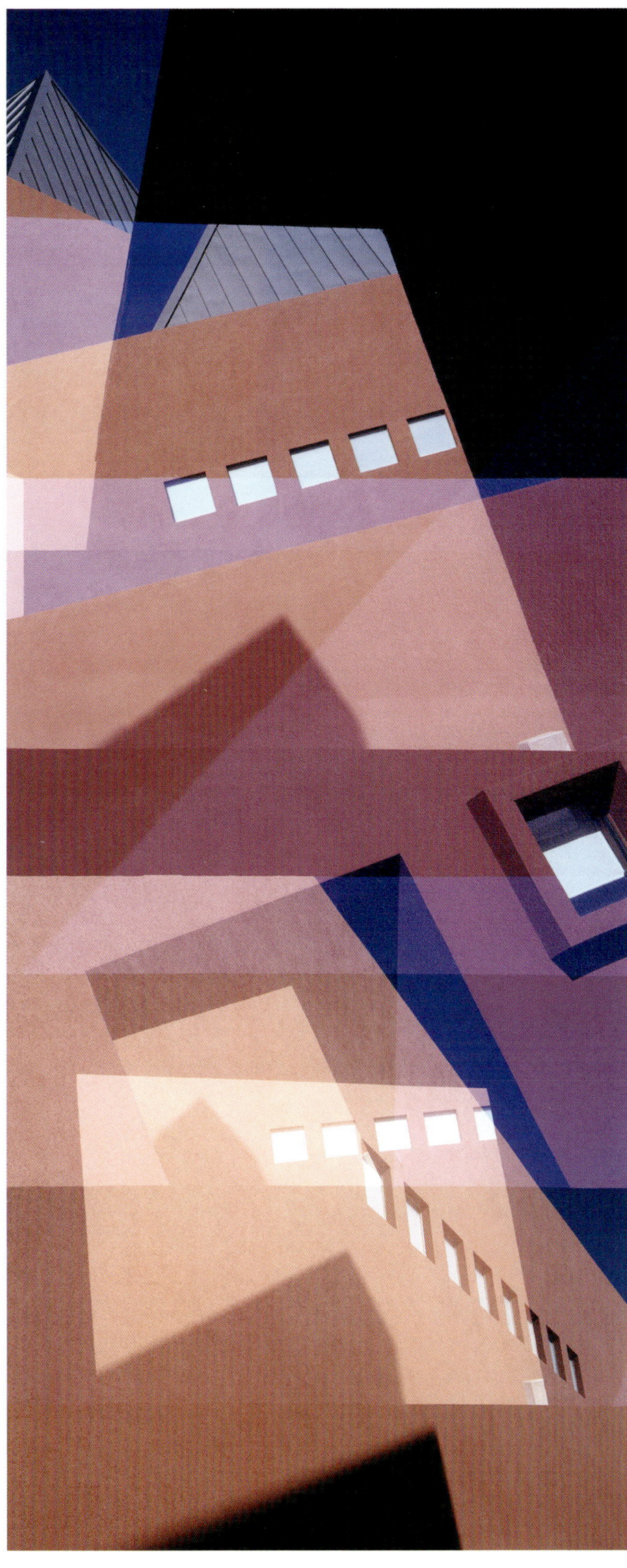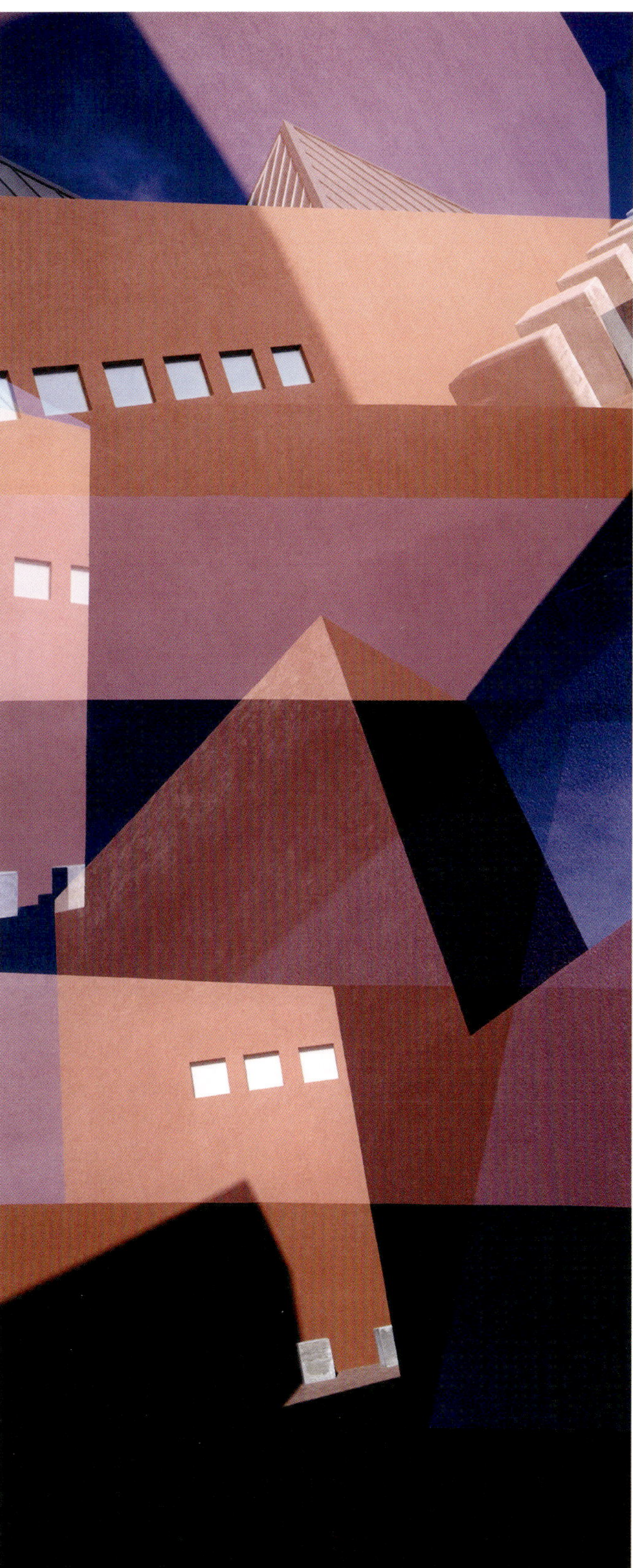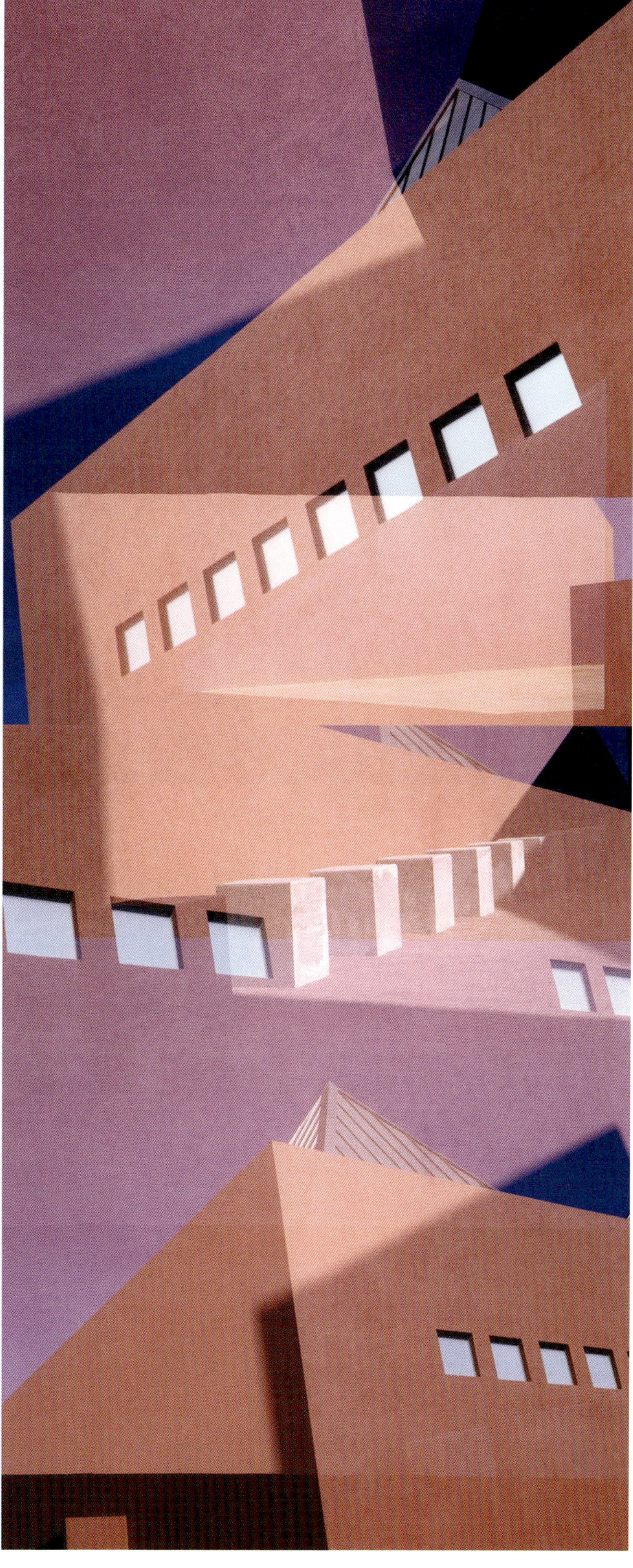

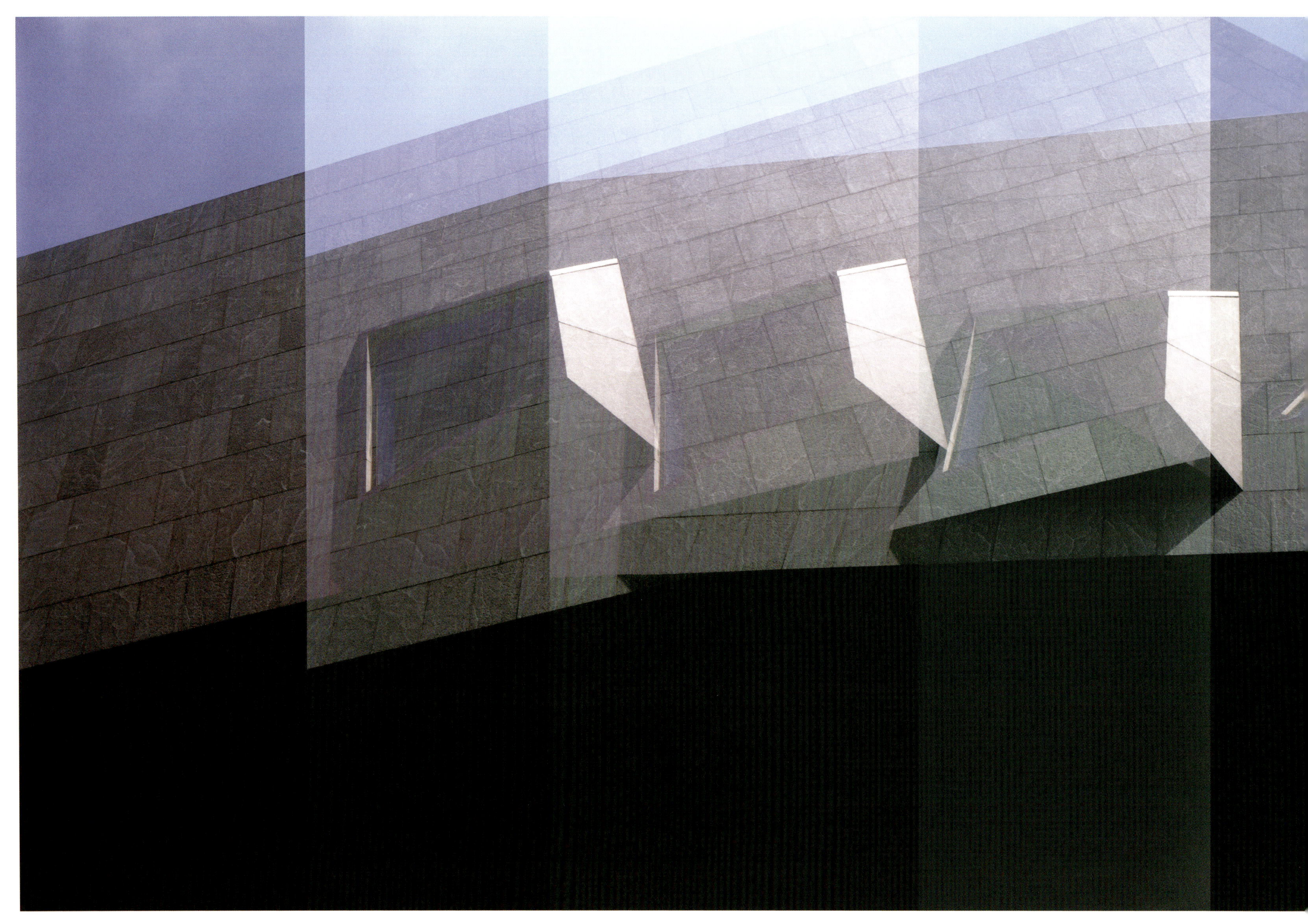

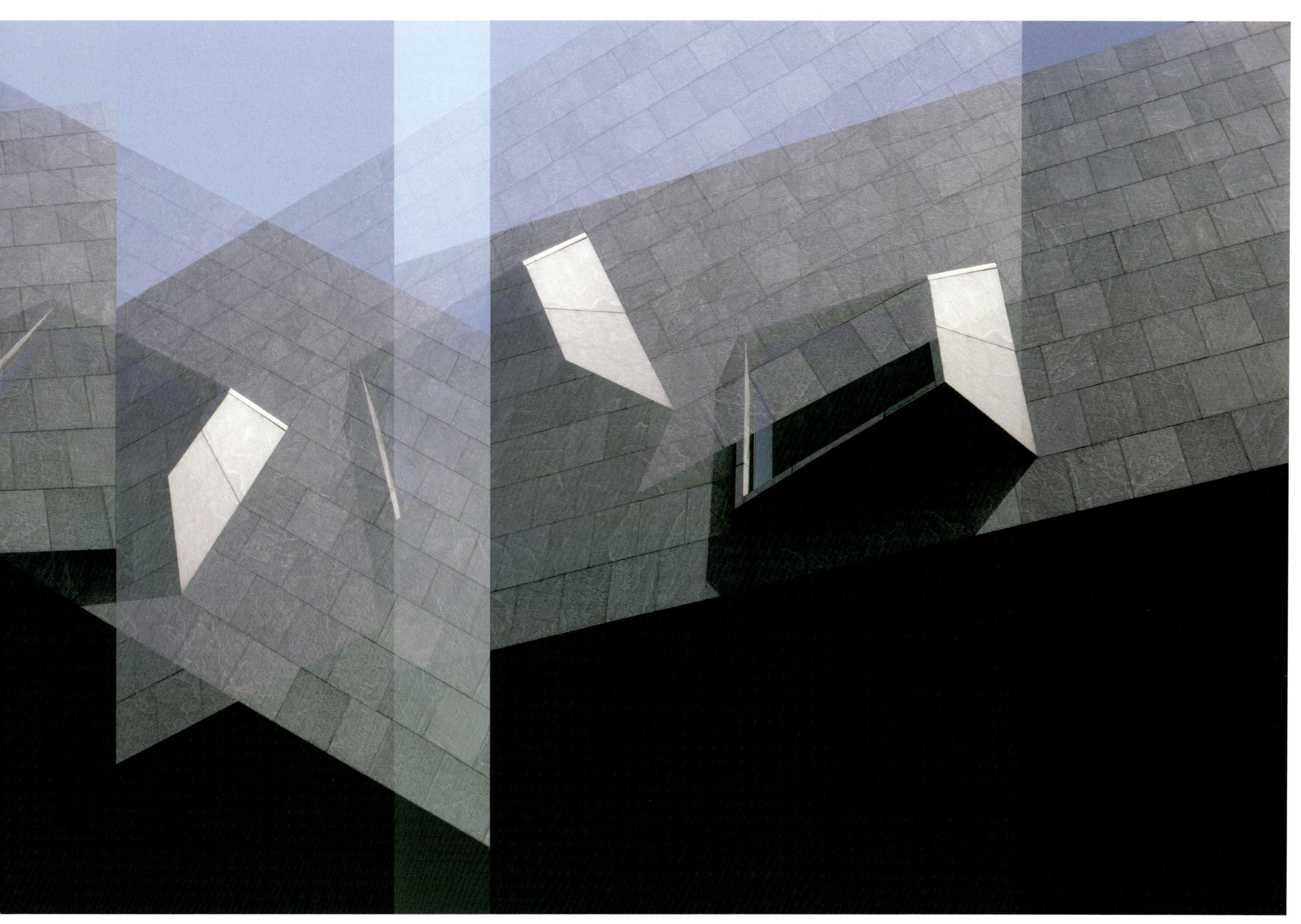

Whitney 9 Color   New York, New York, 2001   ARCHITECT: Marcel Breuer

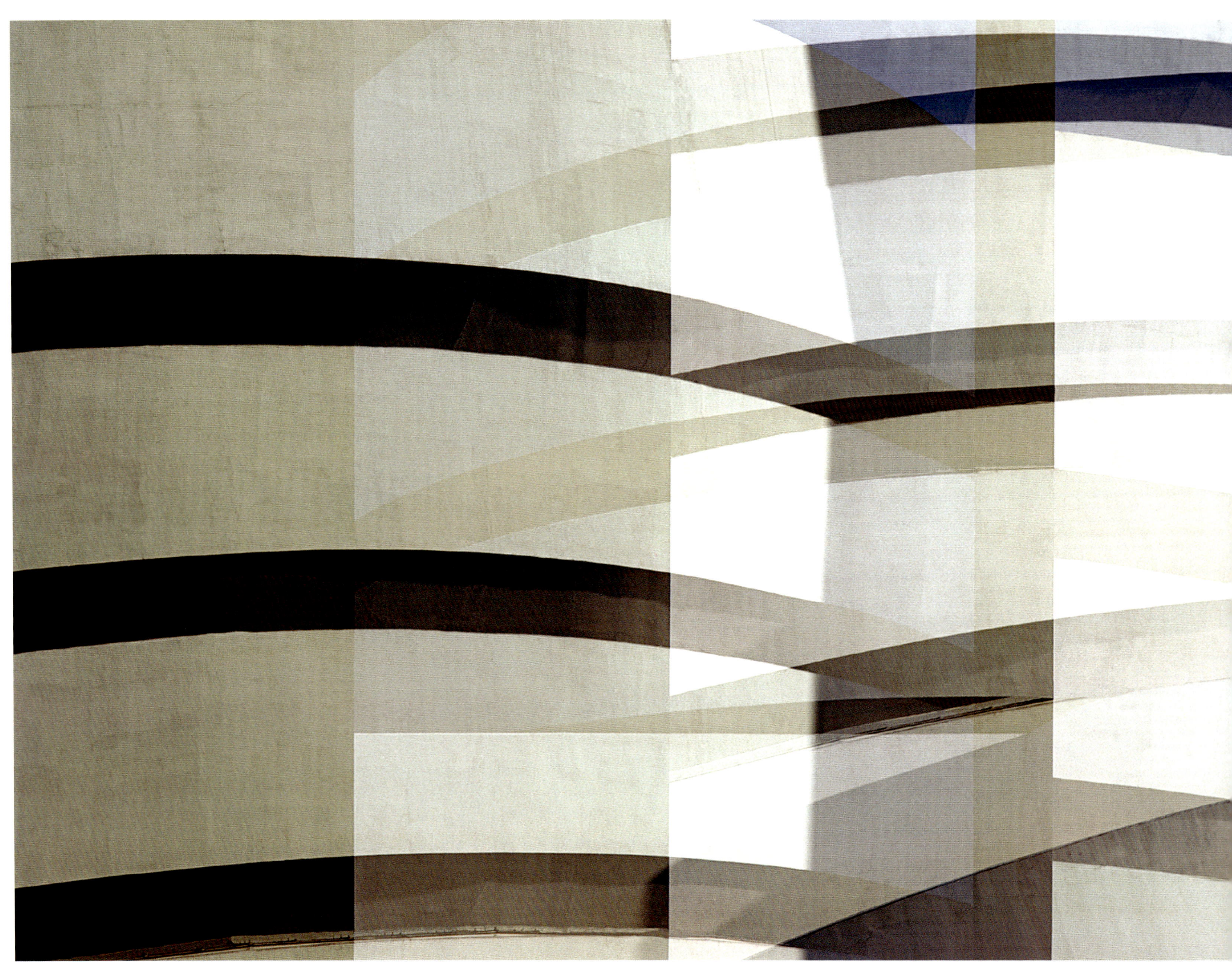

Guggenheim   New York, New York, 1986   ARCHITECT: Frank Lloyd Wright

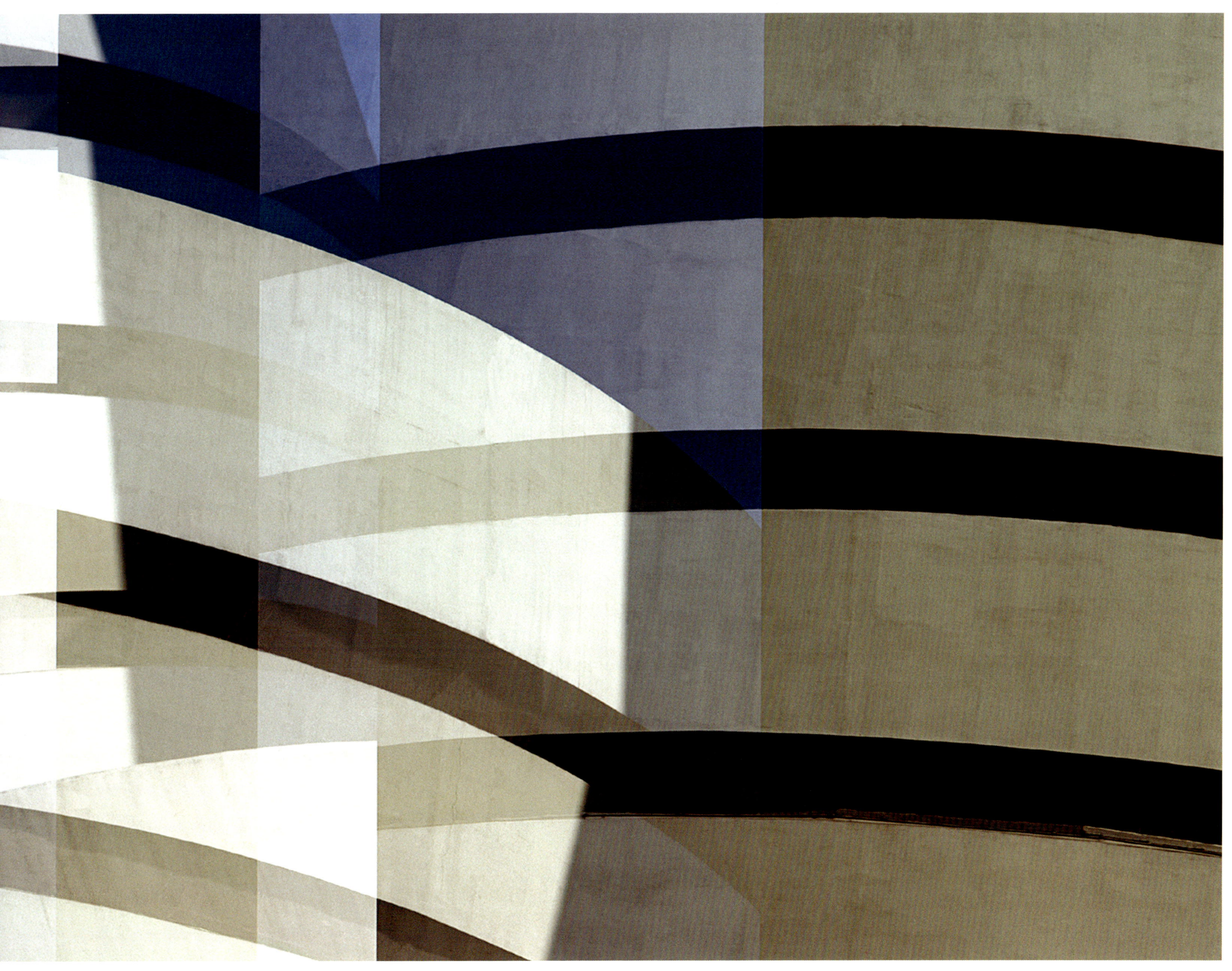

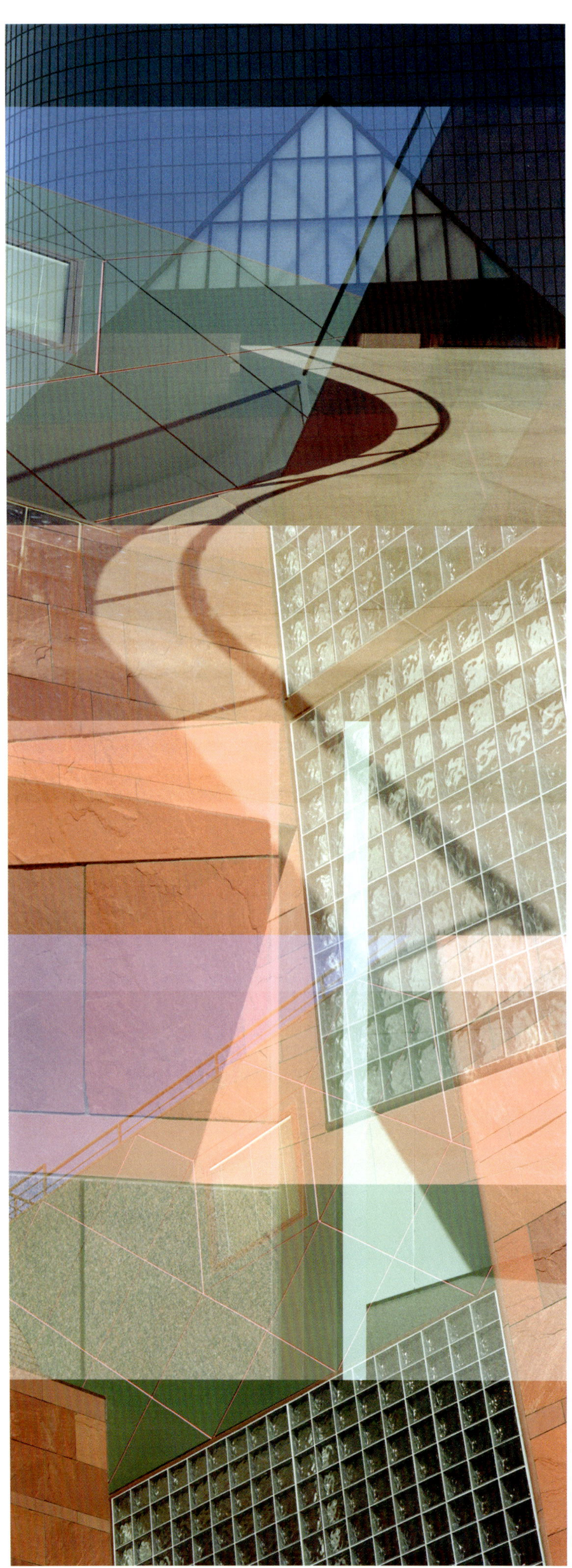

Isozaki's L.A. MOCA Pyramid   Los Angeles, California, 1987   ARCHITECT: Arata Isozaki

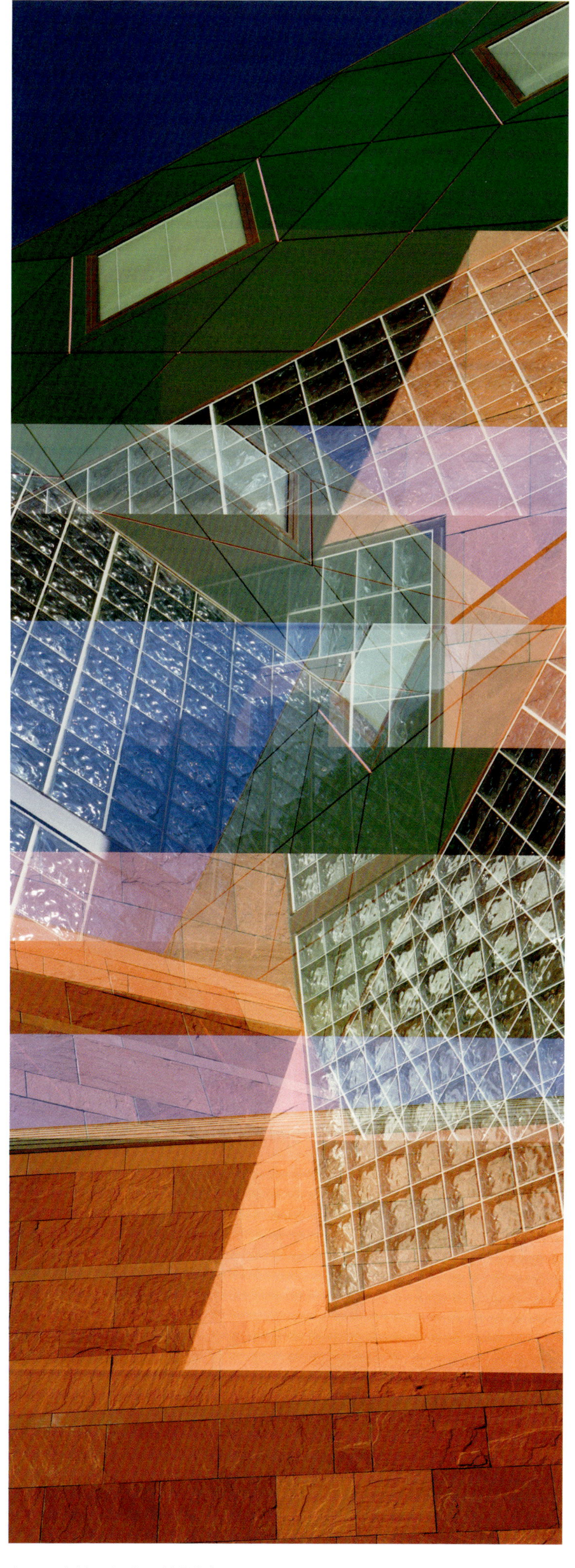

Isozaki's L.A. MOCA Los Angeles, California, 1987 ARCHITECT: Arata Isozaki

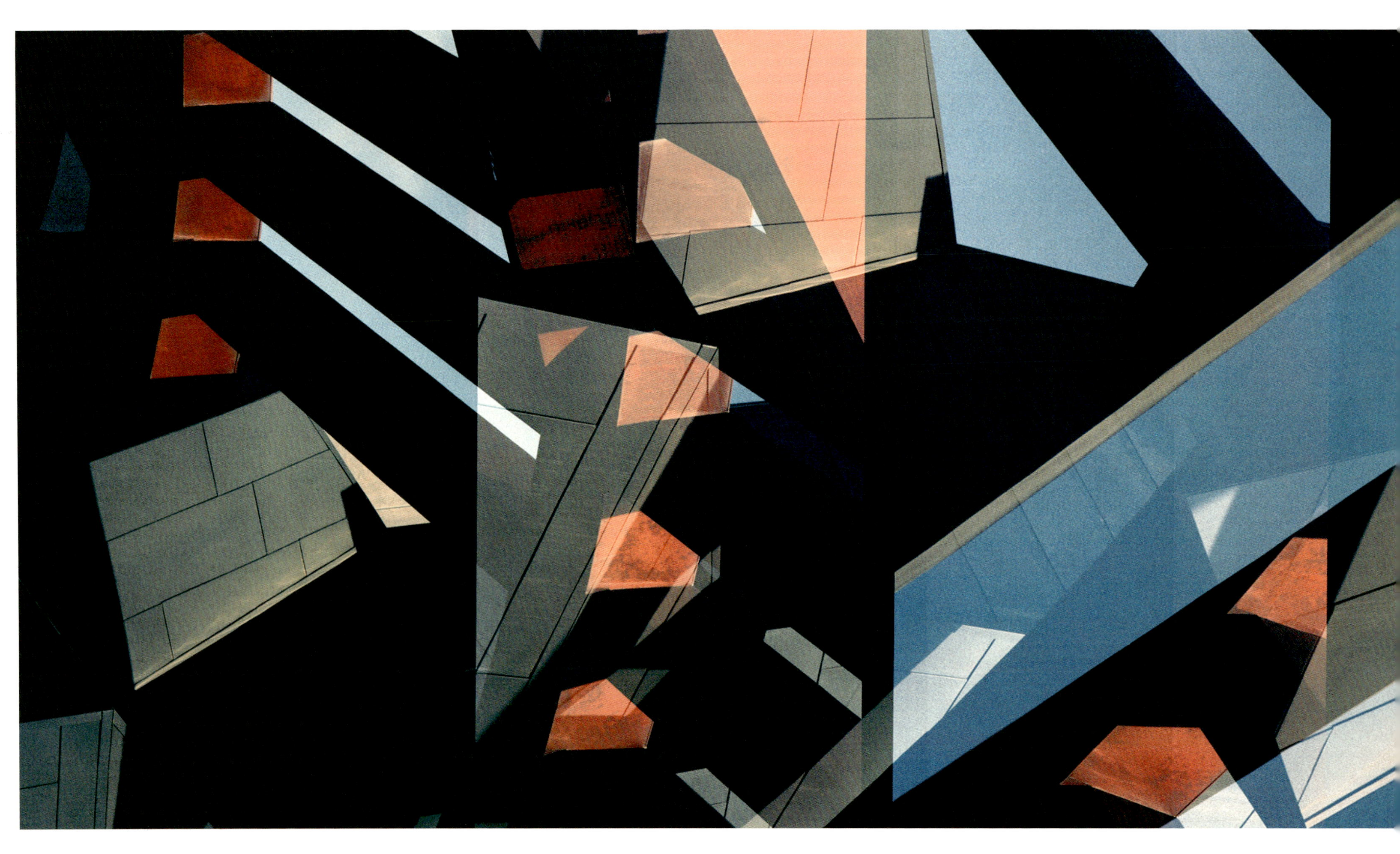

Gehry Irvine Overhang I   Los Angeles, California, 1991   ARCHITECT: Frank O. Gehry & Associates

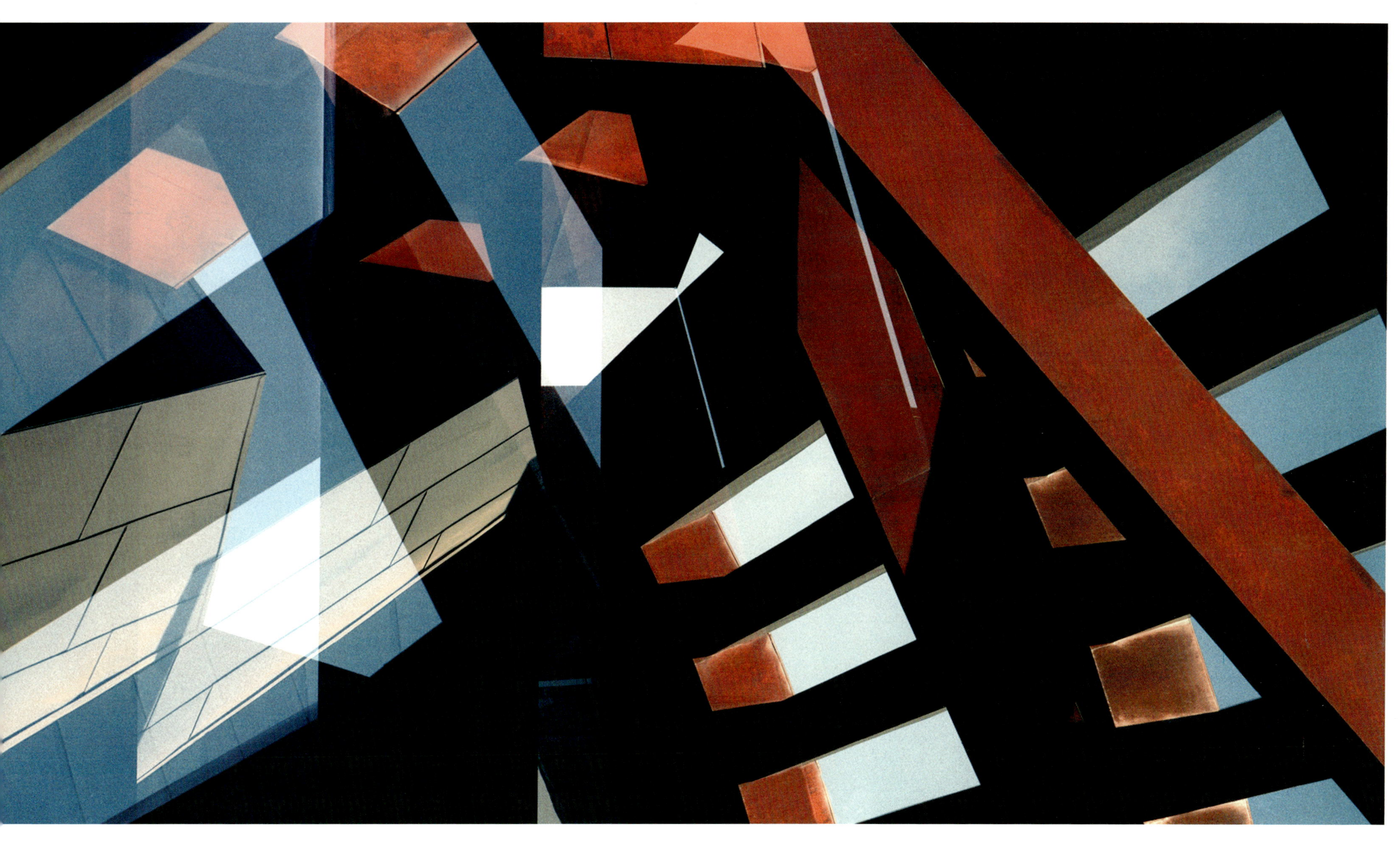

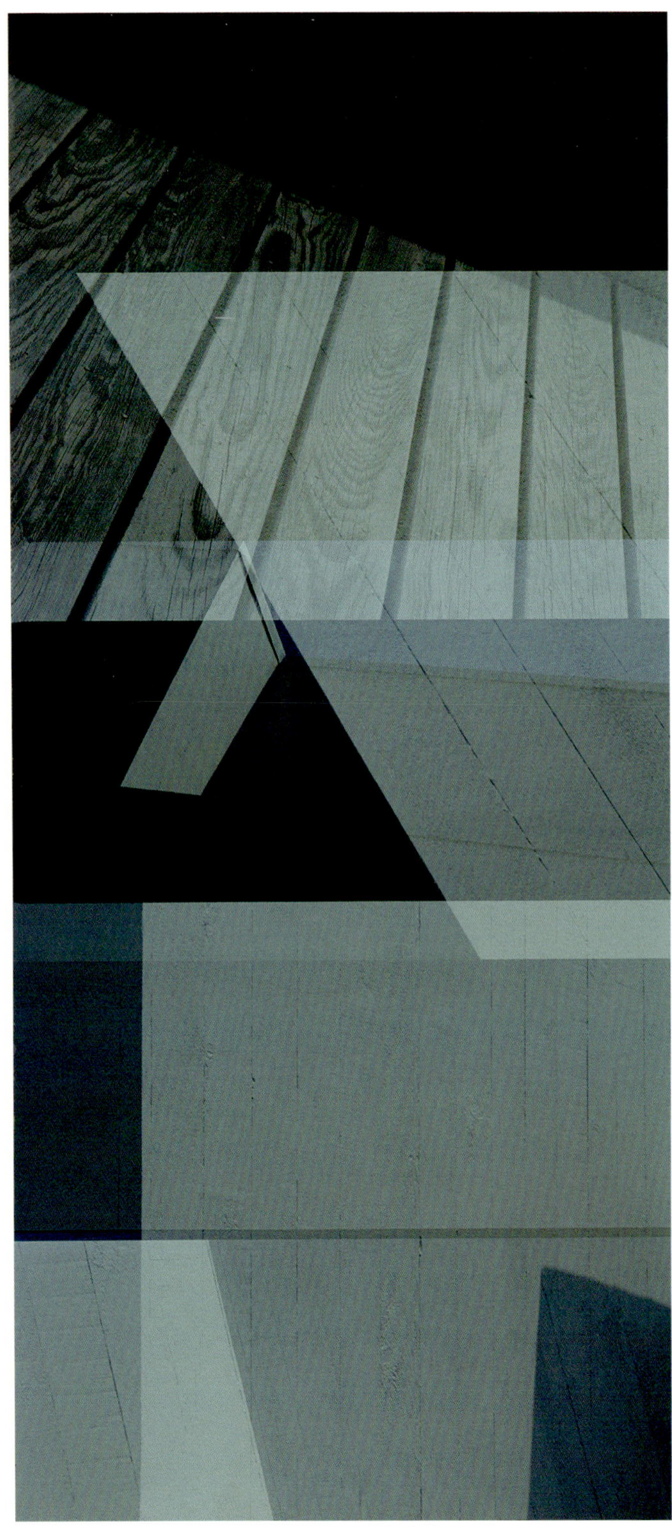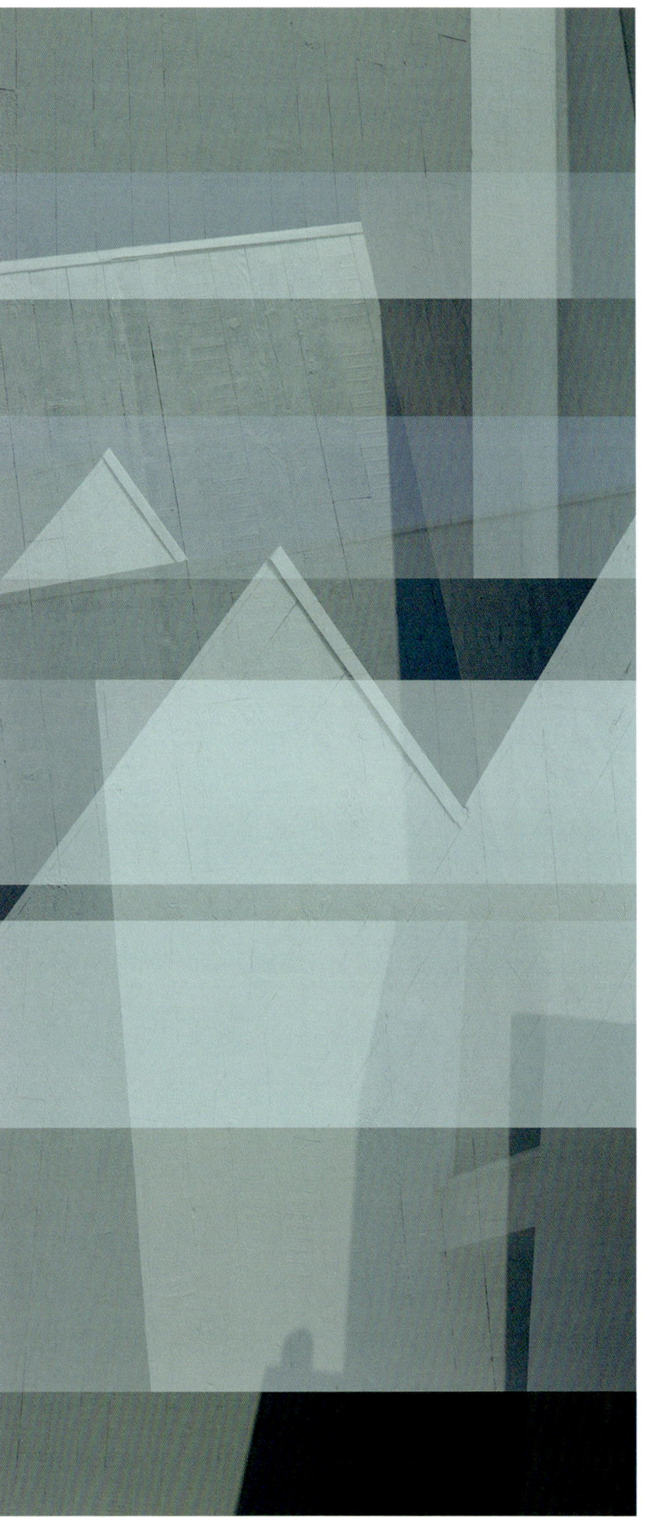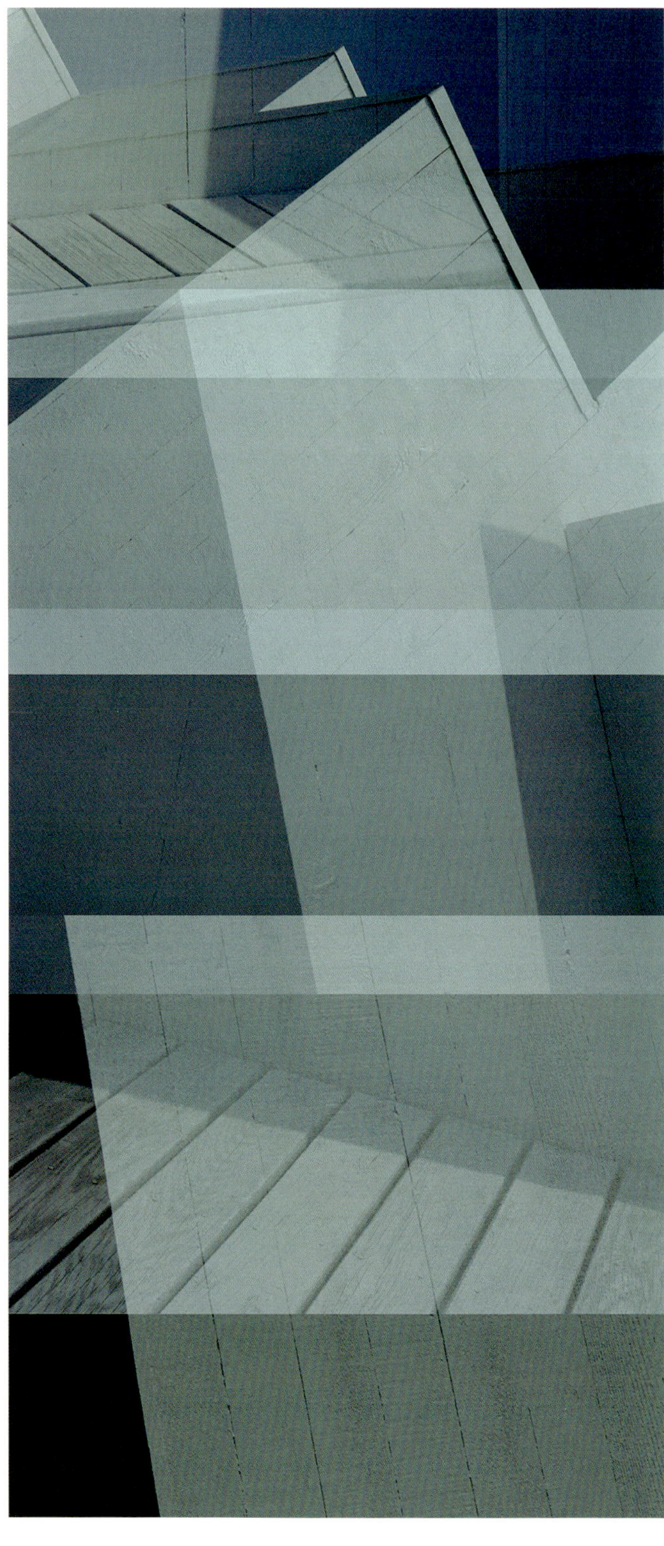

White House Triptych   Amagansett, New York, 1995   ARCHITECT: Don Chappell

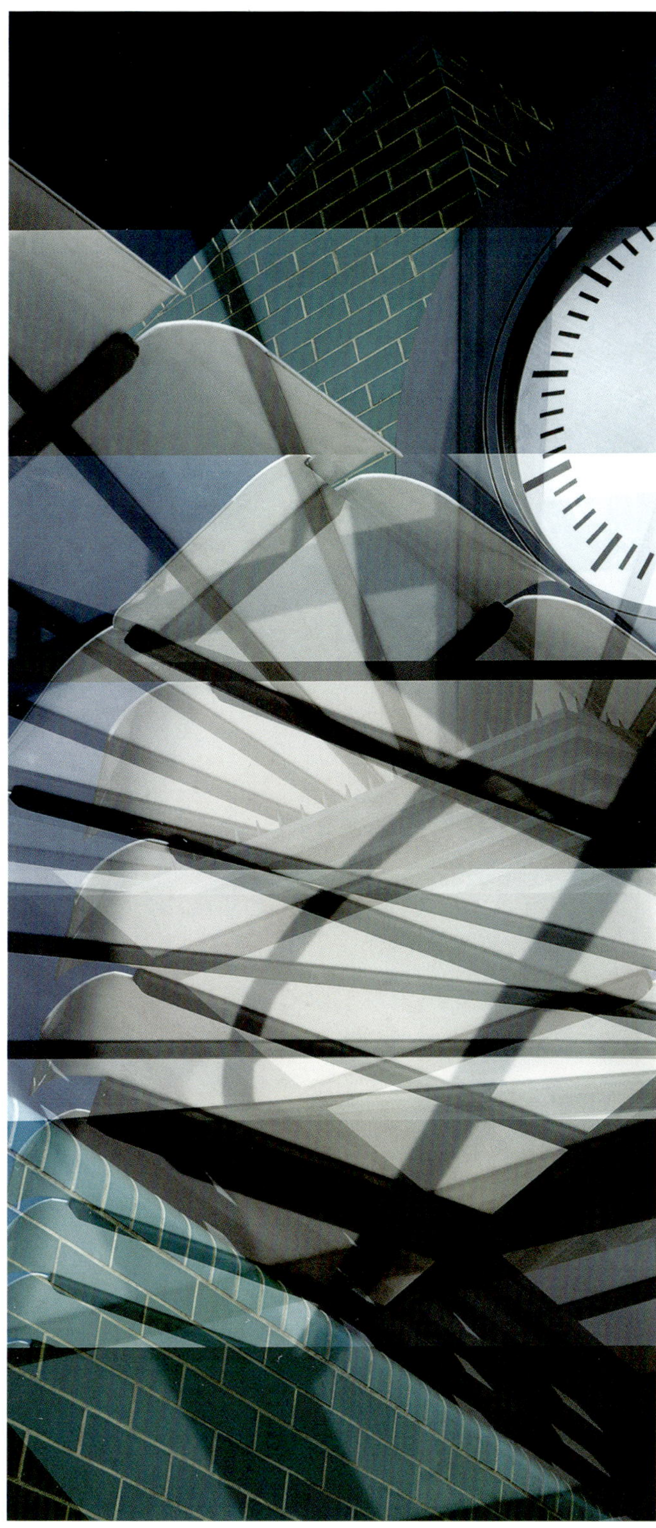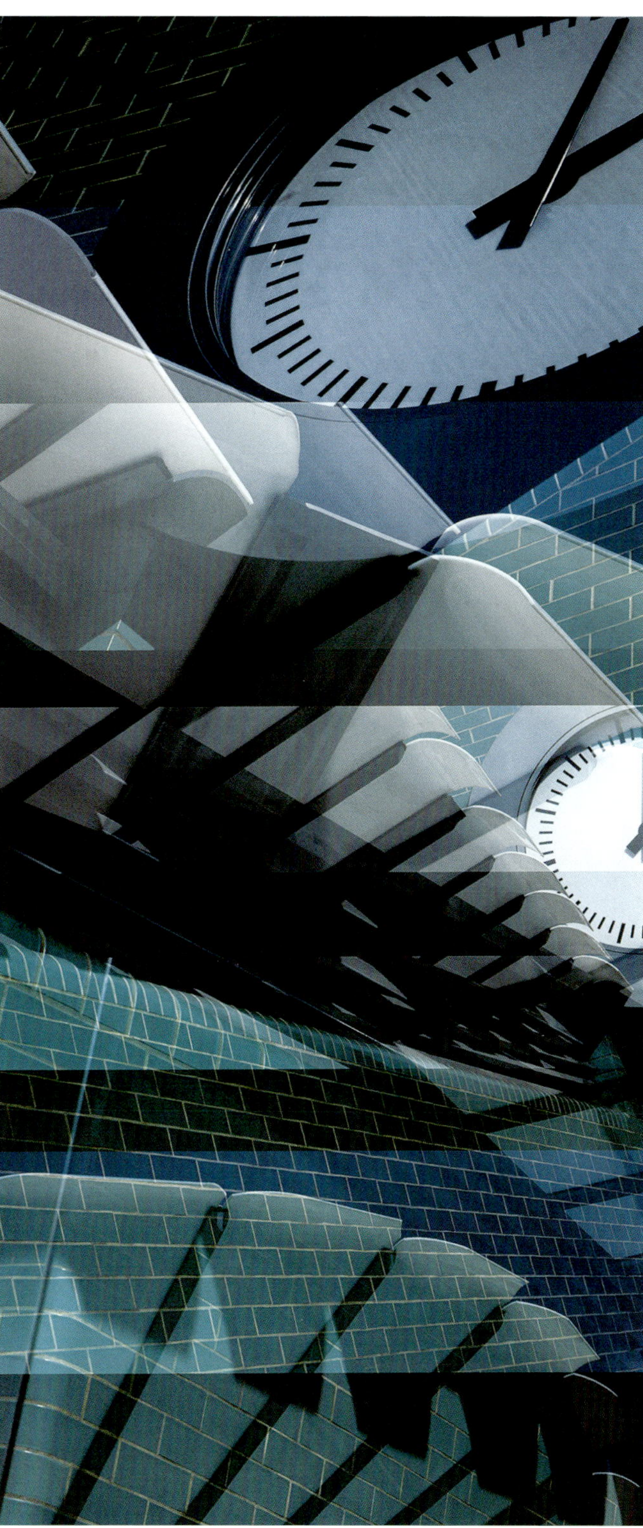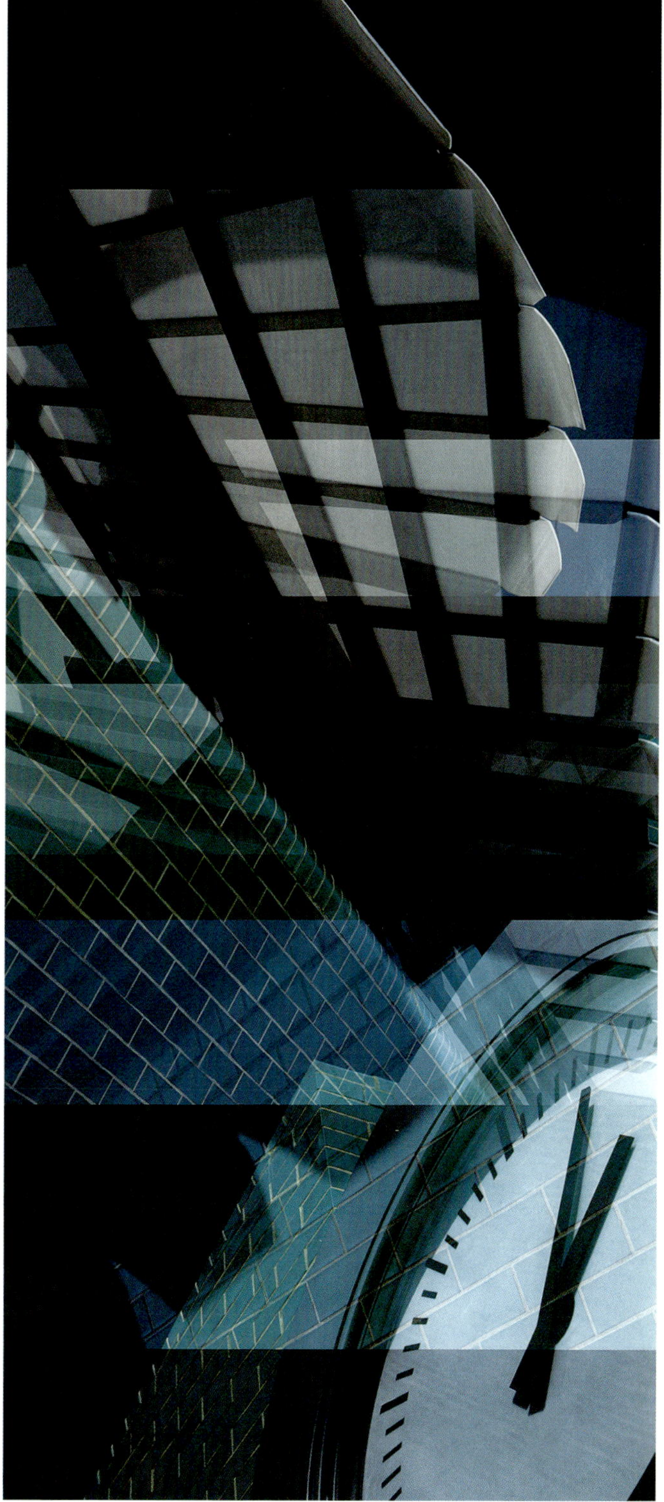

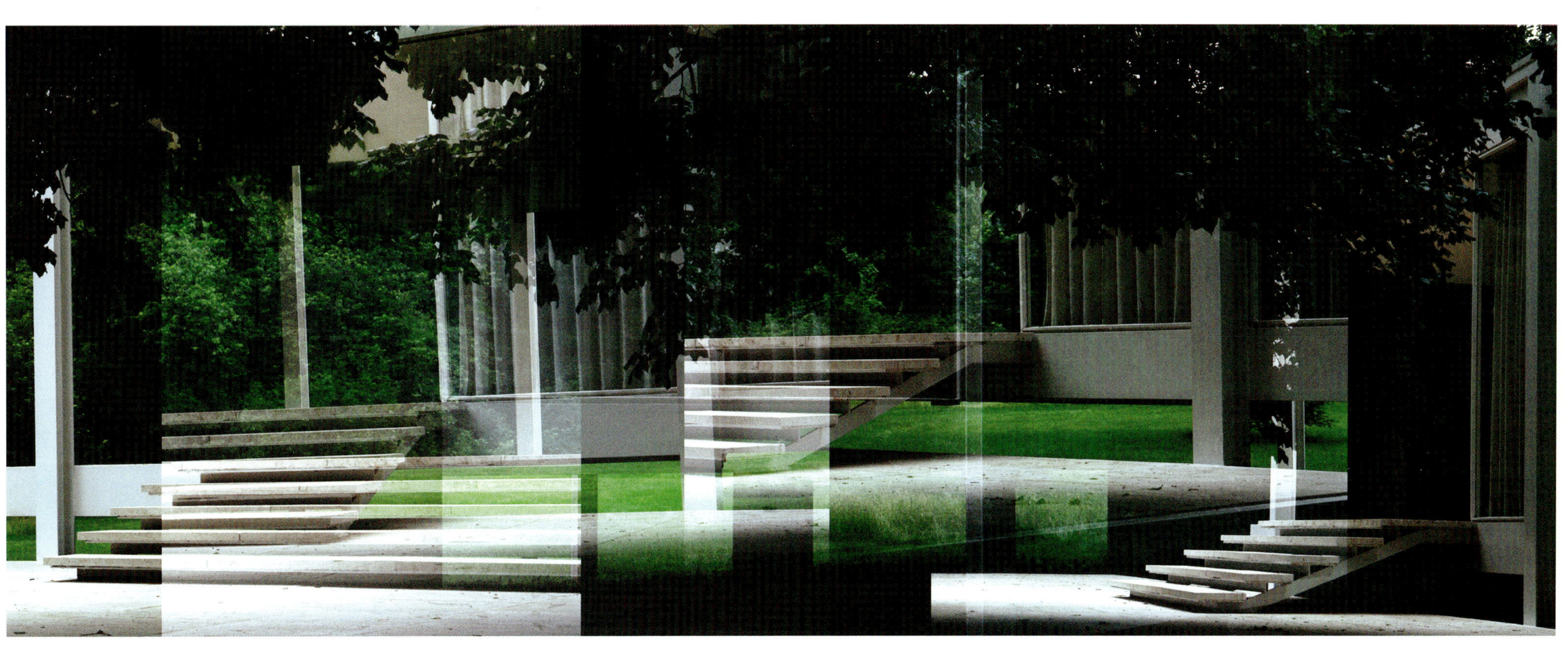

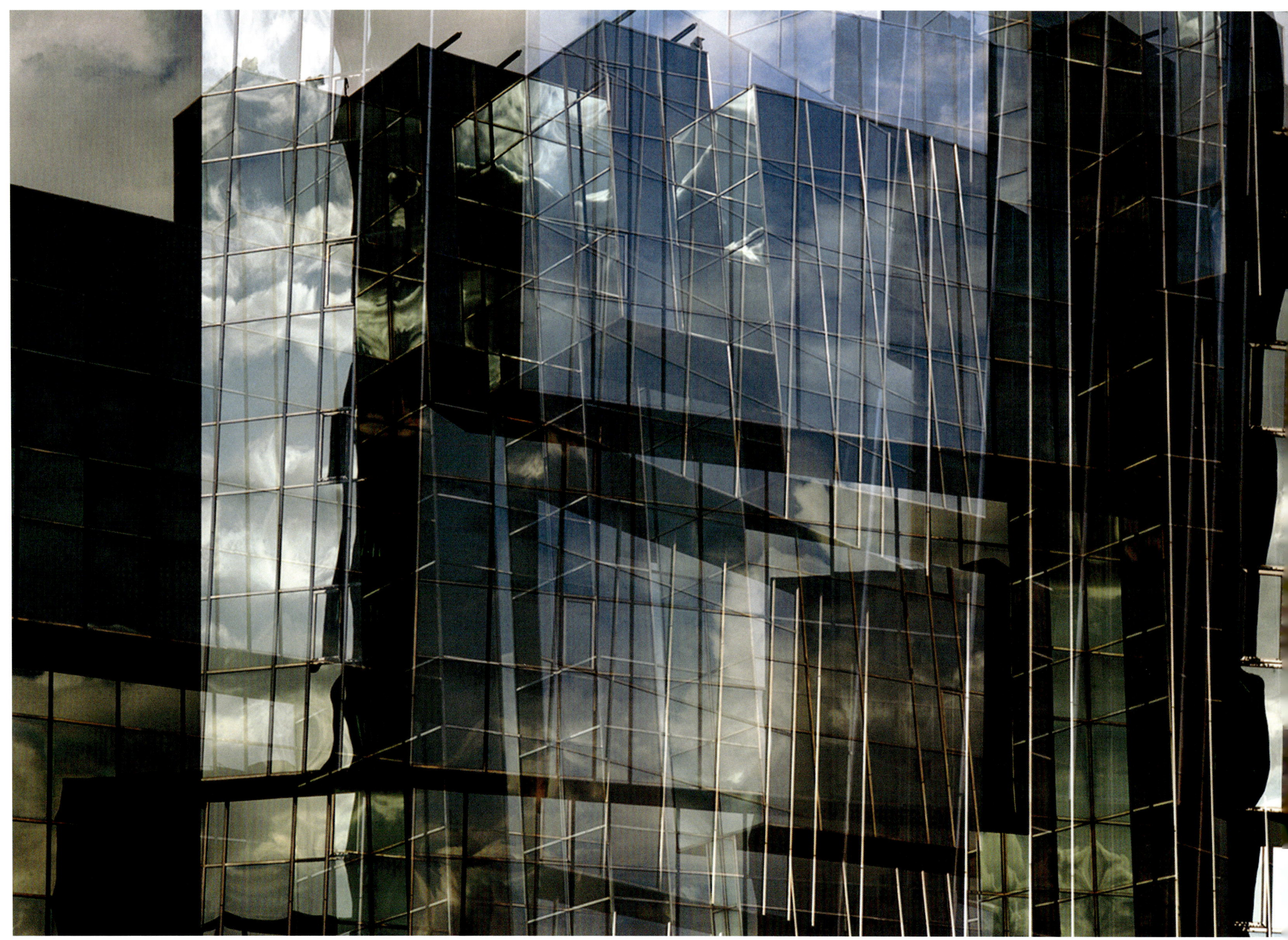

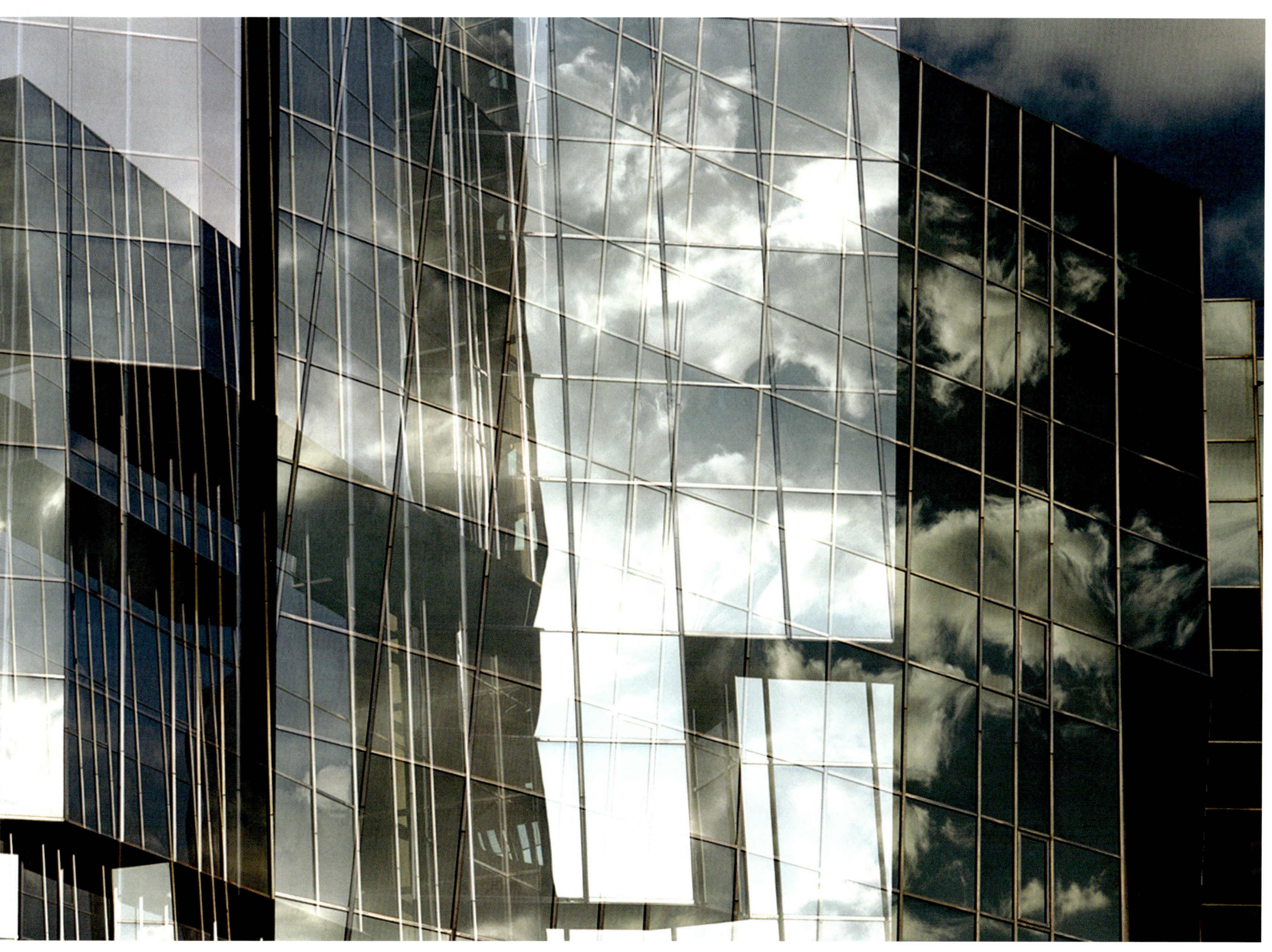

250 Euston Road   London, England, 2000   ARCHITECT: RHWL Partnership

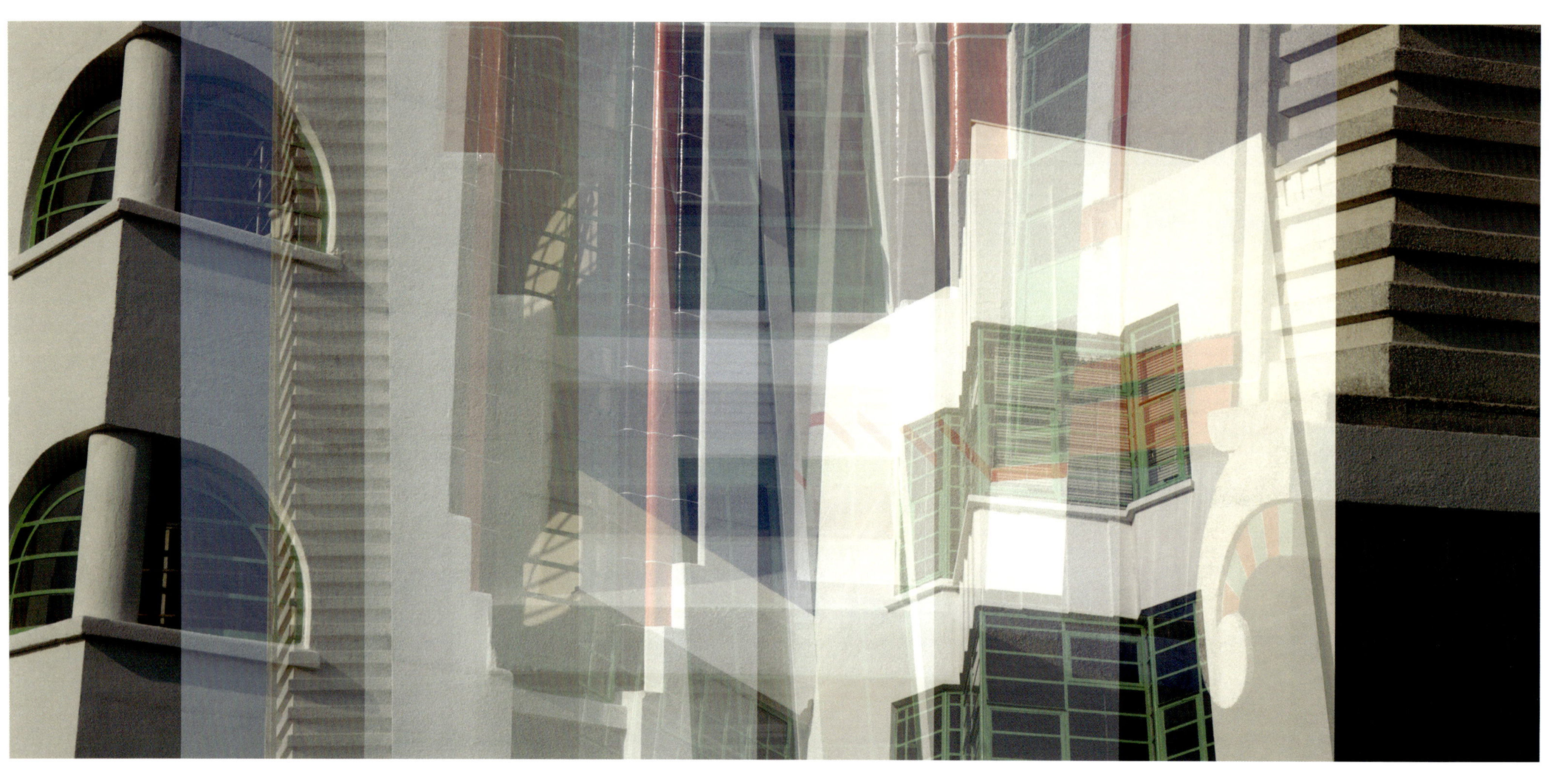

Hoover II RIBA   London, England, 1985   ARCHITECT: Wallis Gilbert & Partners

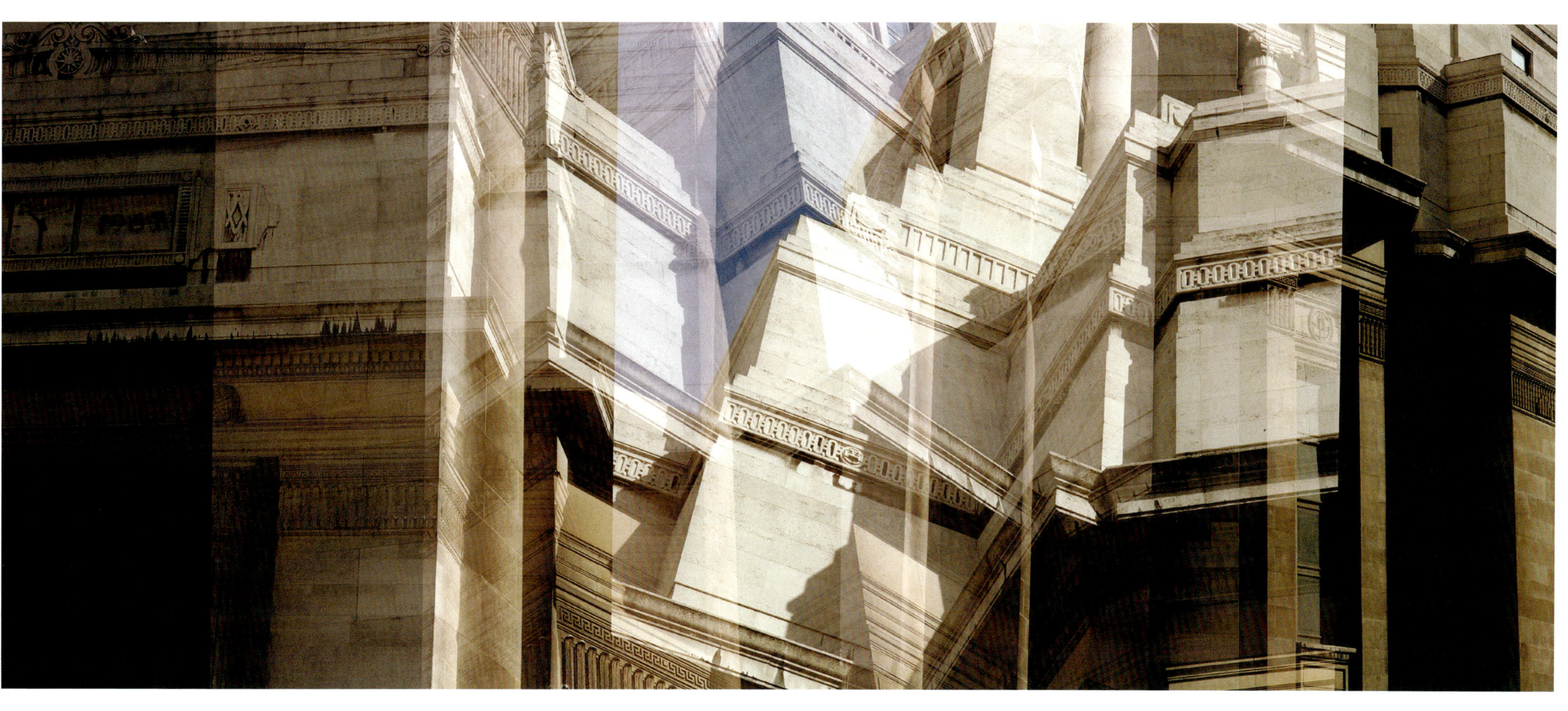

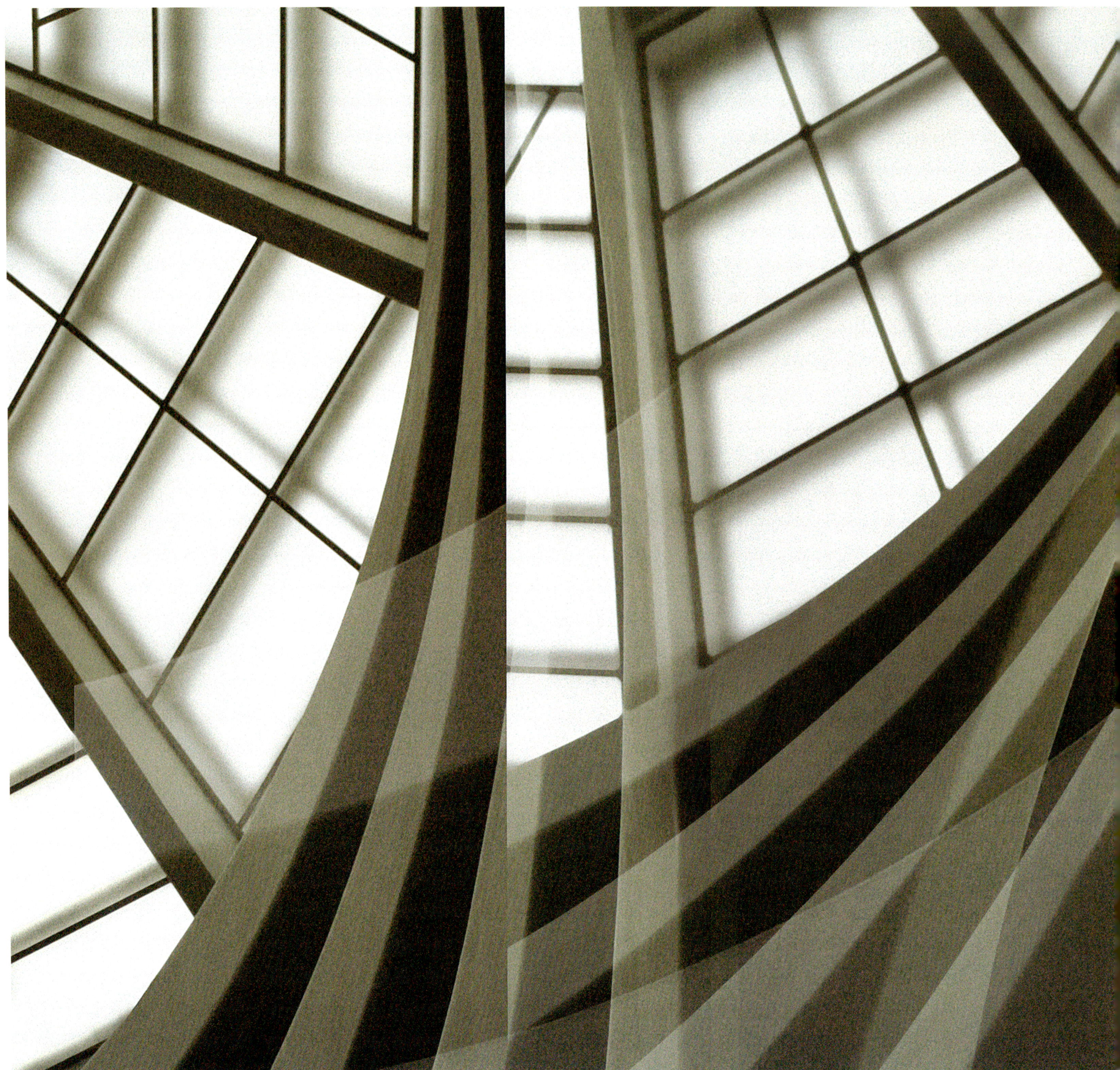

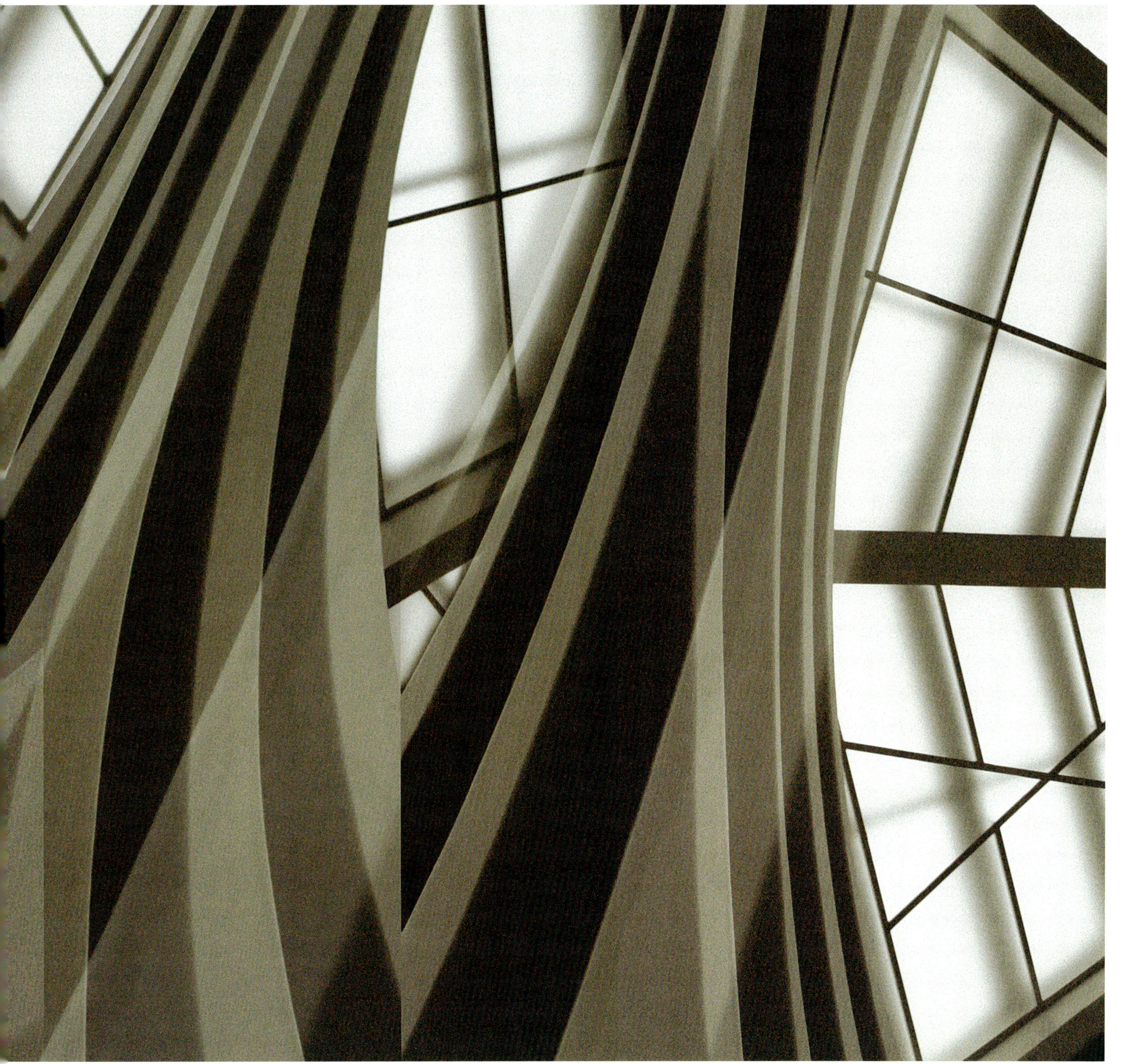

Guggenheim Skylight   New York, New York, 2005   ARCHITECT: Frank Lloyd Wright

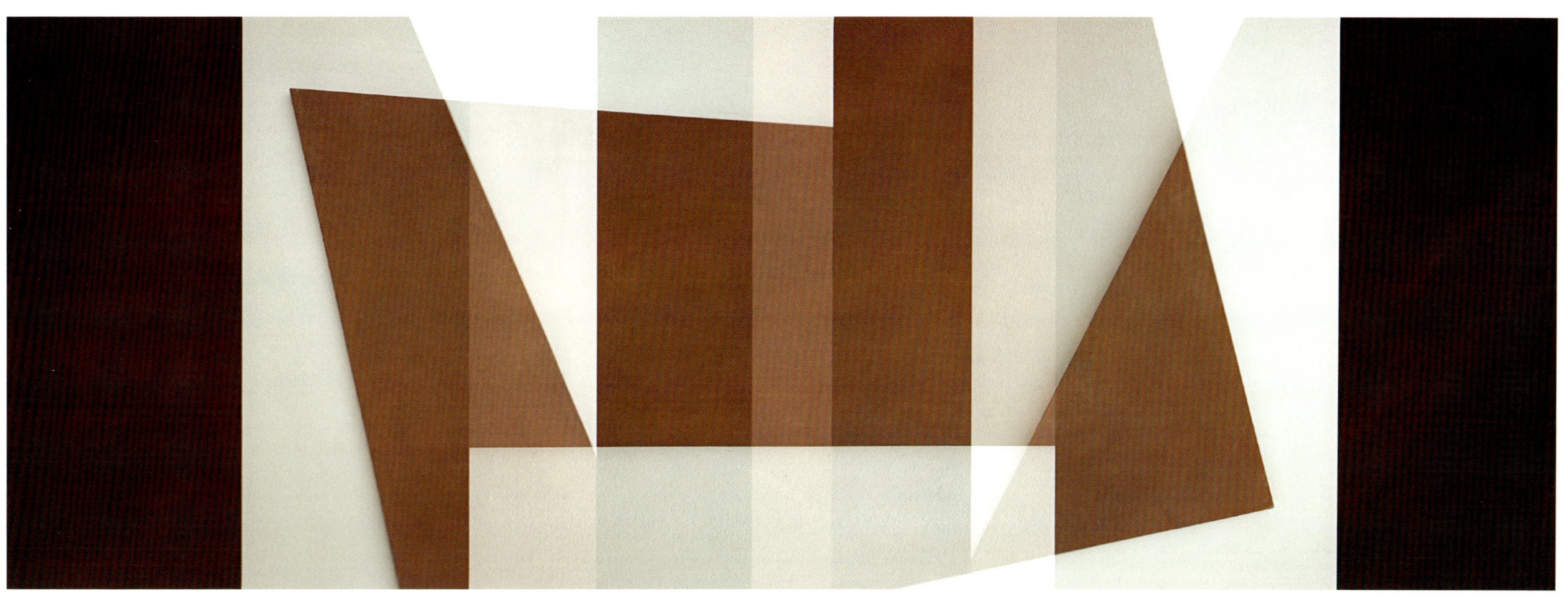

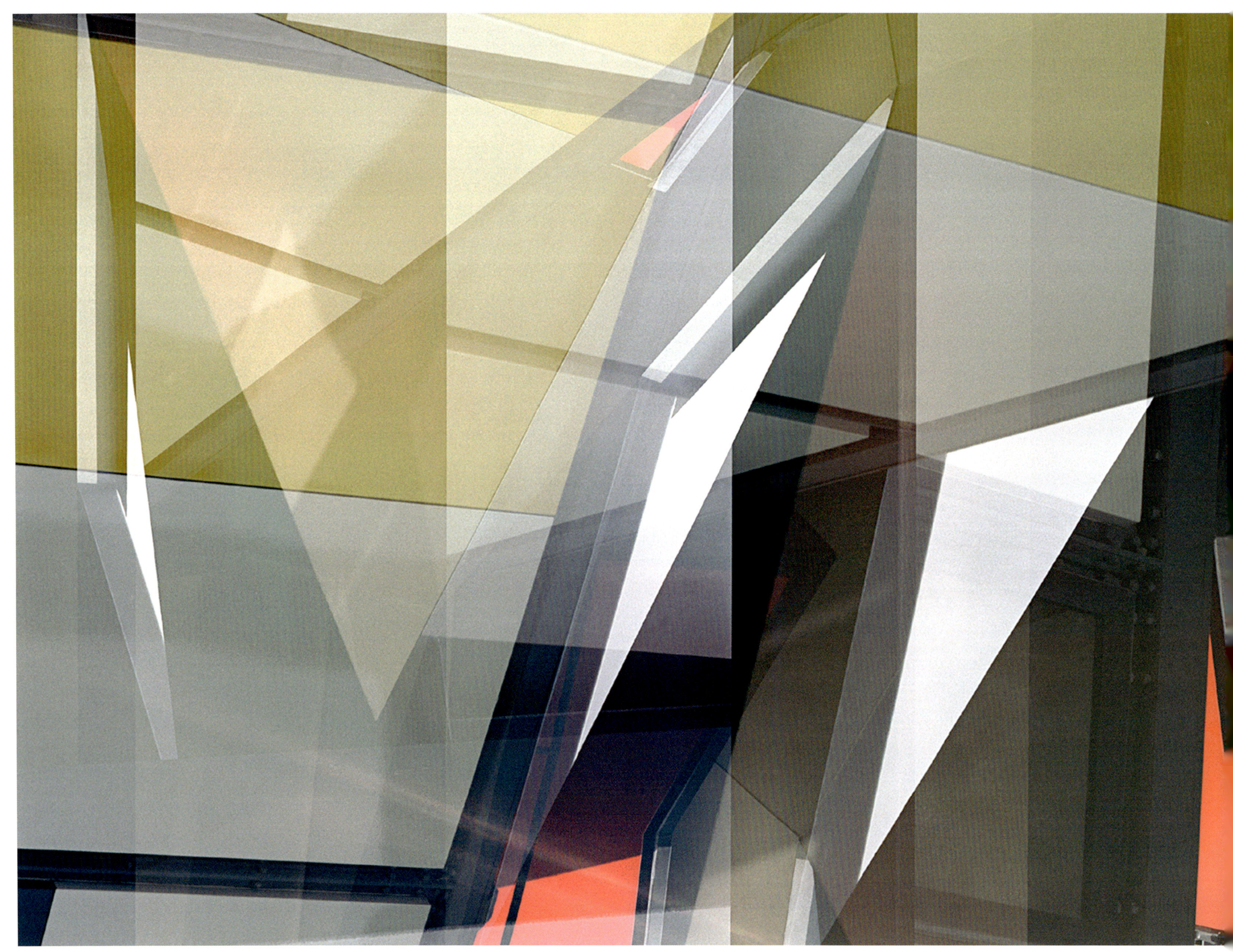

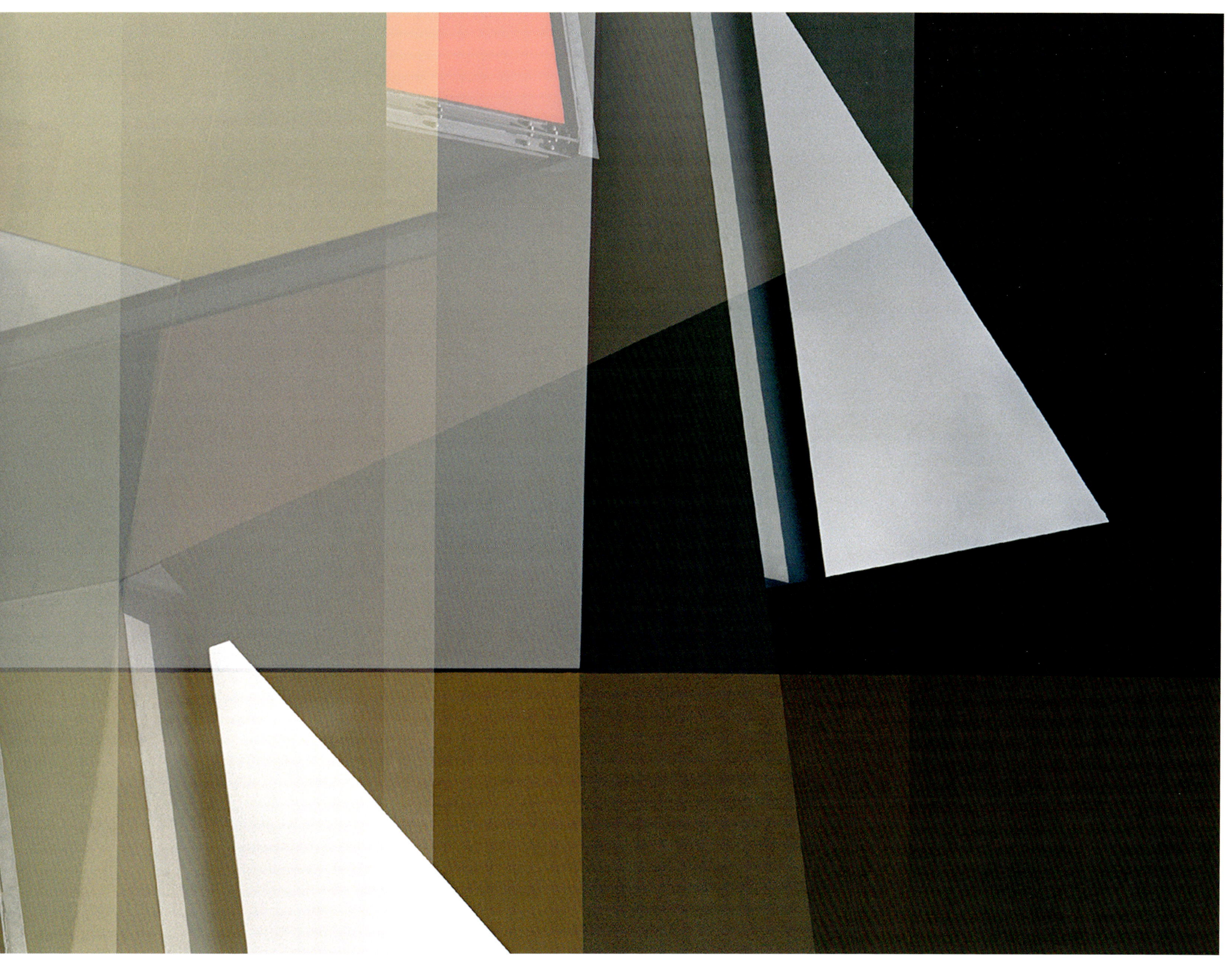

Centre Corbusier   Zurich, Switzwerland, 1988   ARCHITECT: Le Corbusier

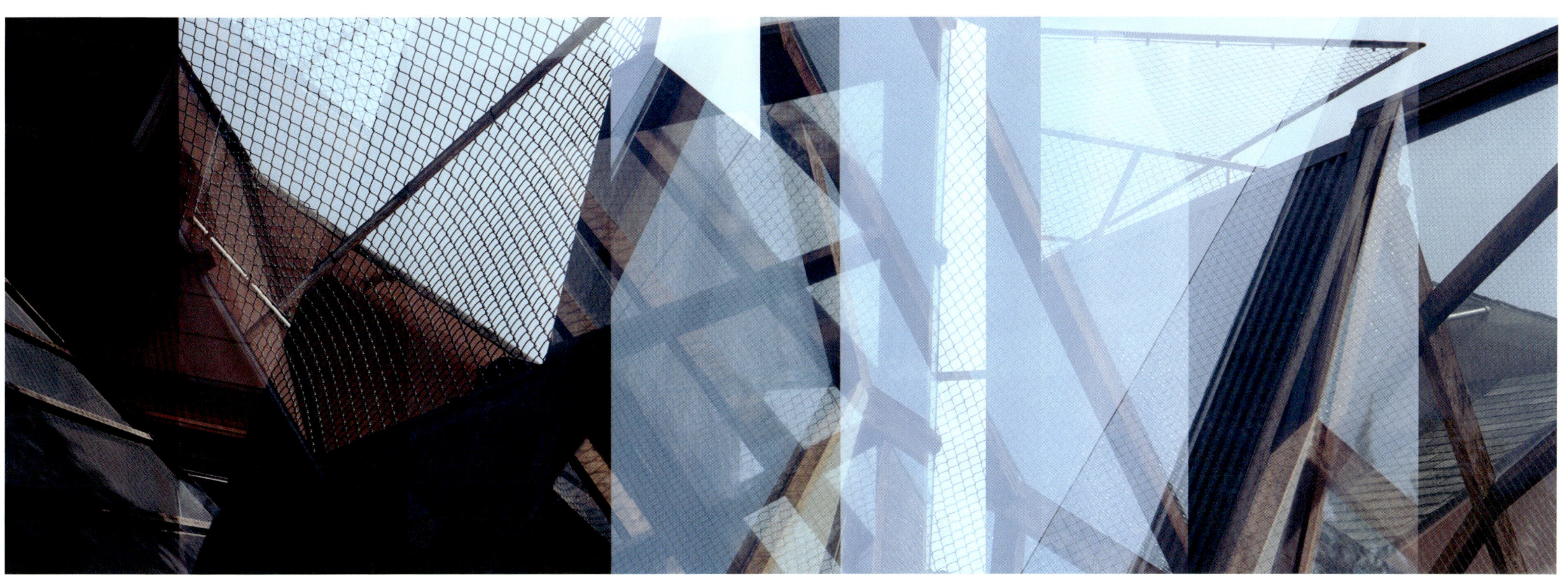

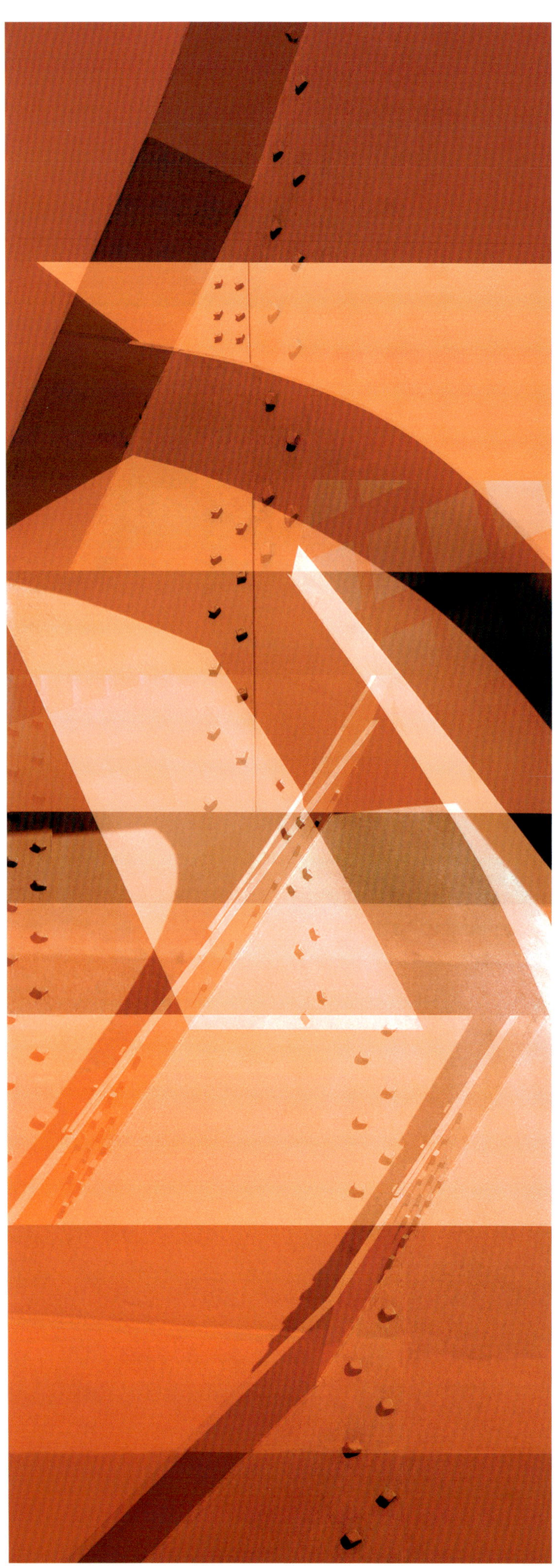

Calder Red   Chicago, Illinois, 1986   ARTIST: Alexander Calder

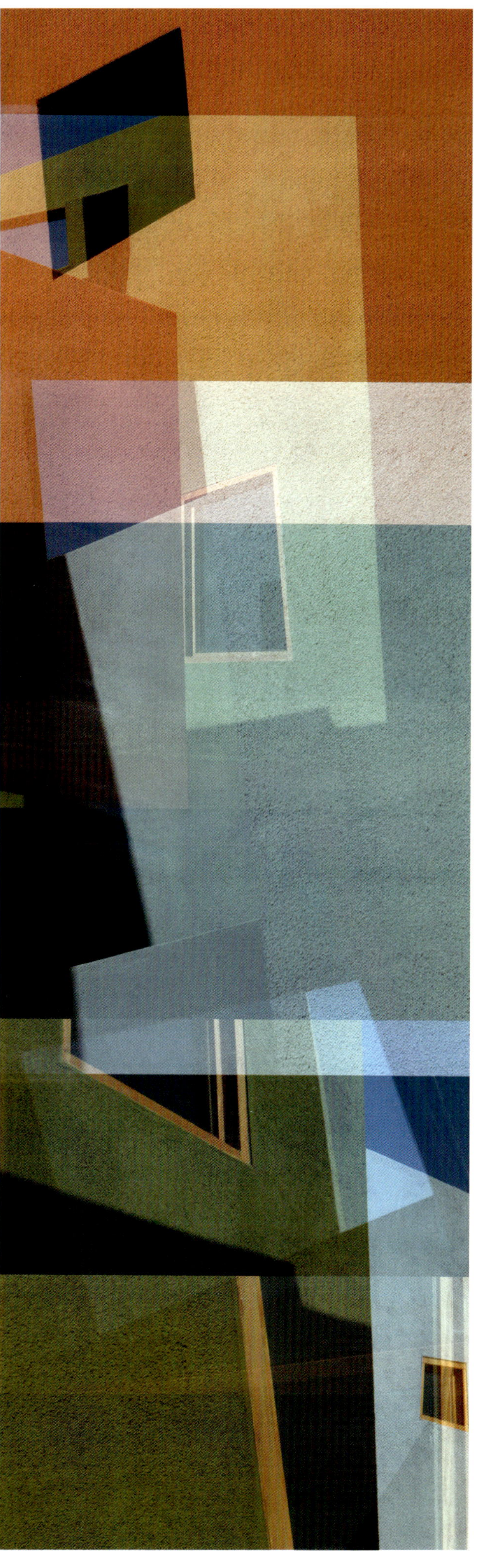

The Monument, Joshua Tree V   Joshua Tree, California, 1992   ARCHITECT: Josh Schweitzer

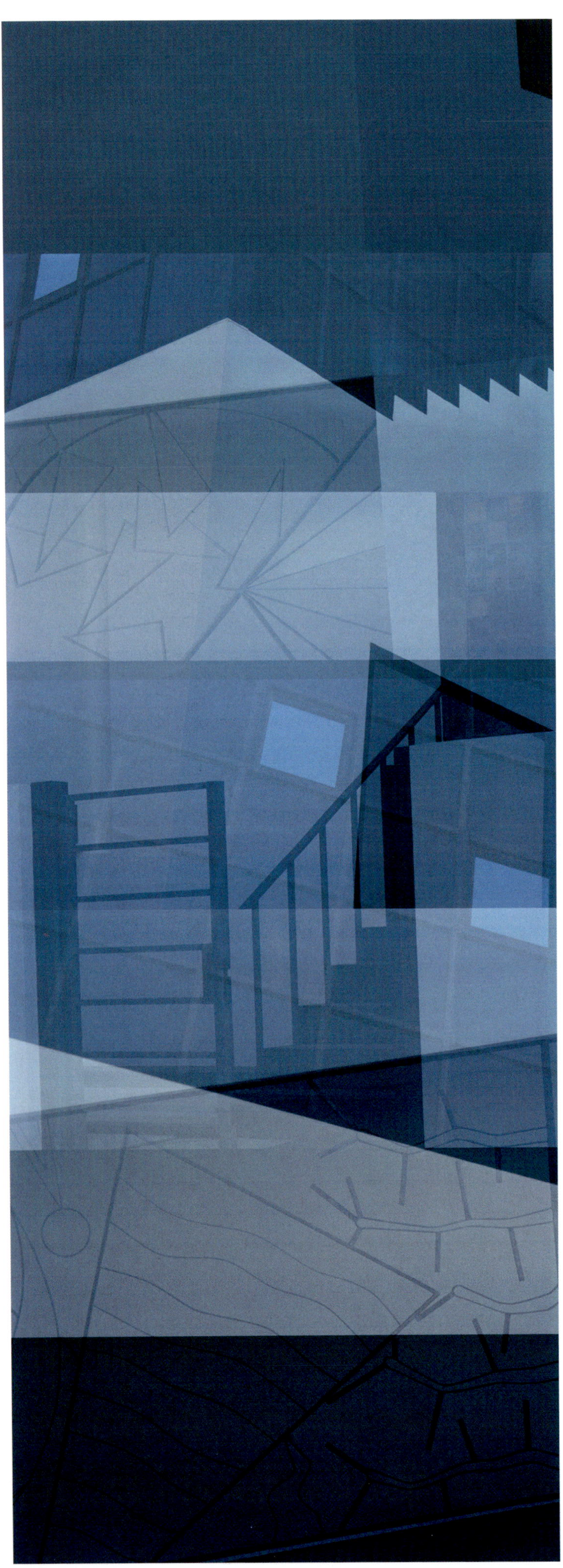

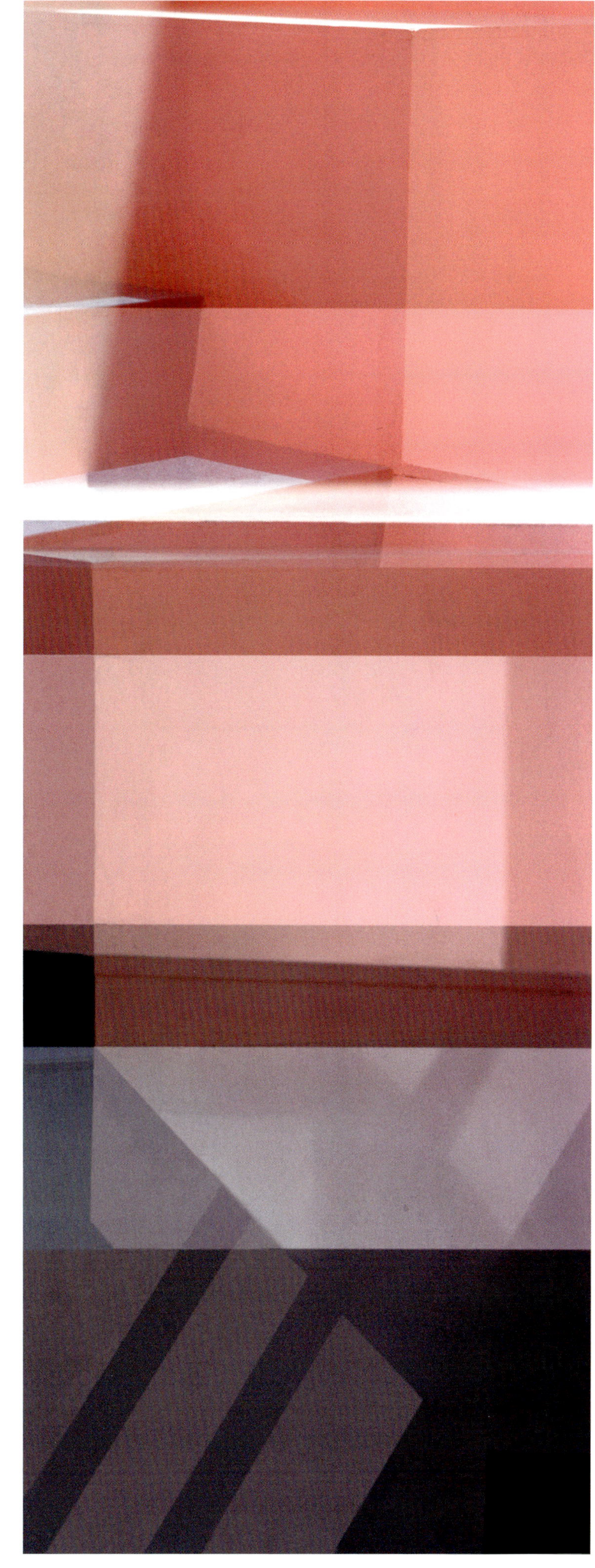

Fobney II Pink 6   Reading, England, 1988   ARCHITECT: Terry Farrell

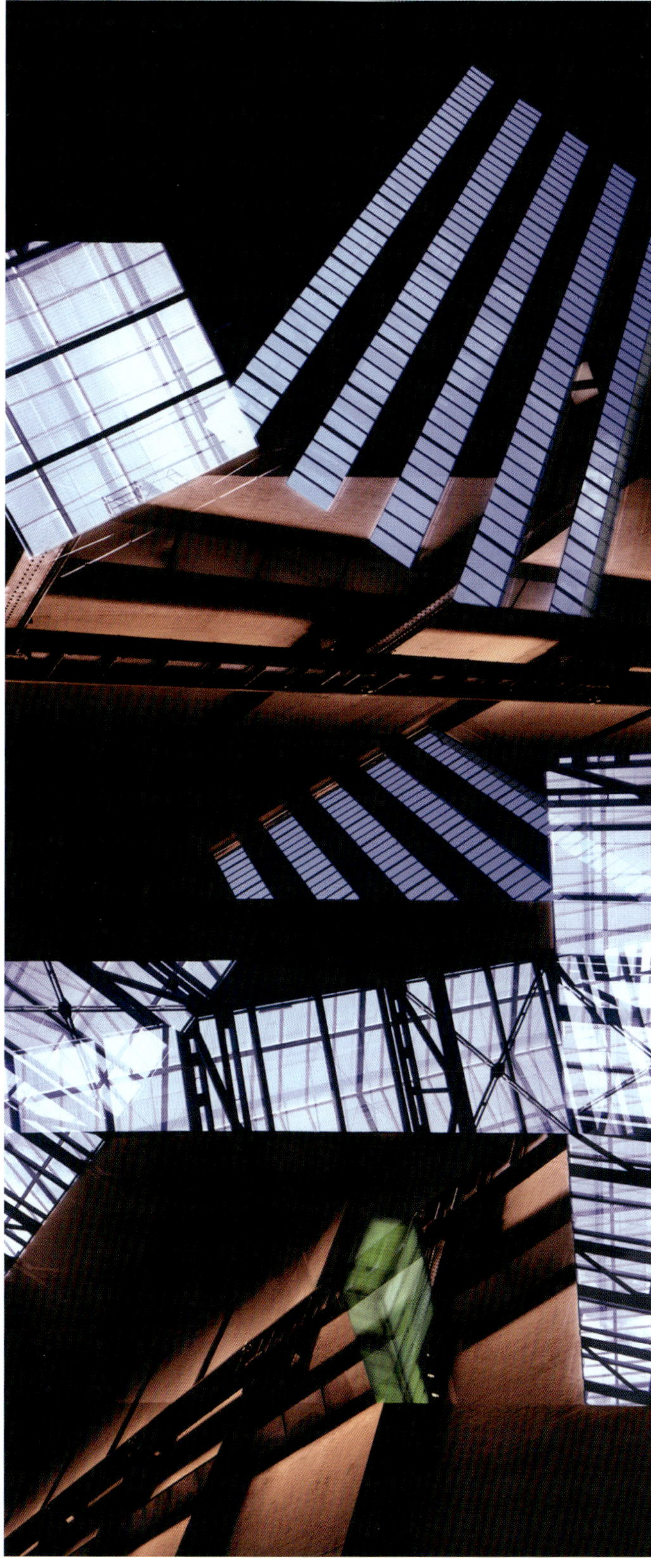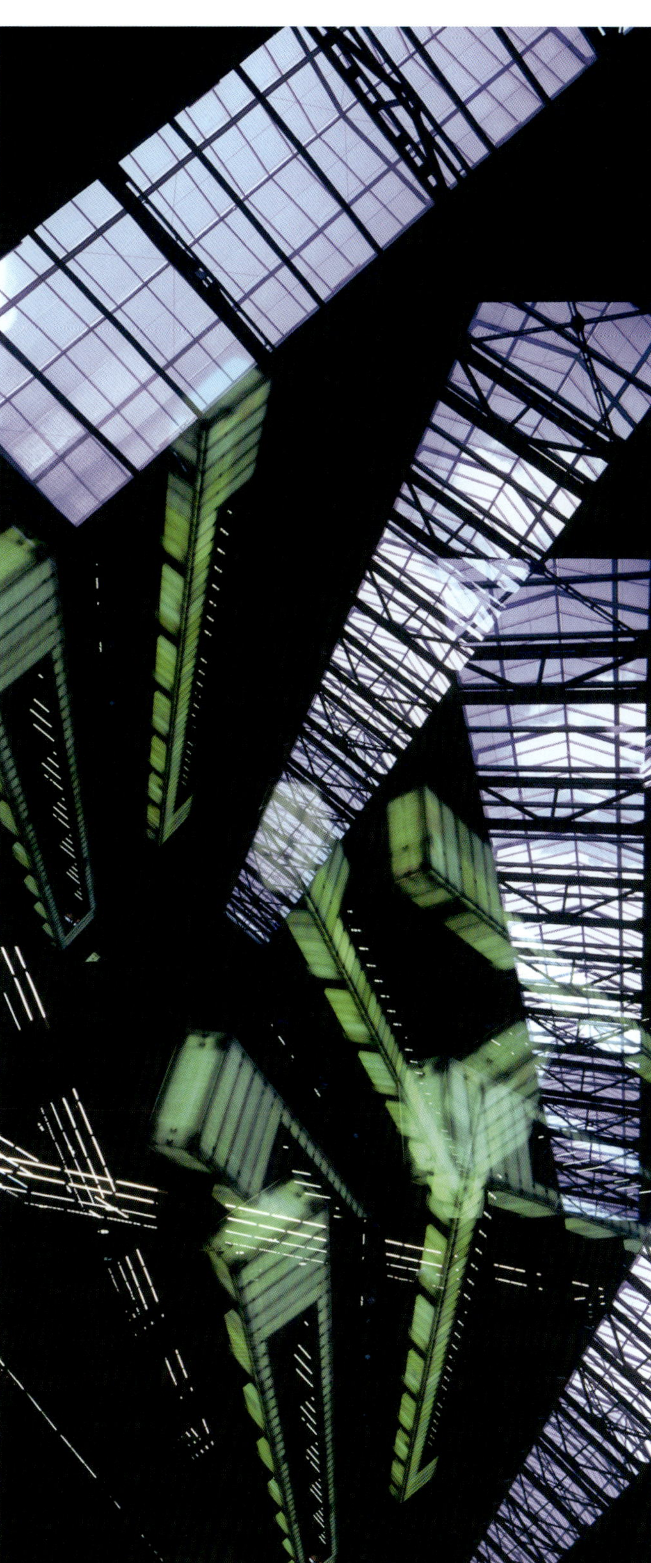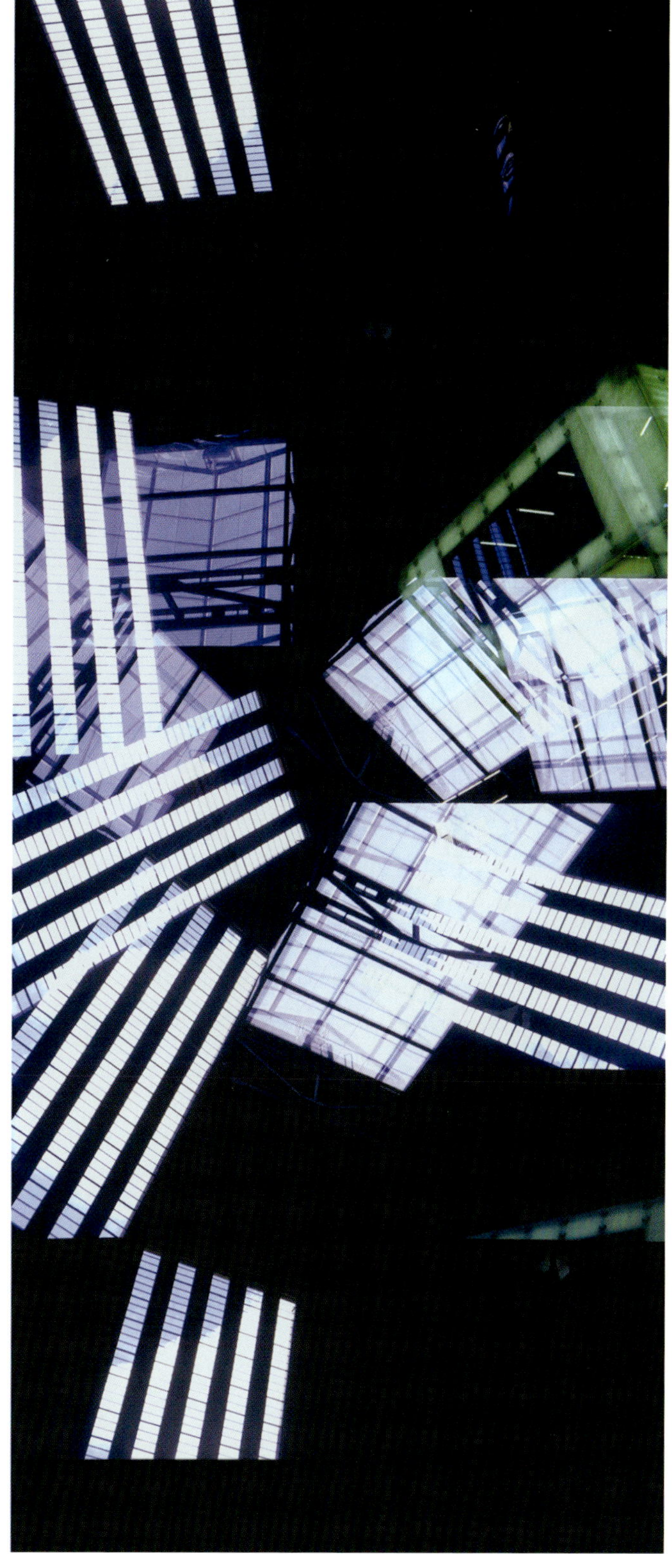

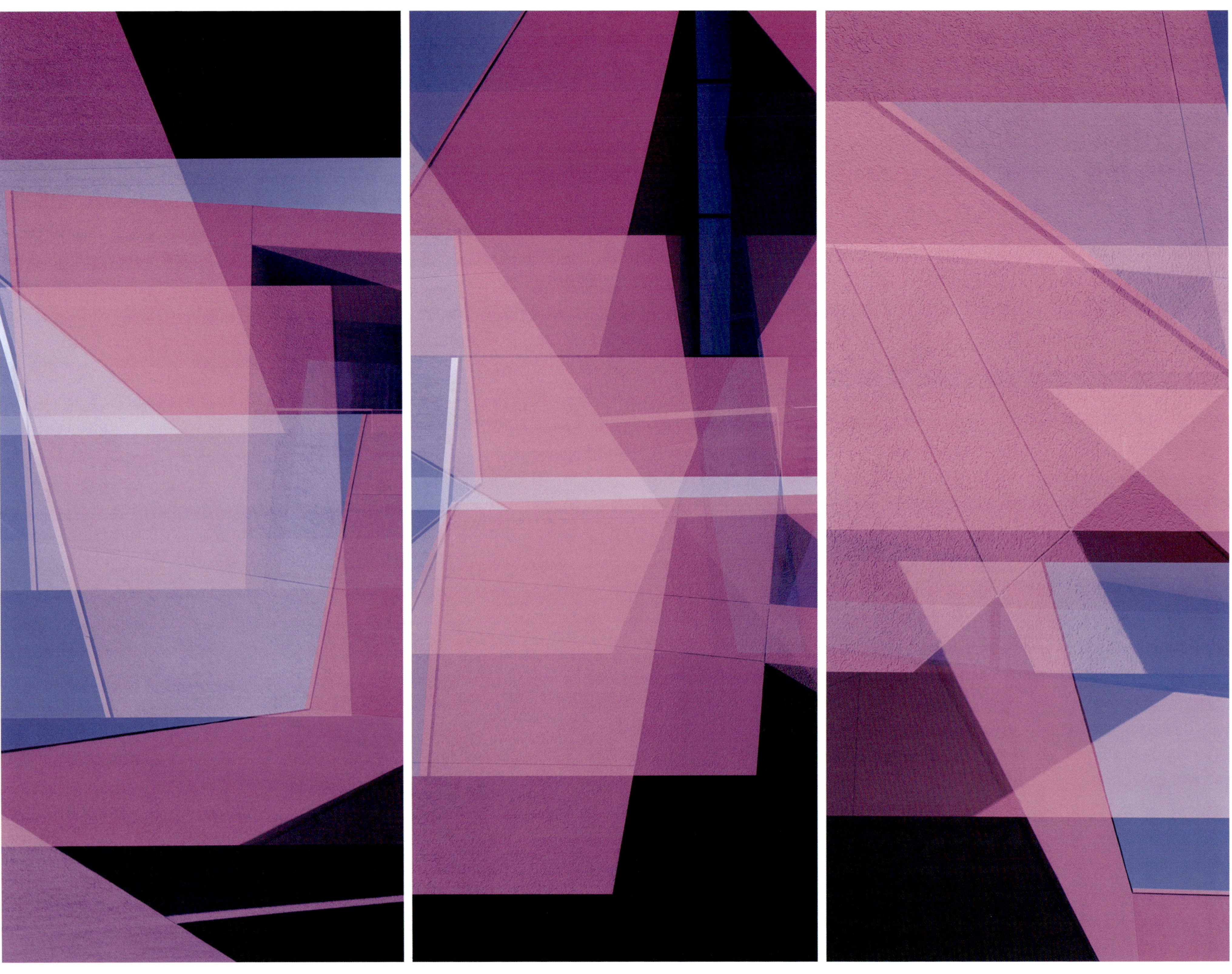

Blood Bank Triptych Alburquerque, New Mexico, 1997 ARCHITECT: Antoine Predock

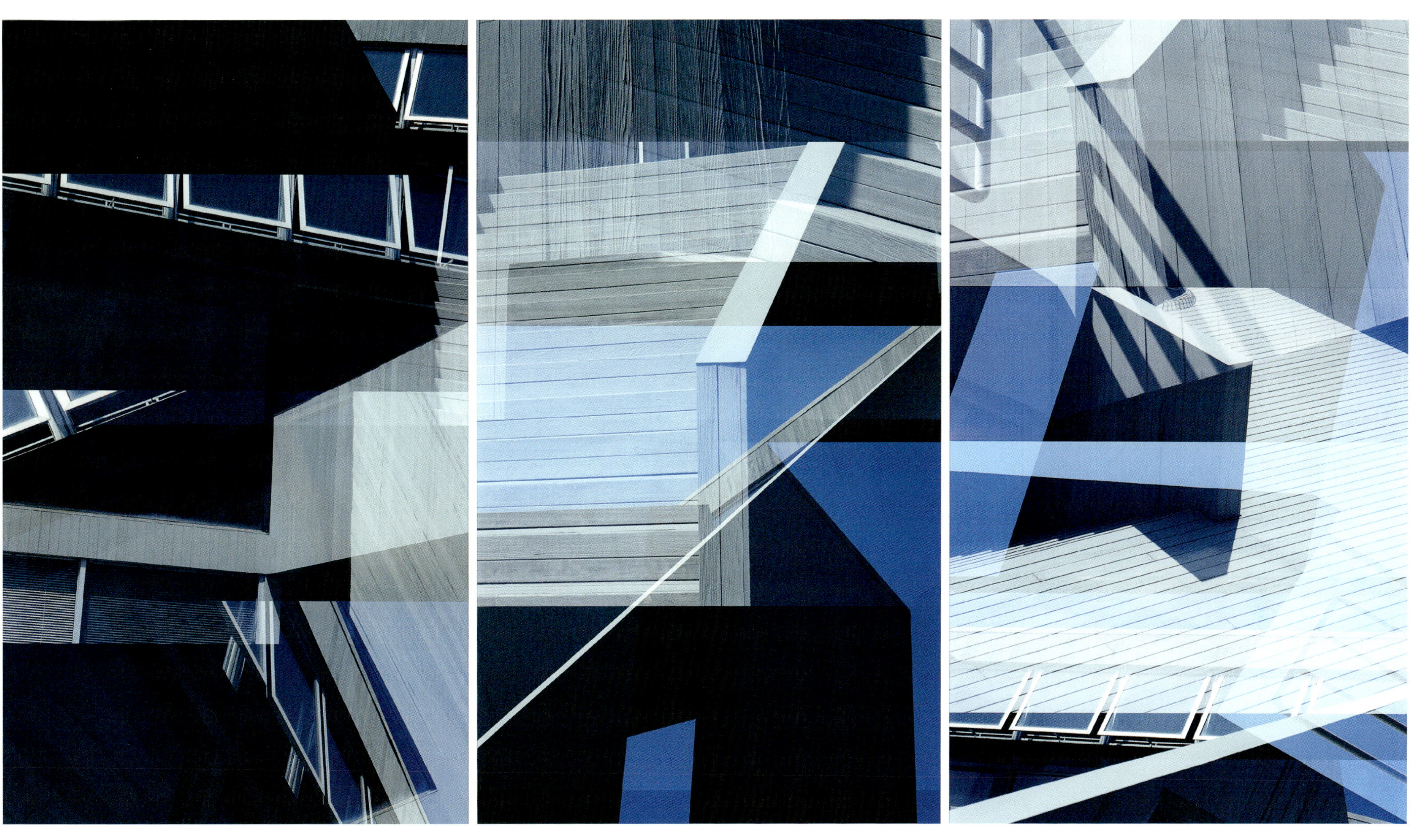

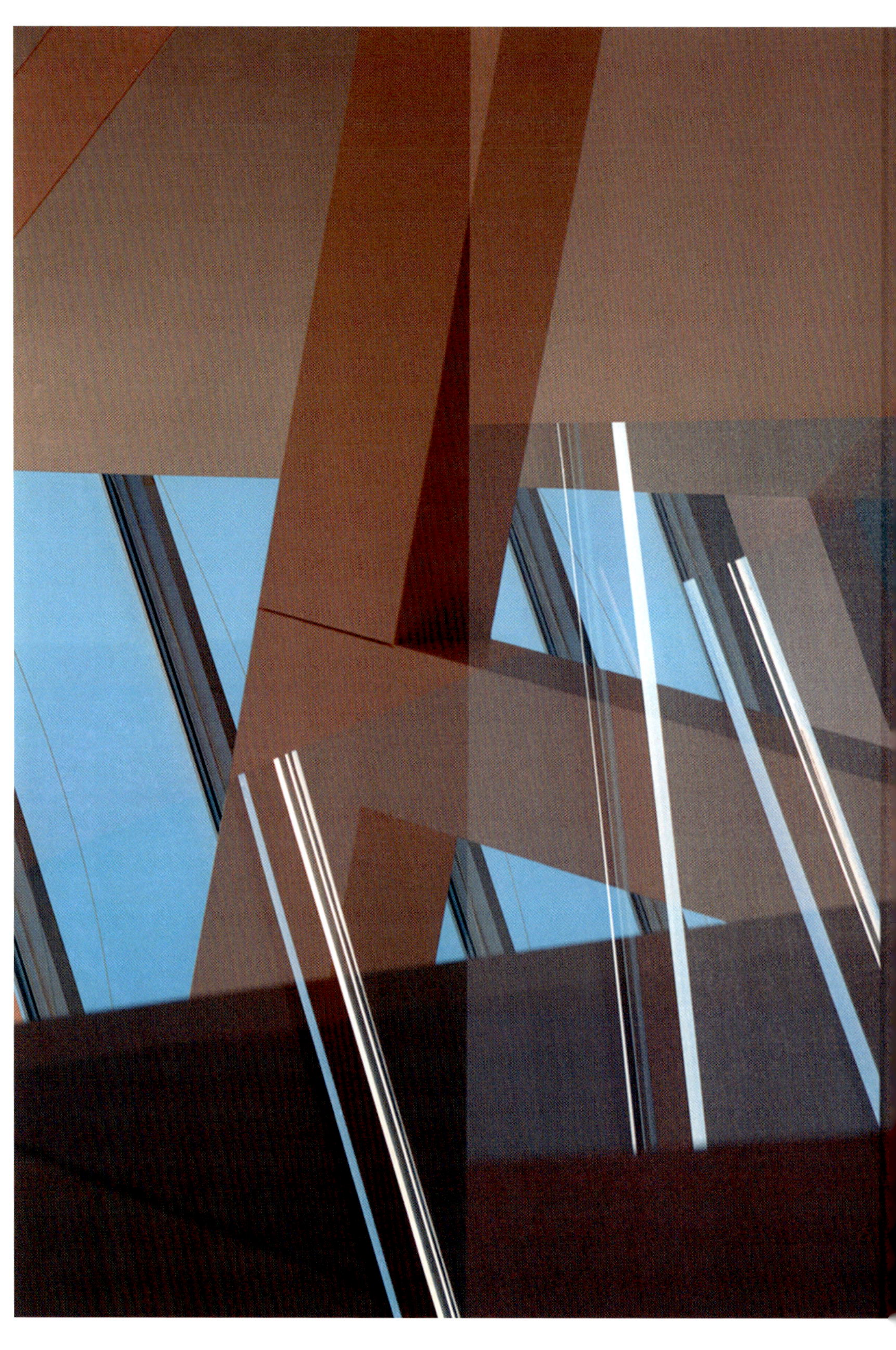

Columbia Library Pink   New York, New York, 1985   ARCHITECT: Cain, Farrell & Bell

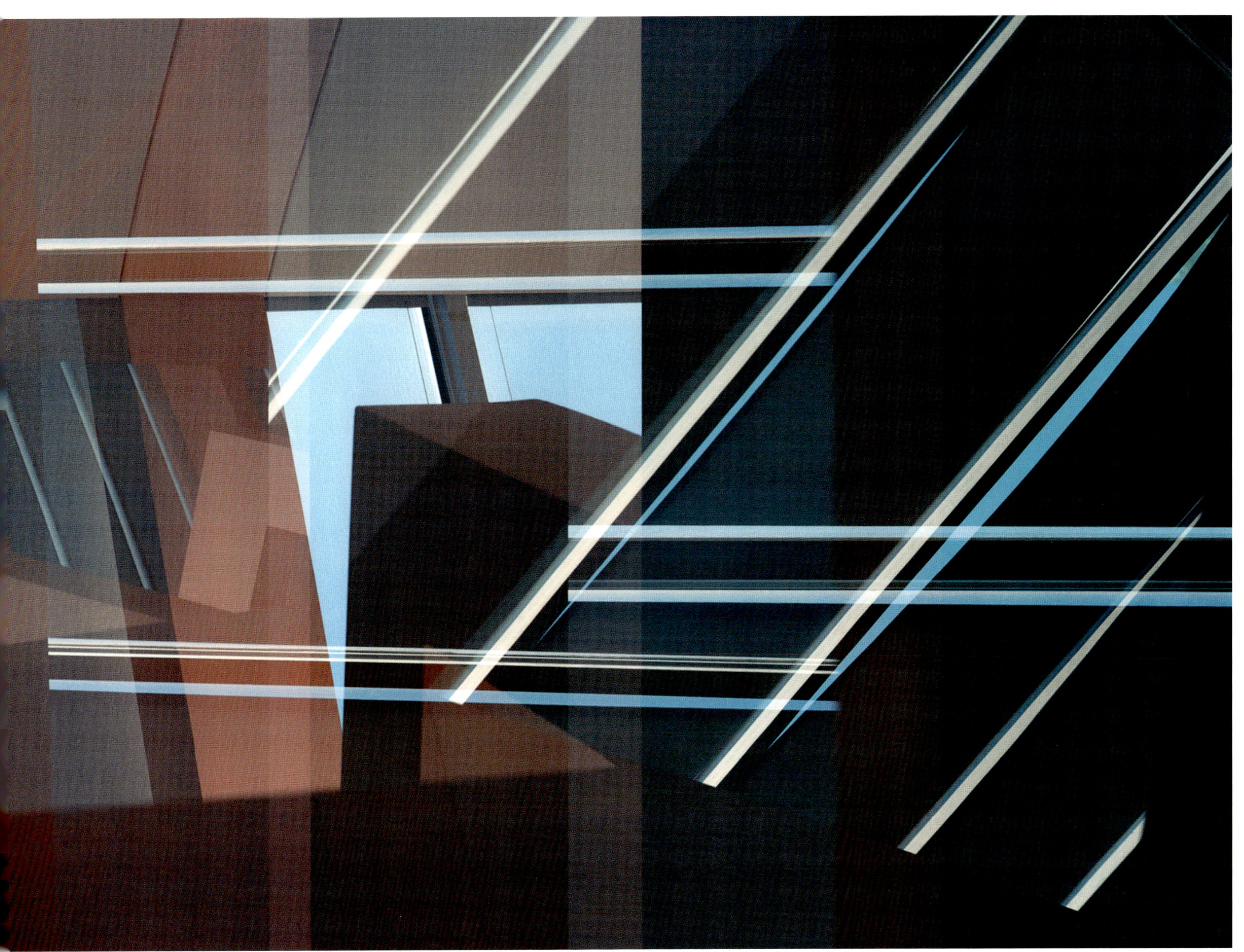

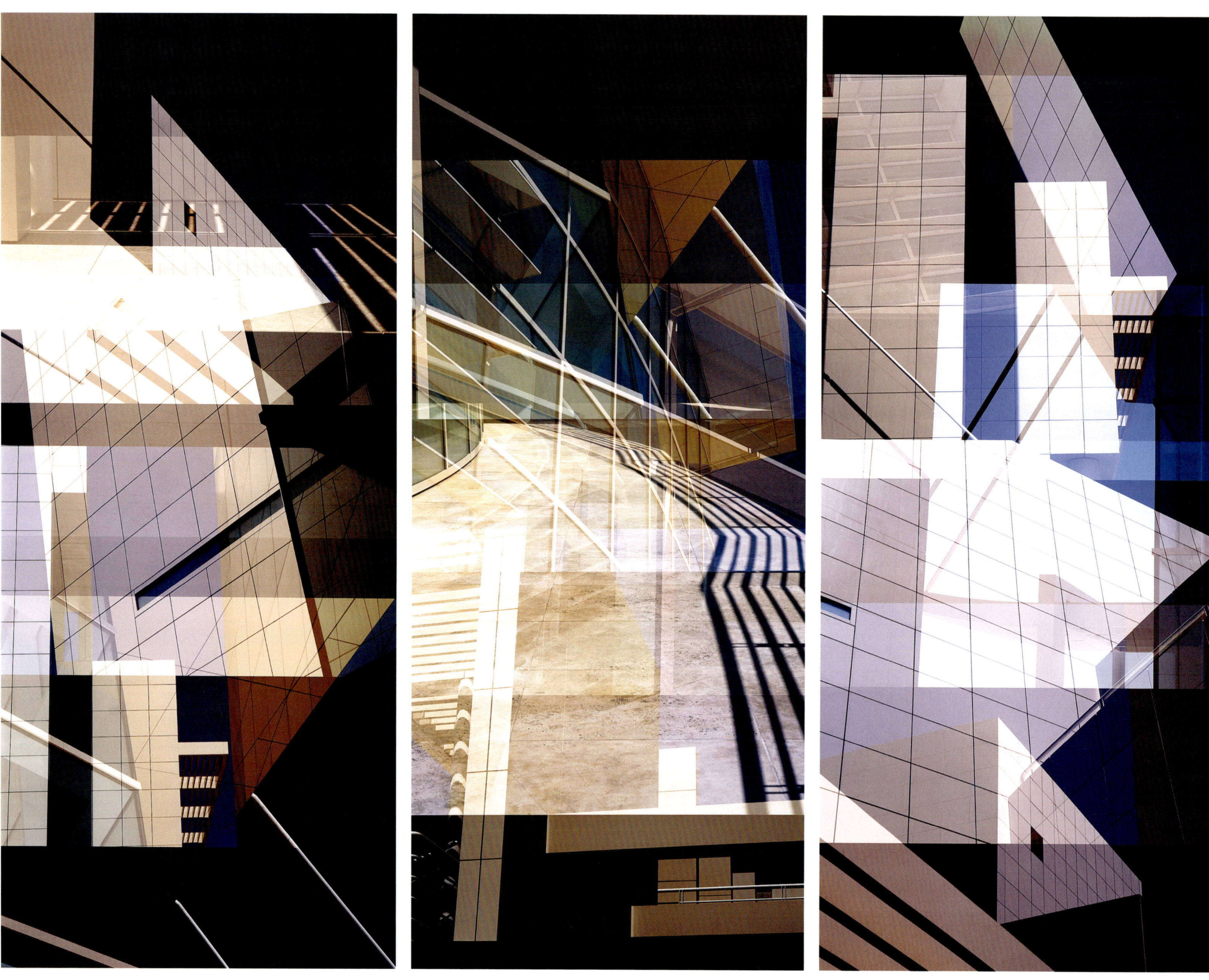

Getty Stone Triptych   Los Angeles, California, 1997   ARCHITECT: Richard Meier

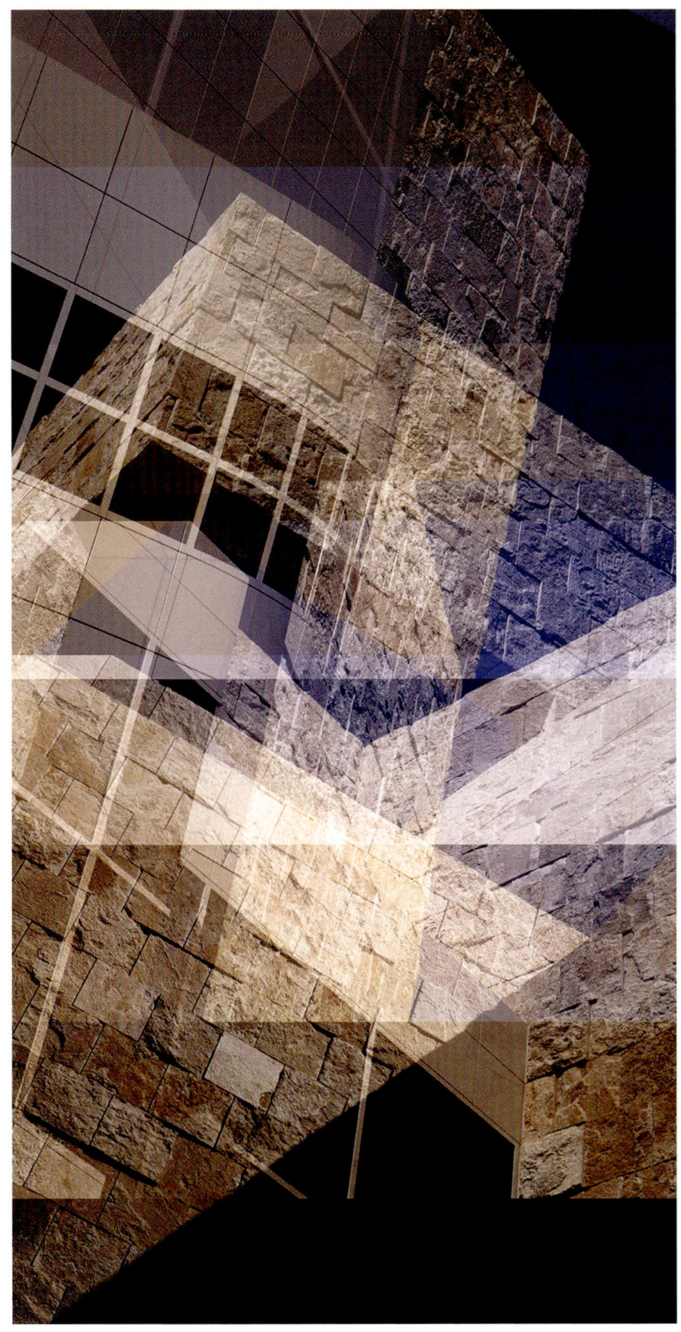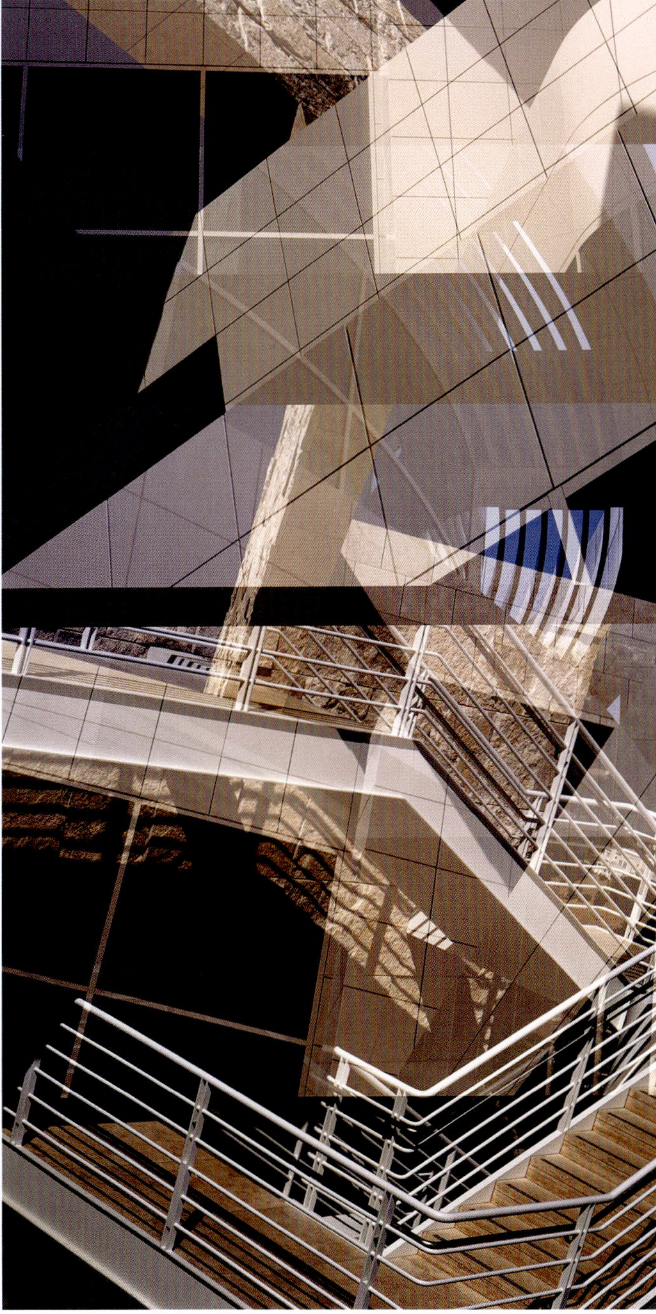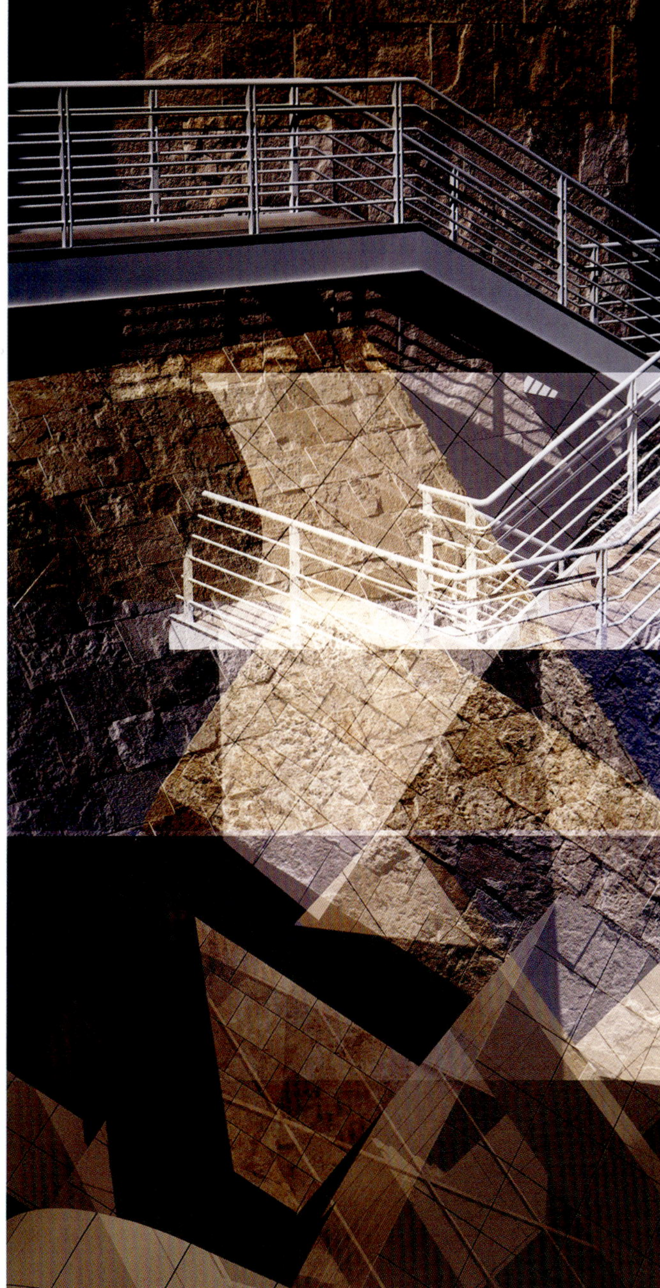

Getty Entrance Triptych   Los Angeles, California, 1997   ARCHITECT: Richard Meier

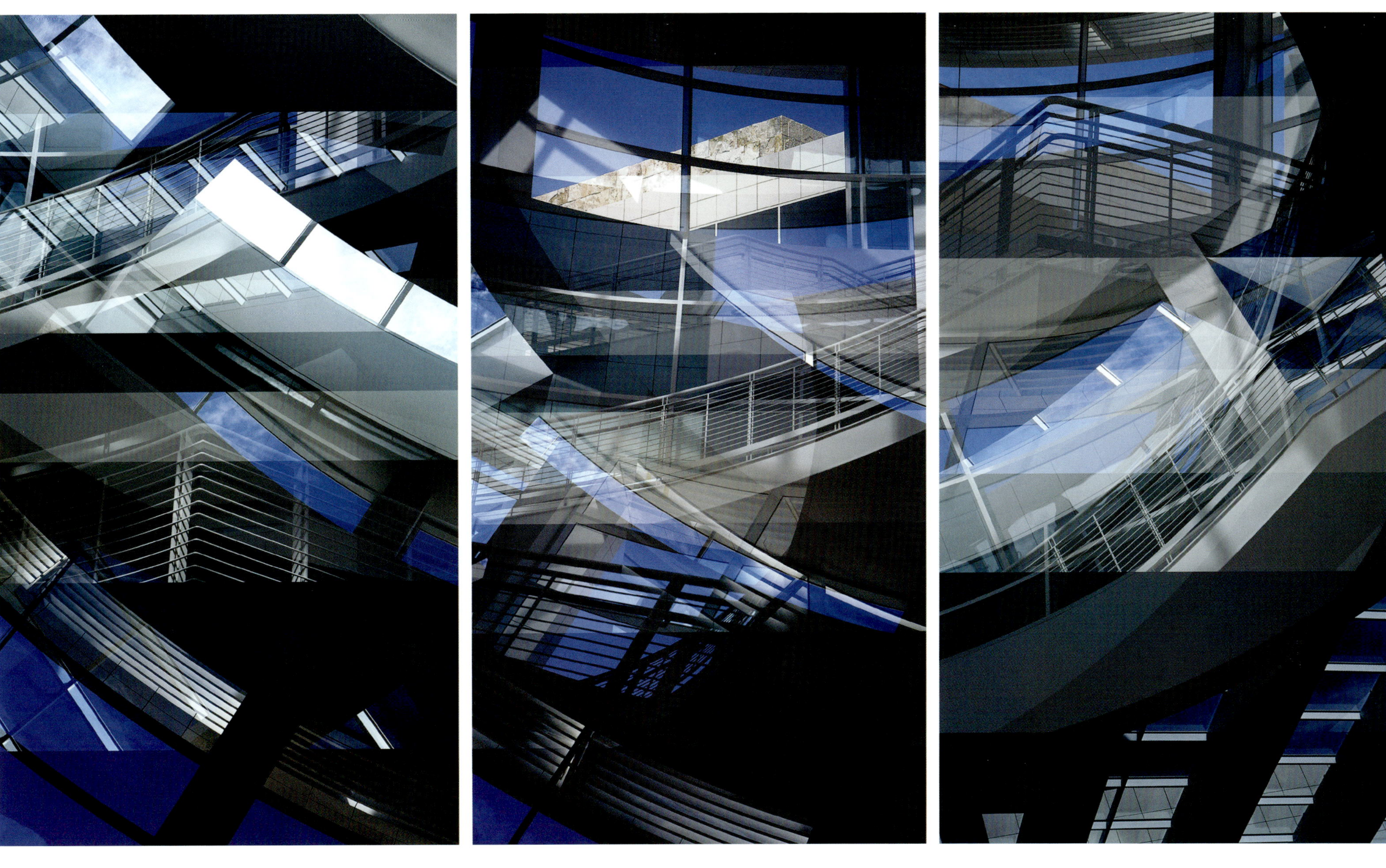

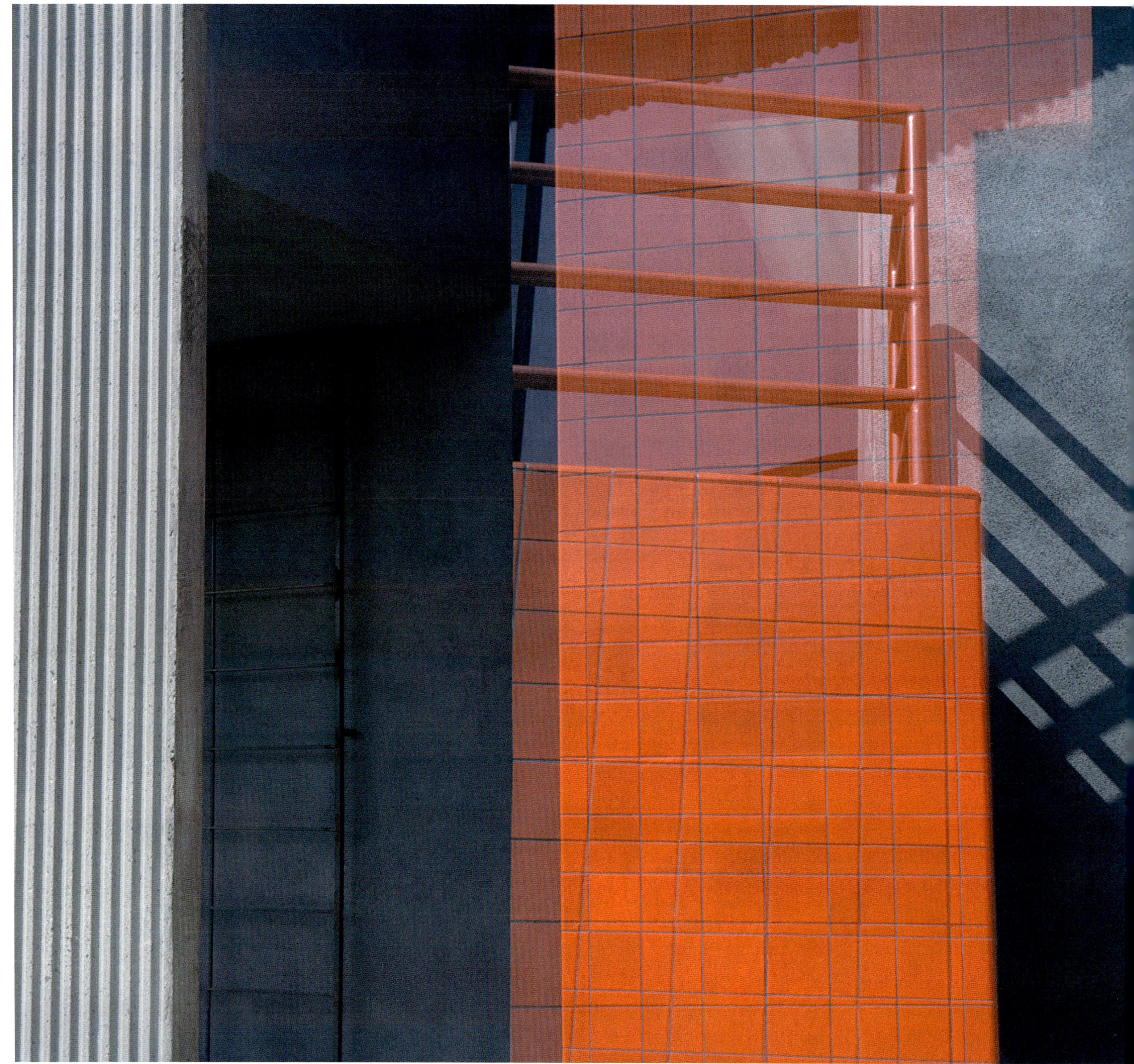

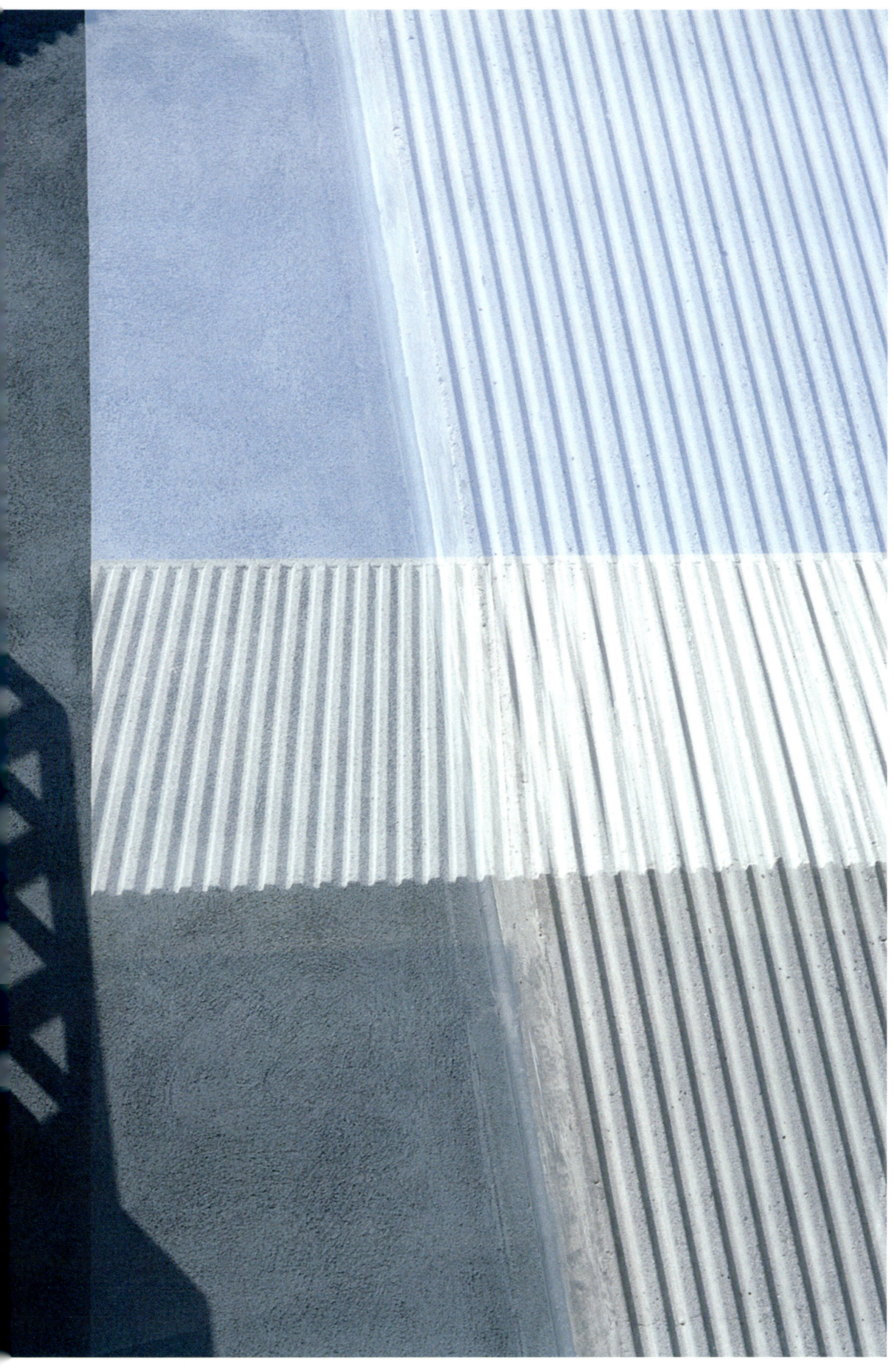

L.A. Warehouse H   Los Angeles, California, 1984   ARCHITECT: Claudia Carol (Barasch Architects)

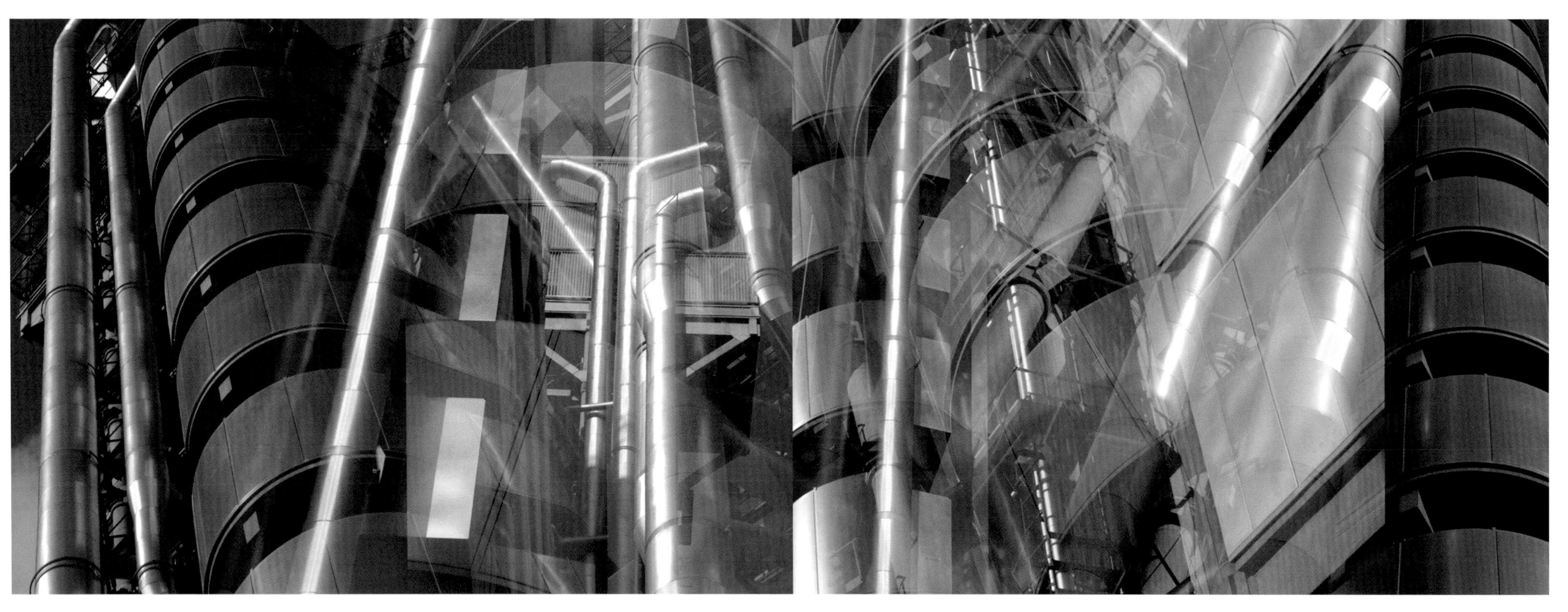

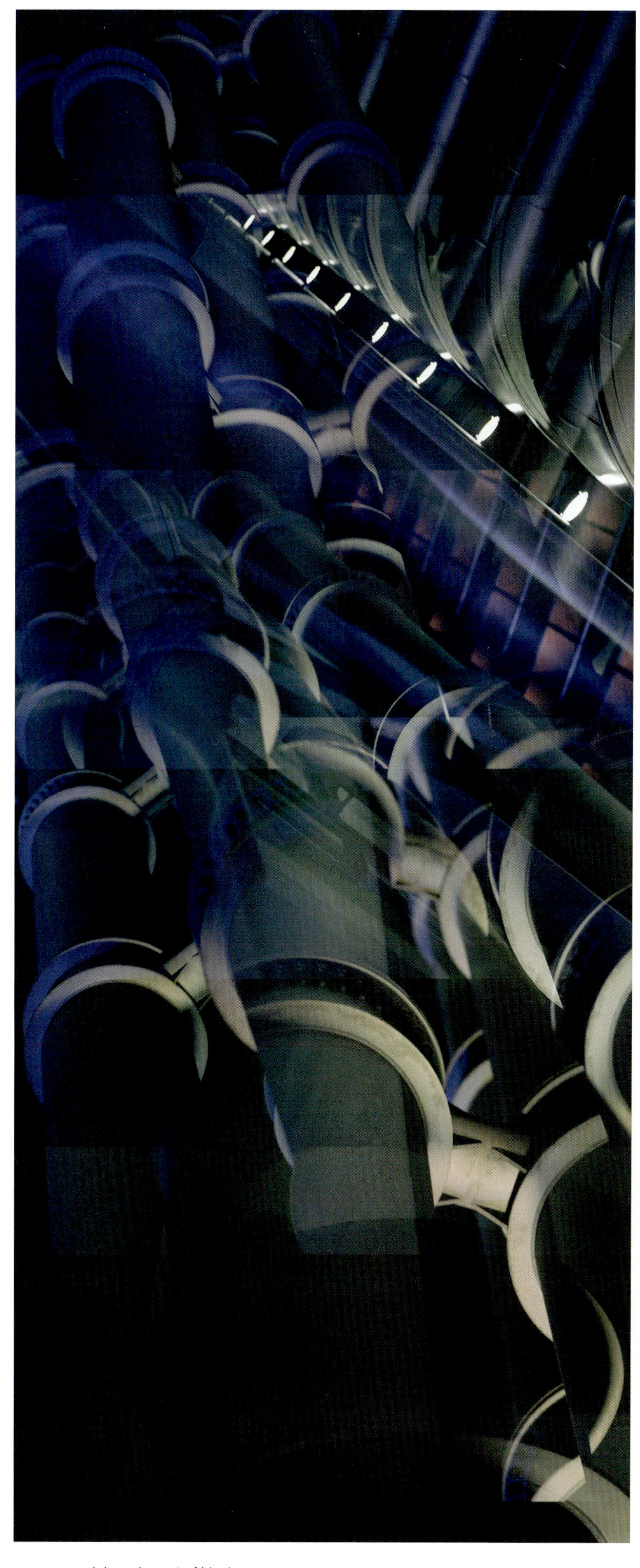

Lloyds at Night   London, England, 1986   ARCHITECT: Richard Rogers Partnership

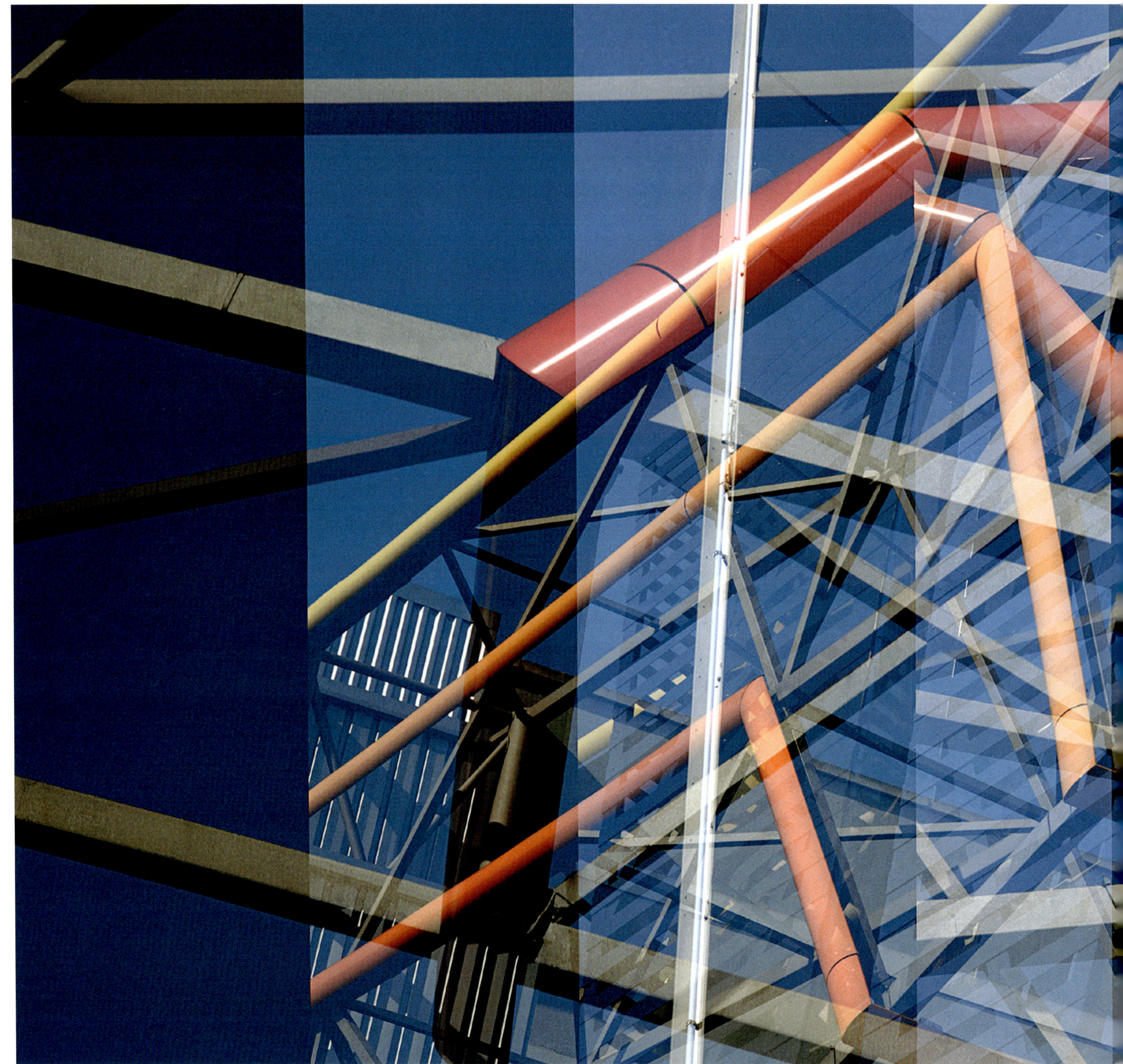

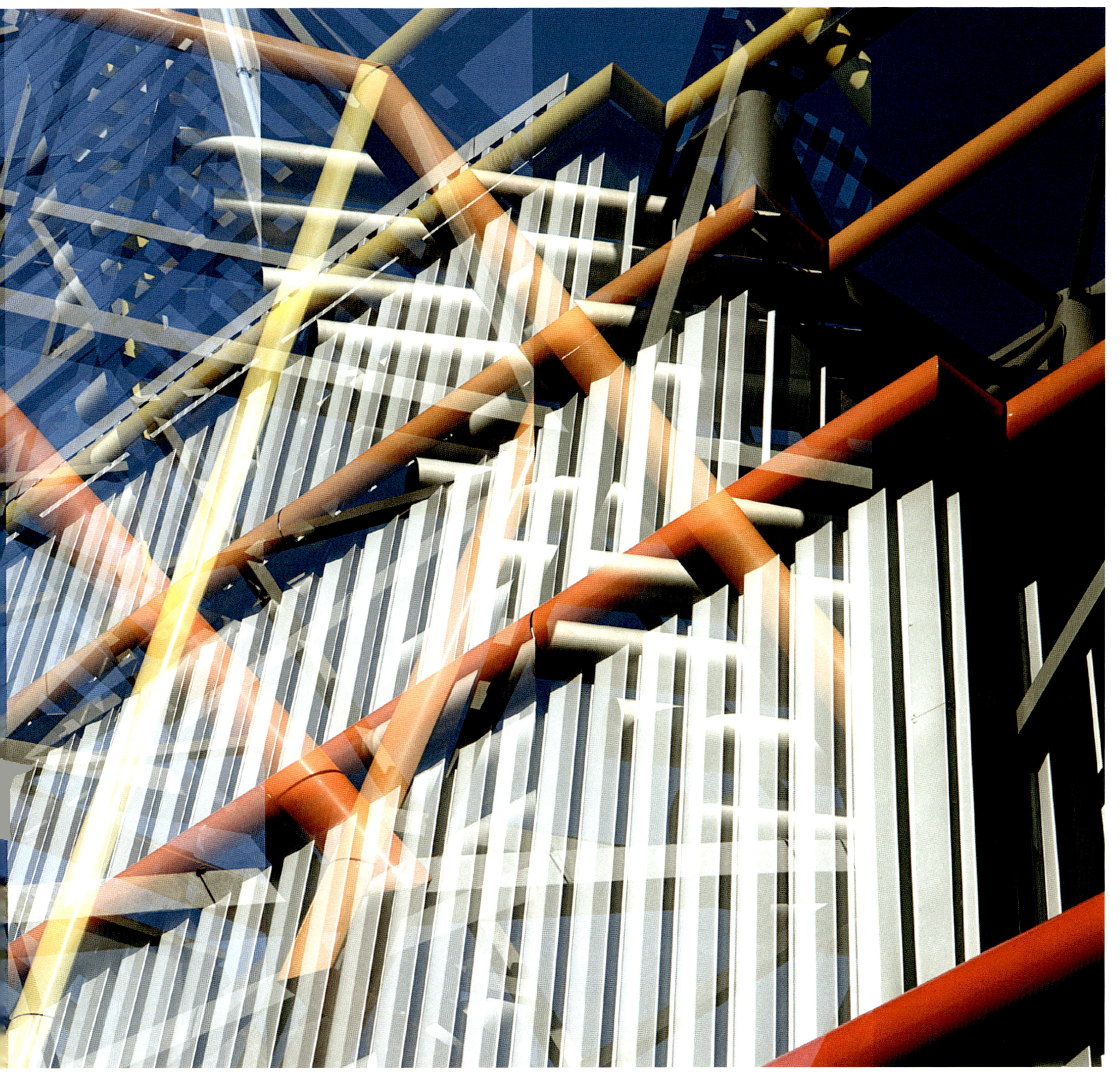

TVAM   London, England, 1985   ARCHITECT: Terry Farrell

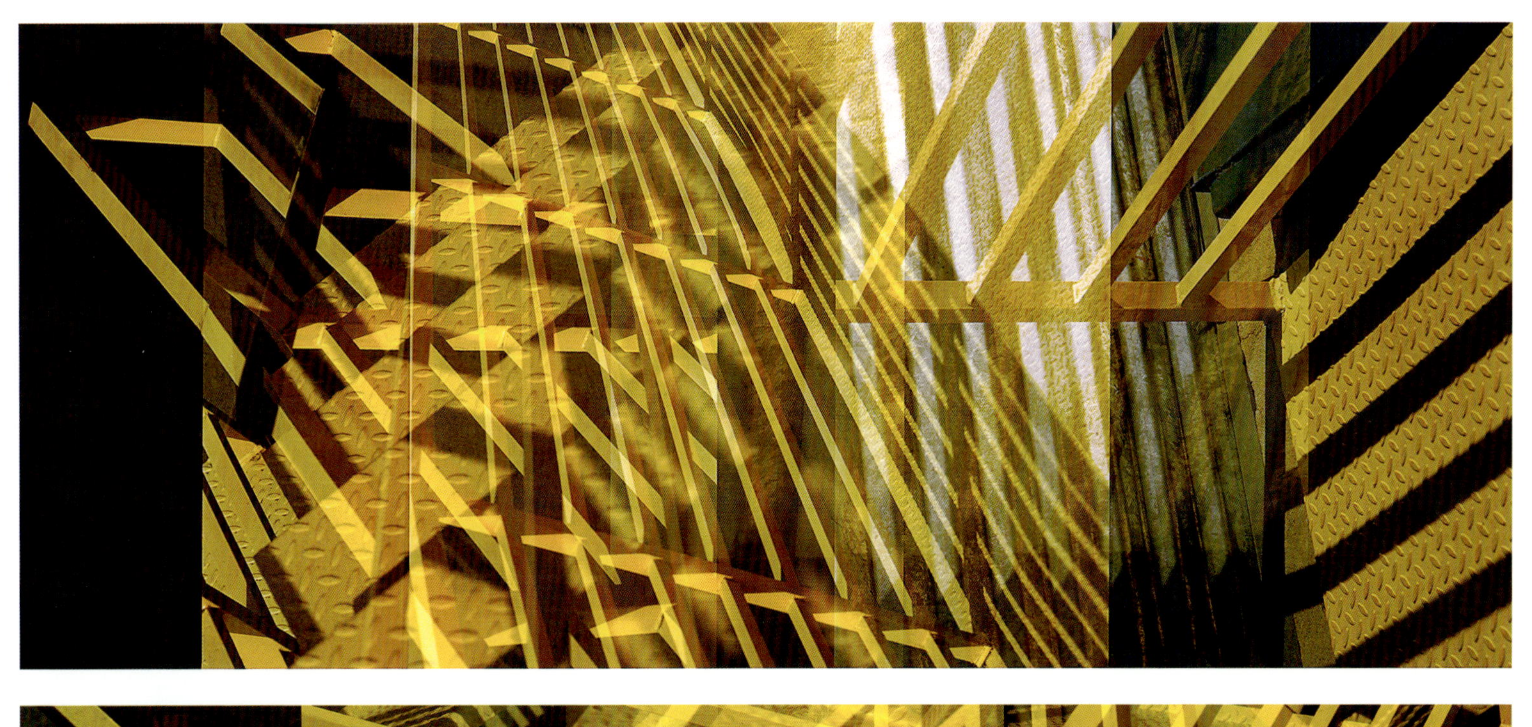

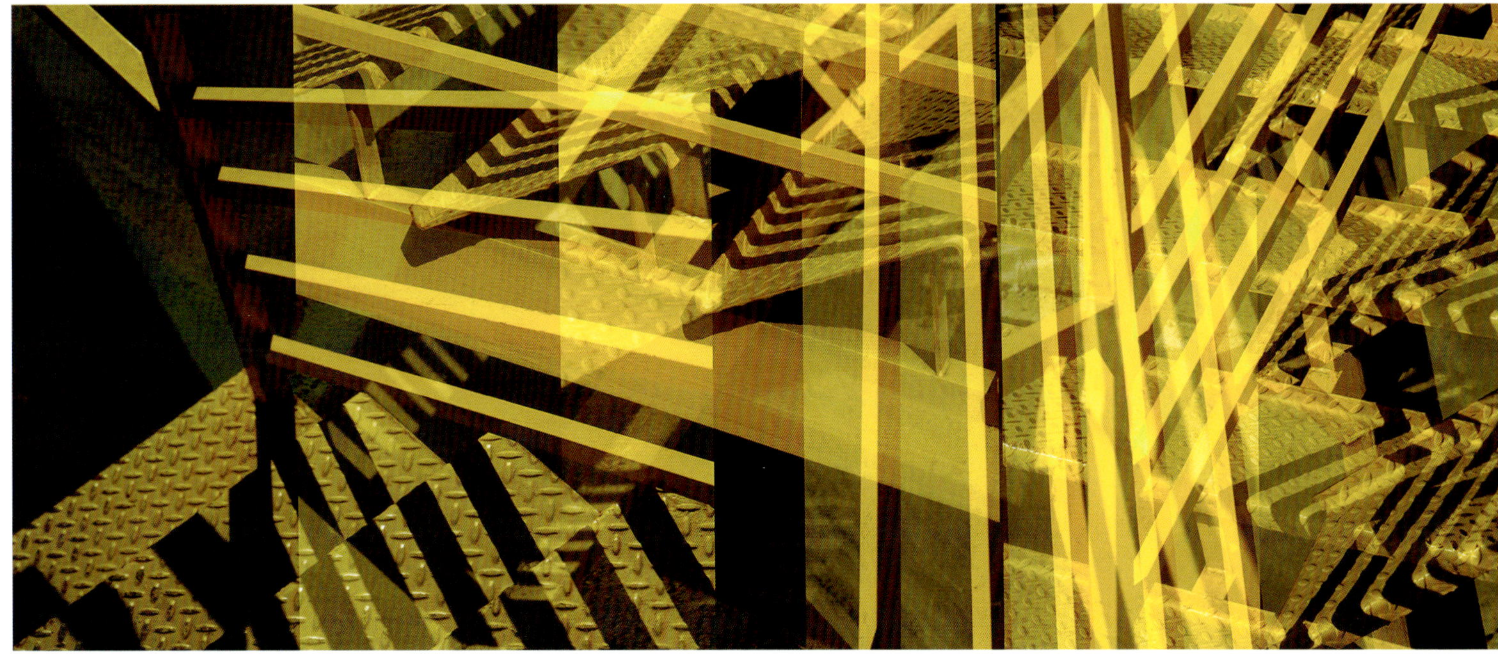

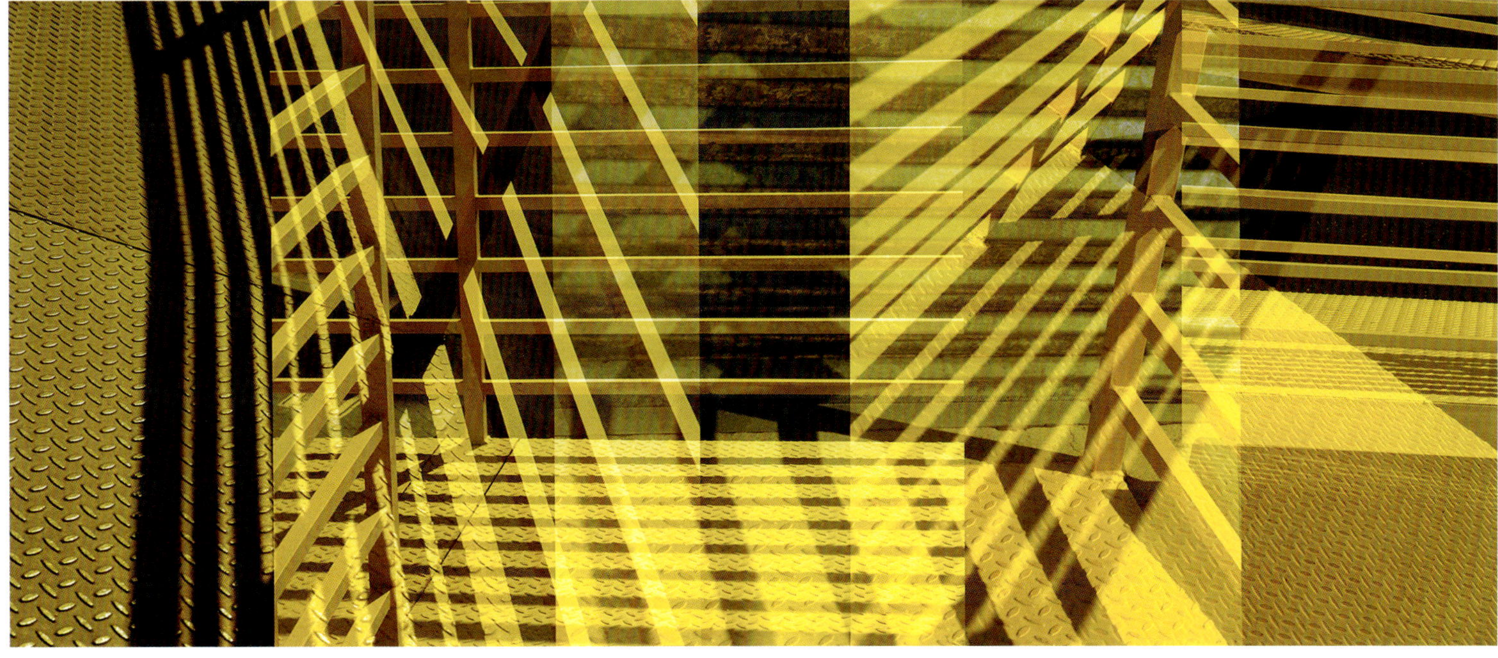

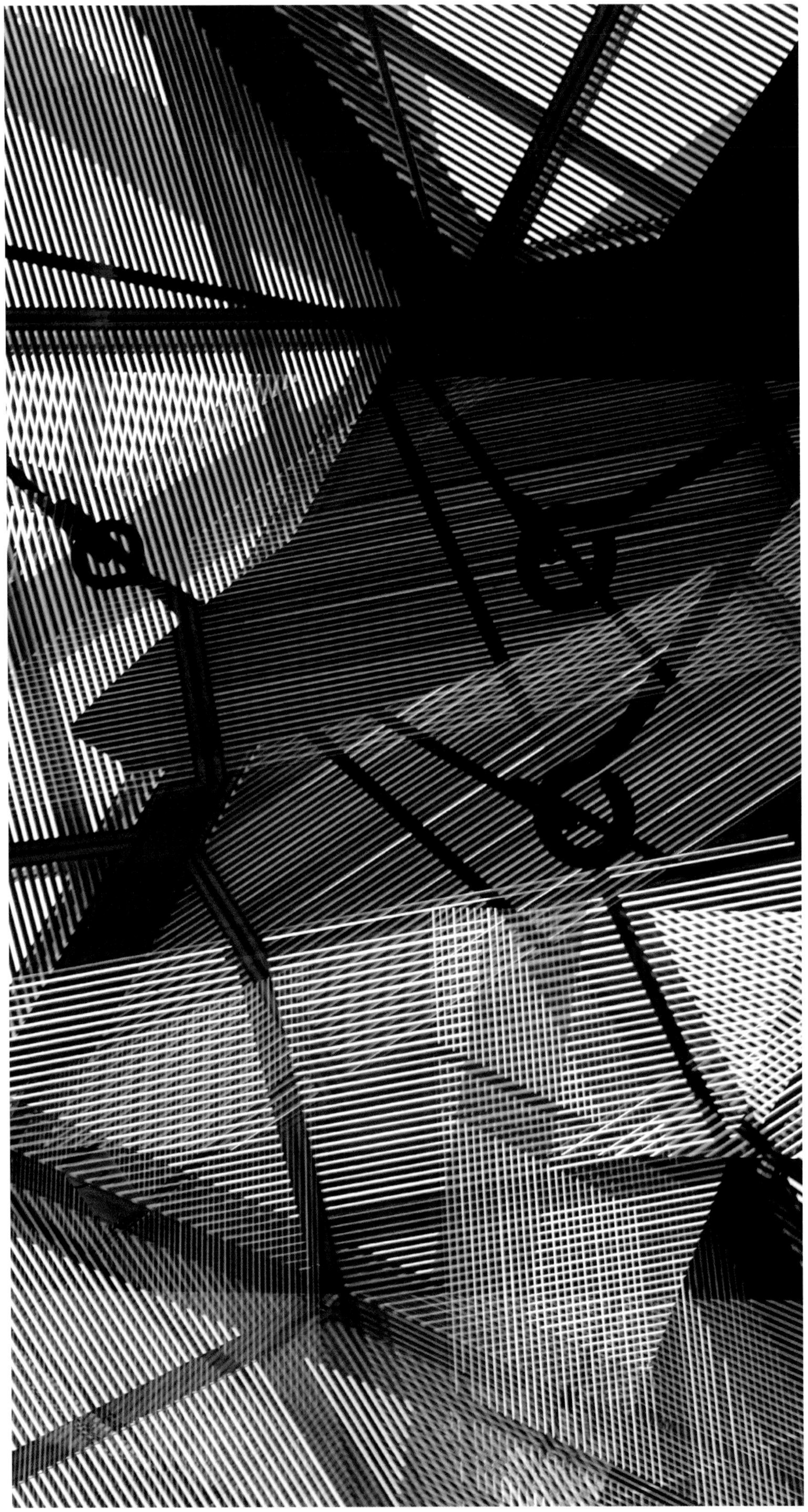

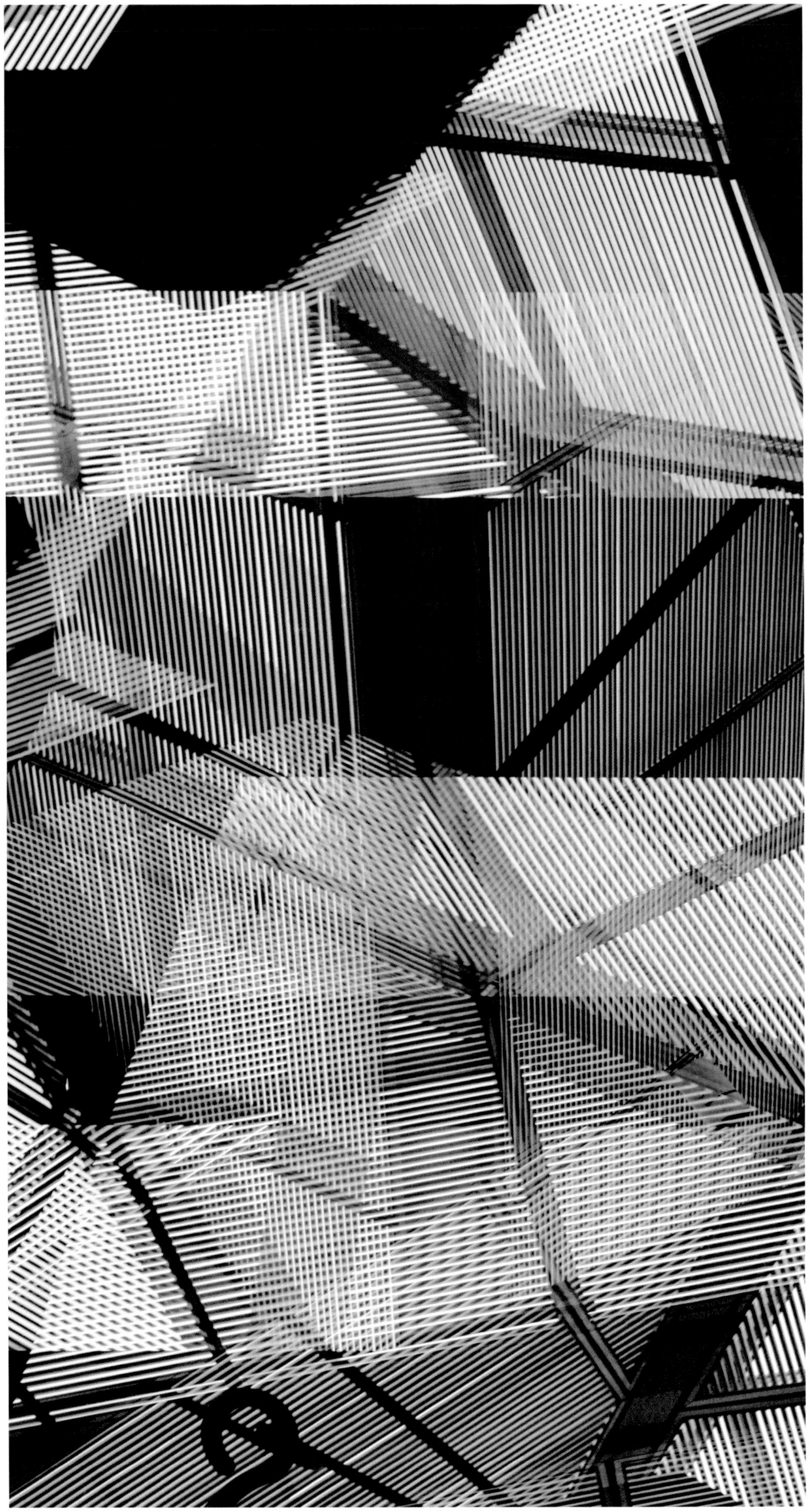

Left to right, above and opposite: Washington National Gallery Extension I, III, IV, V Washington, D.C., 1988 ARCHITECT: I. M. Pei

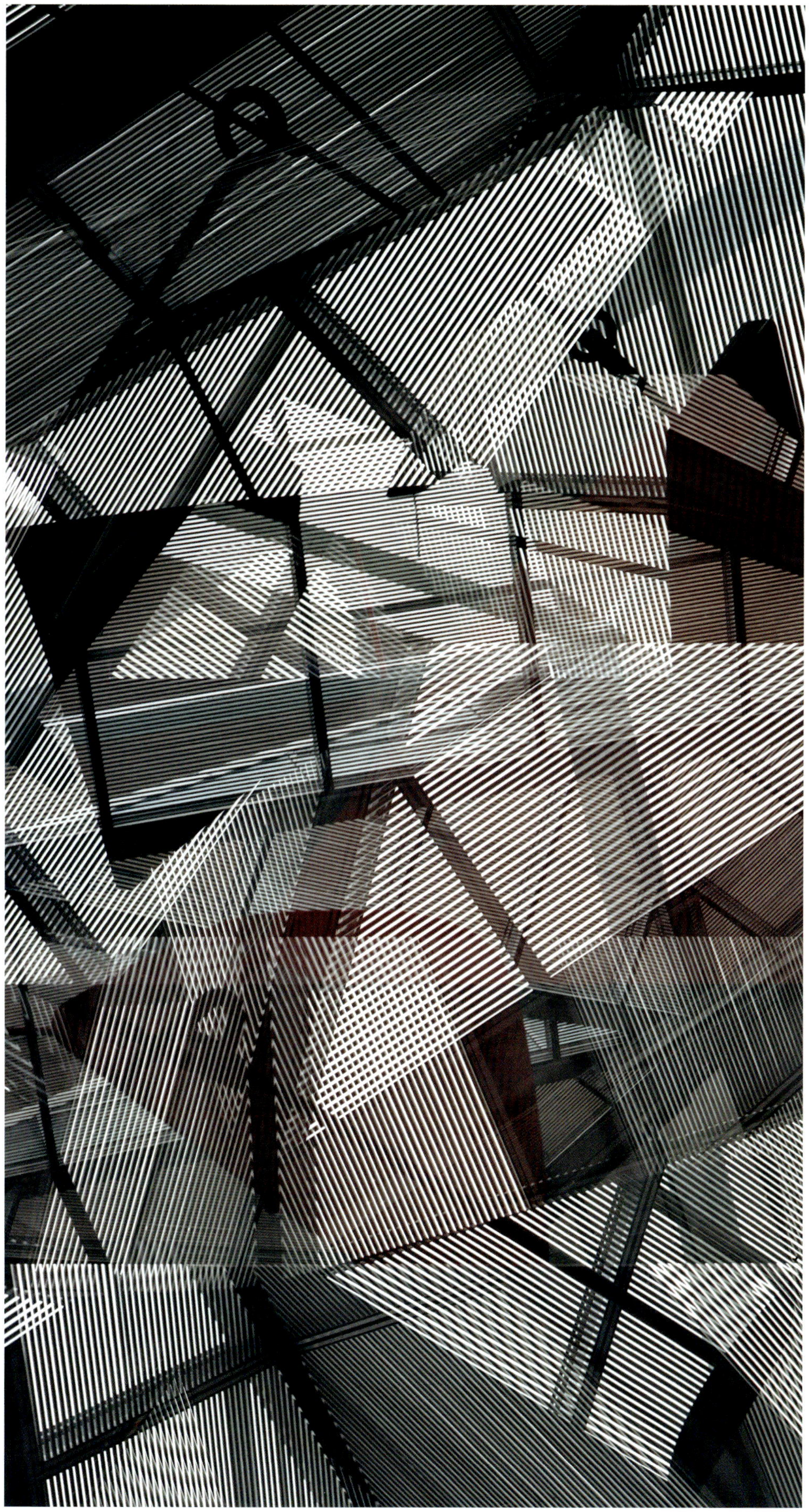

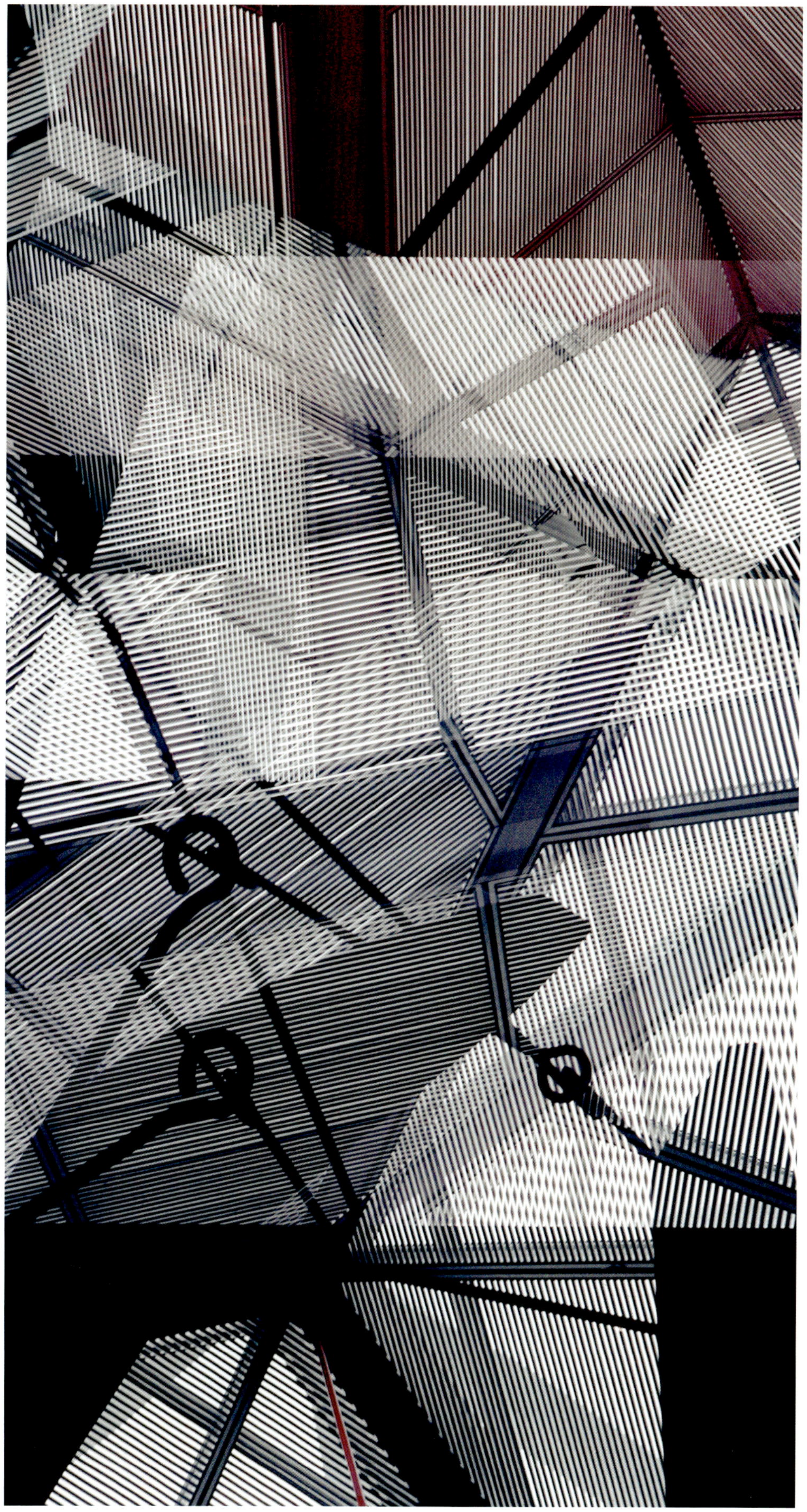

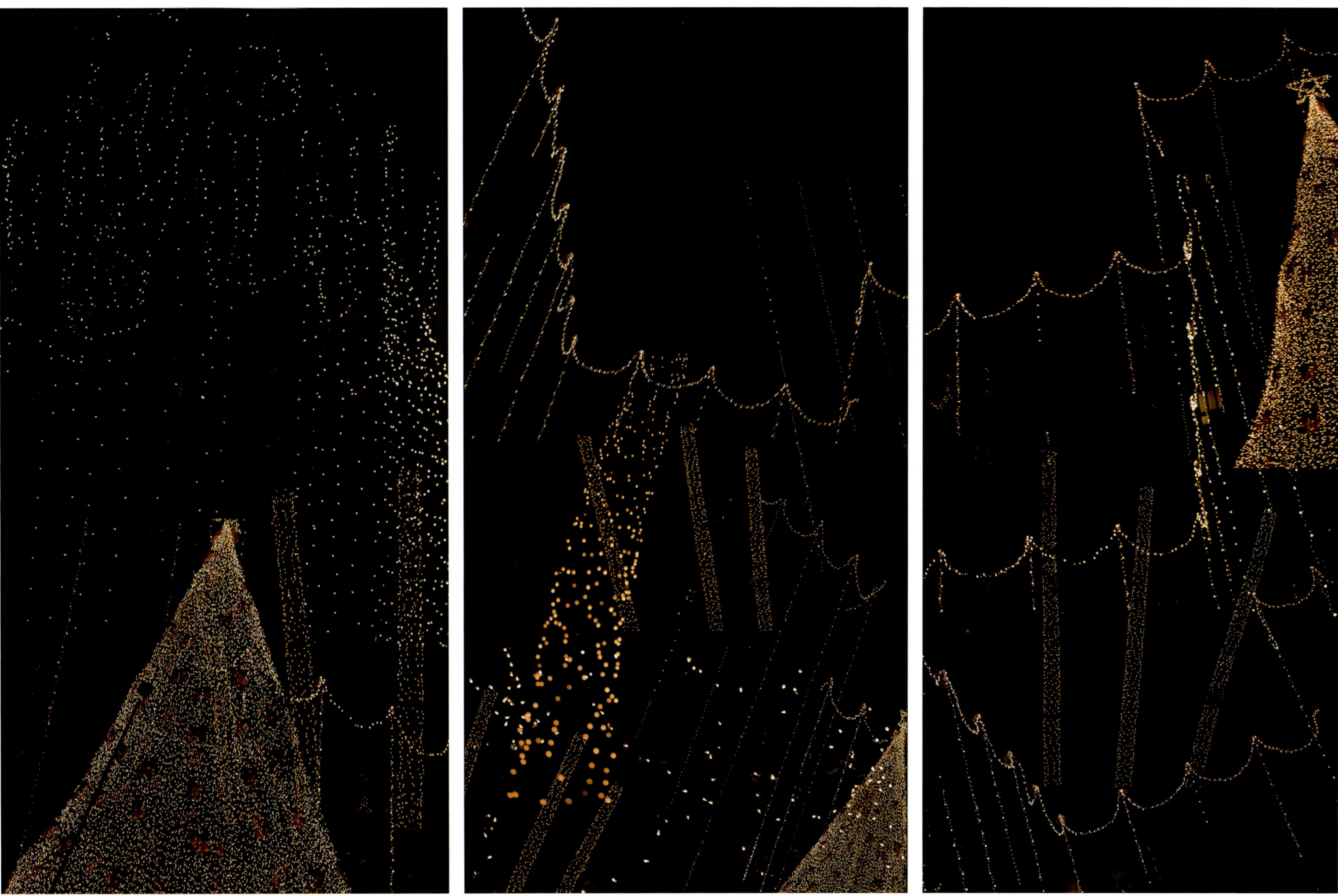

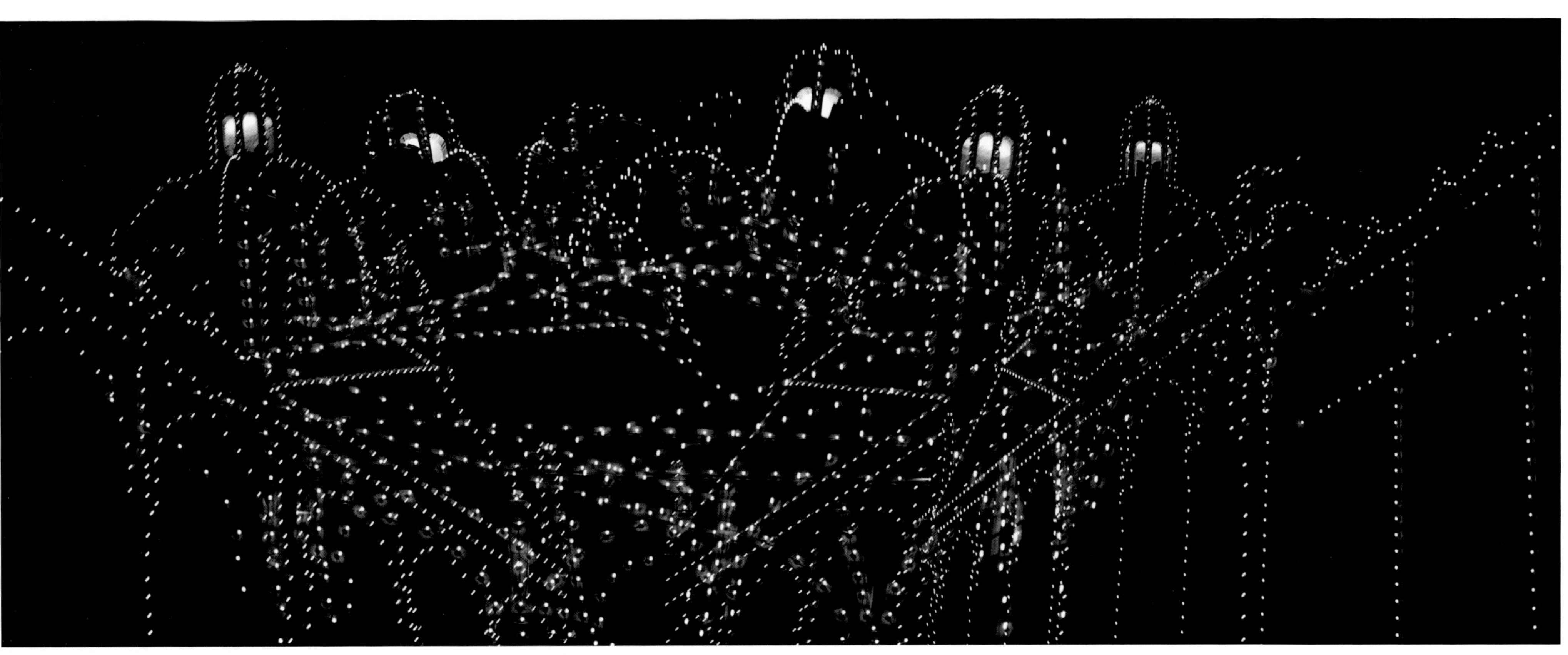

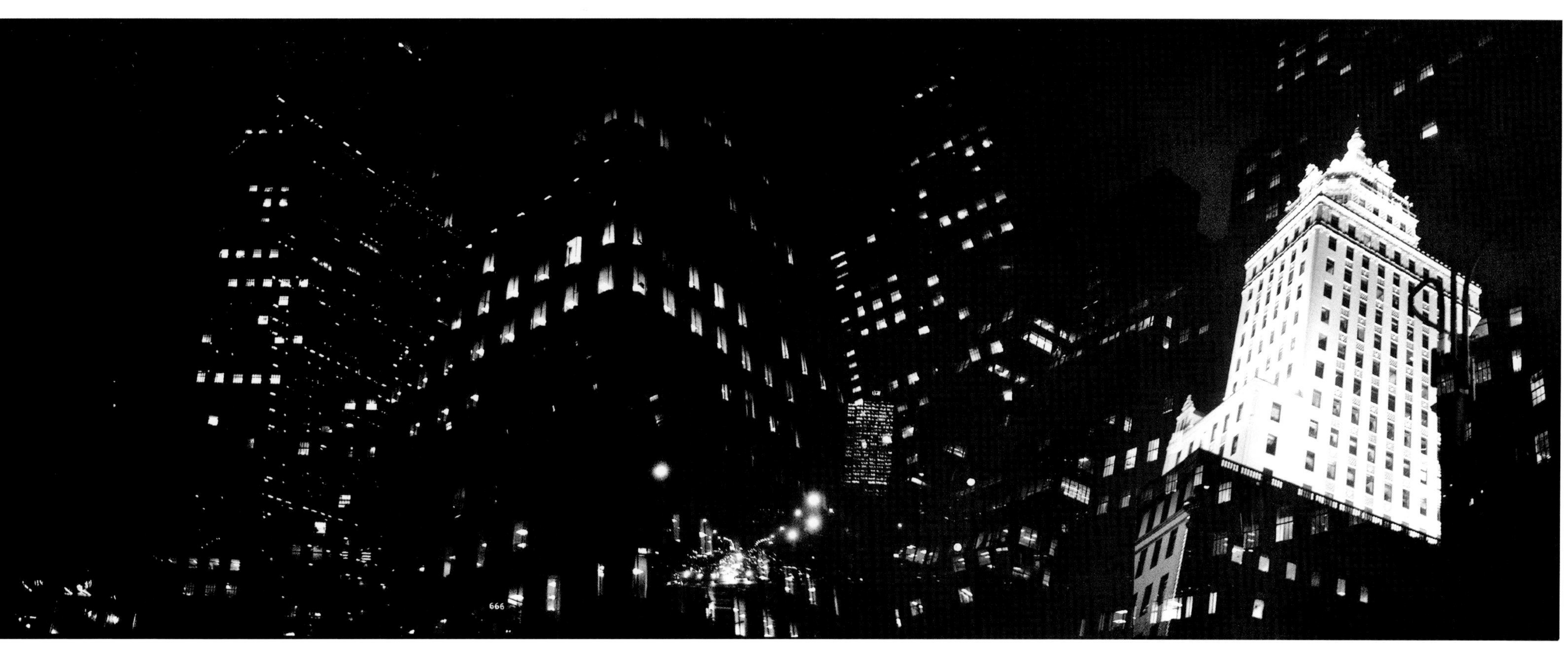

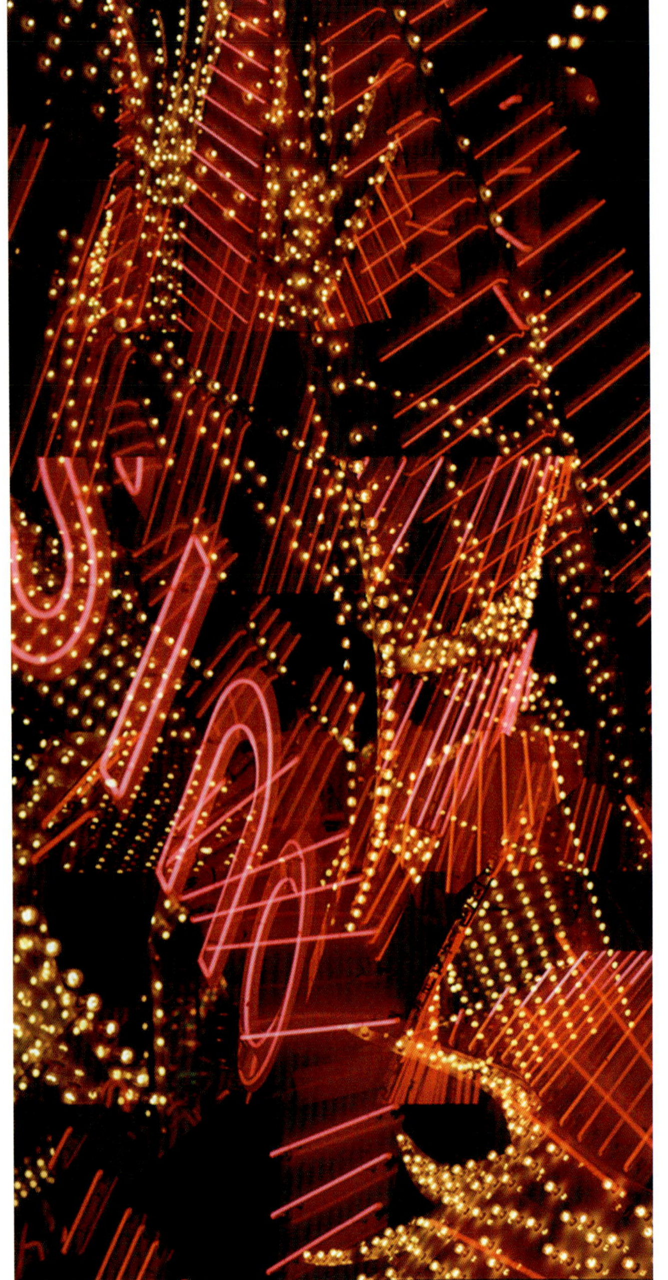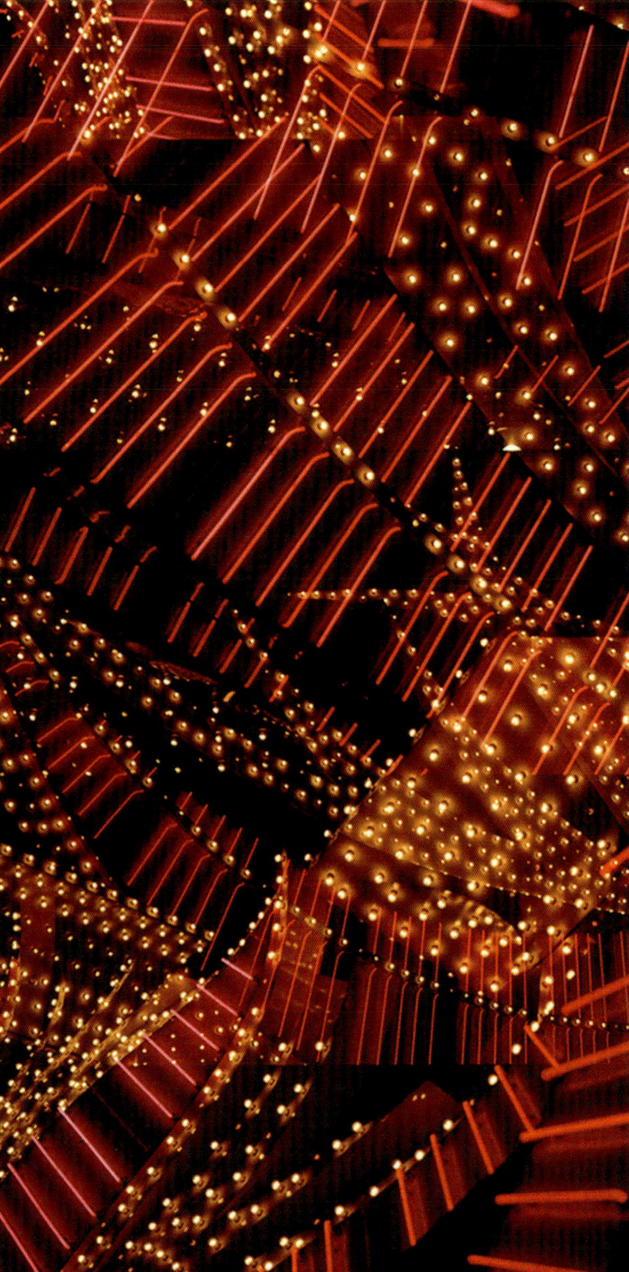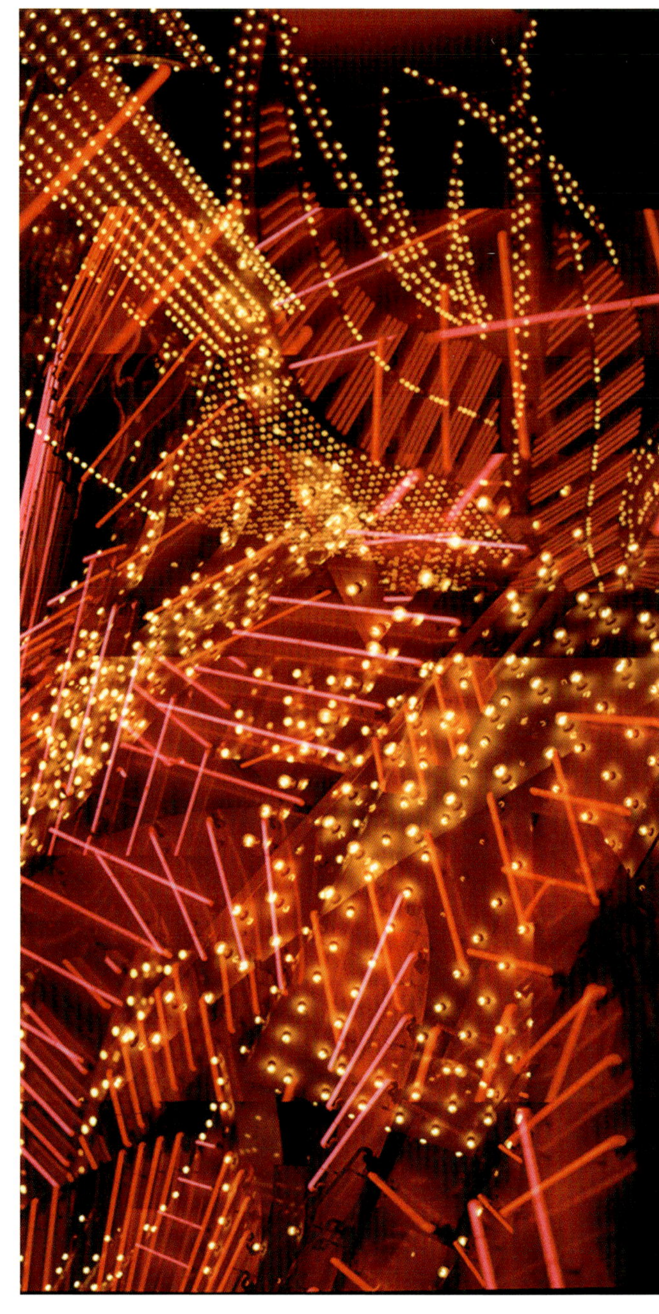

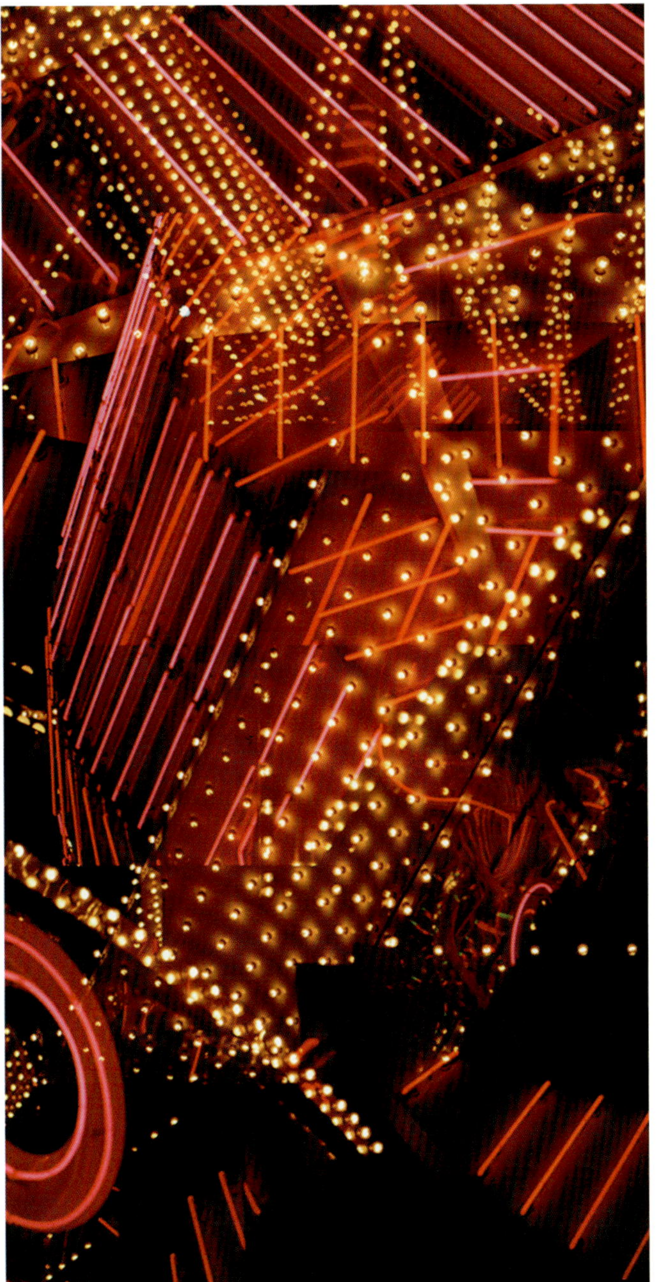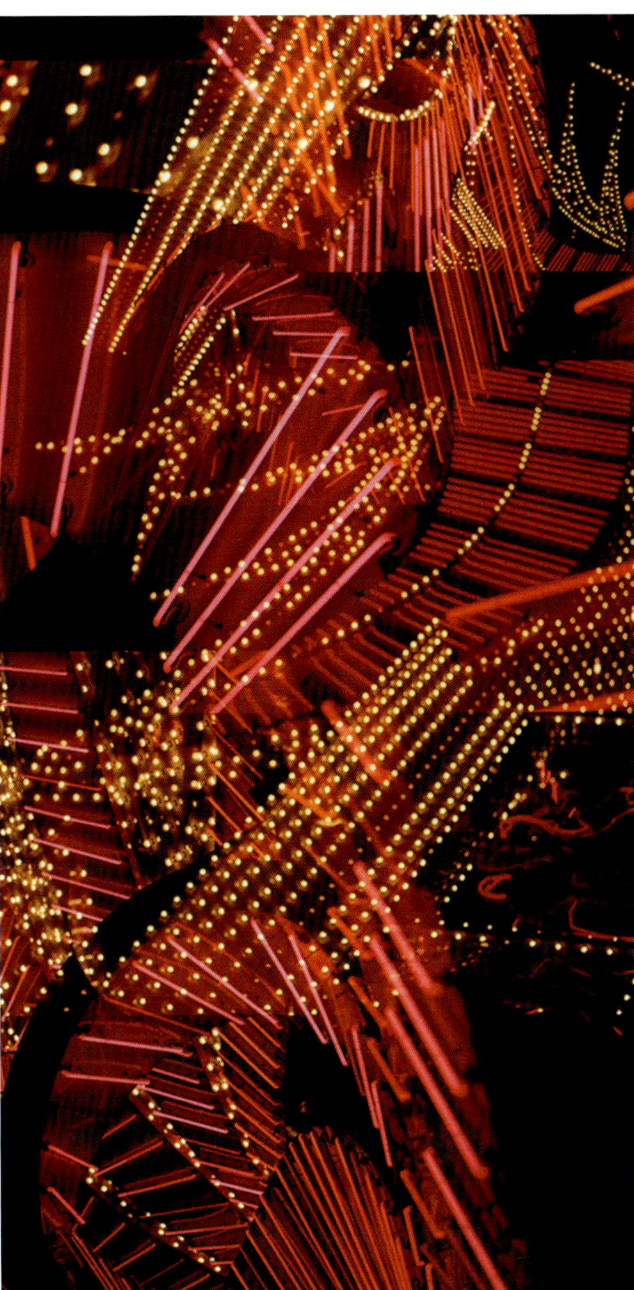

Las Vegas Flamingo Pentaptych   Las Vegas, Nevada, 1995   ARCHITECT: Heath and Company (neon)

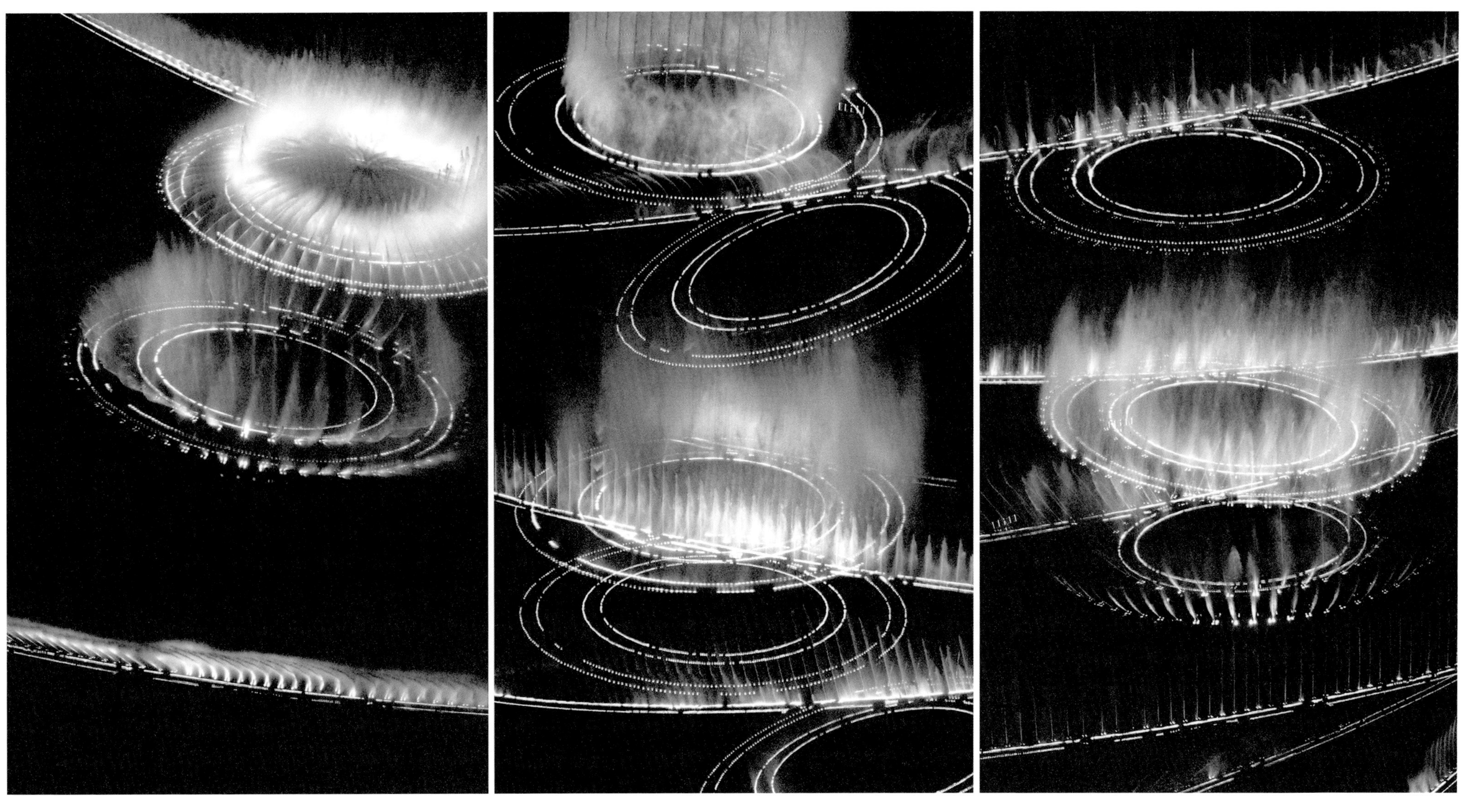

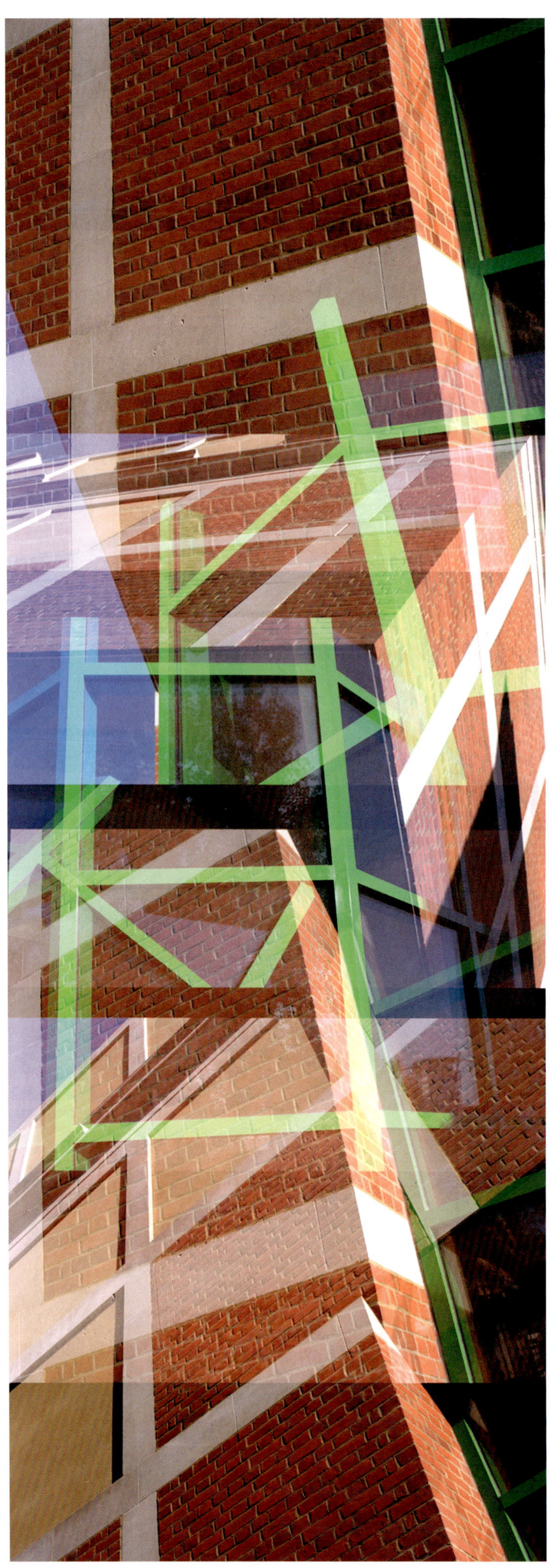

Tate Extension | X's   London, England, 1986   ARCHITECT: James Stirling

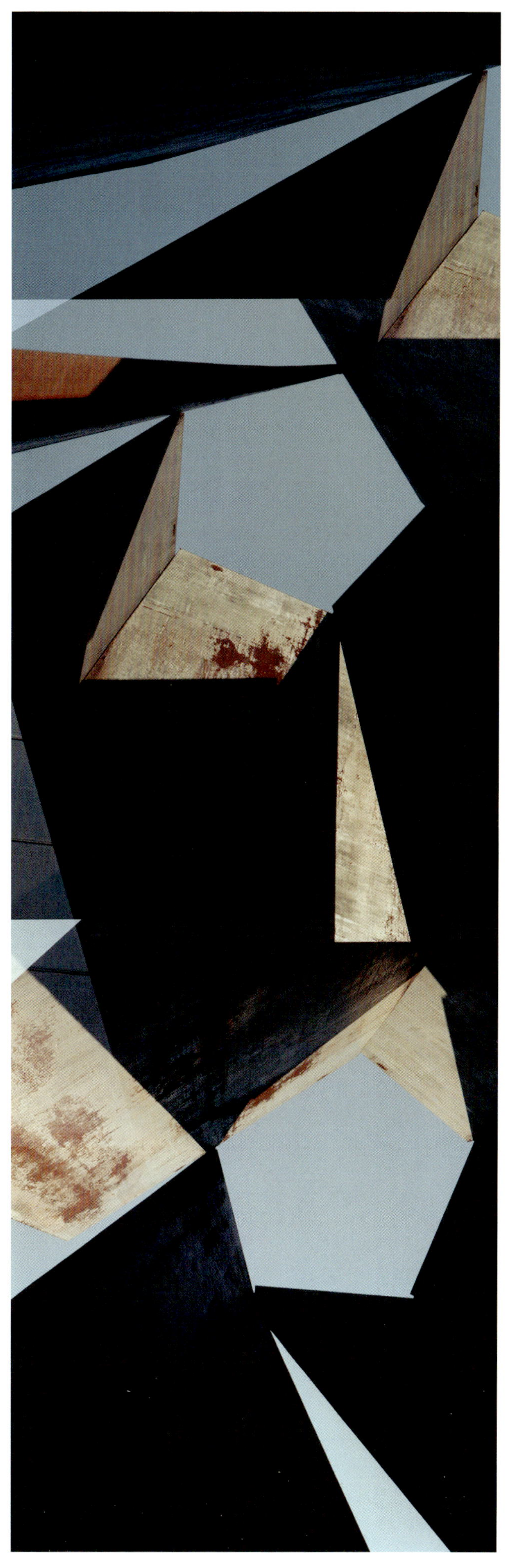

Serra Broadgate   London, England, 1988   ARTIST: Richard Serra

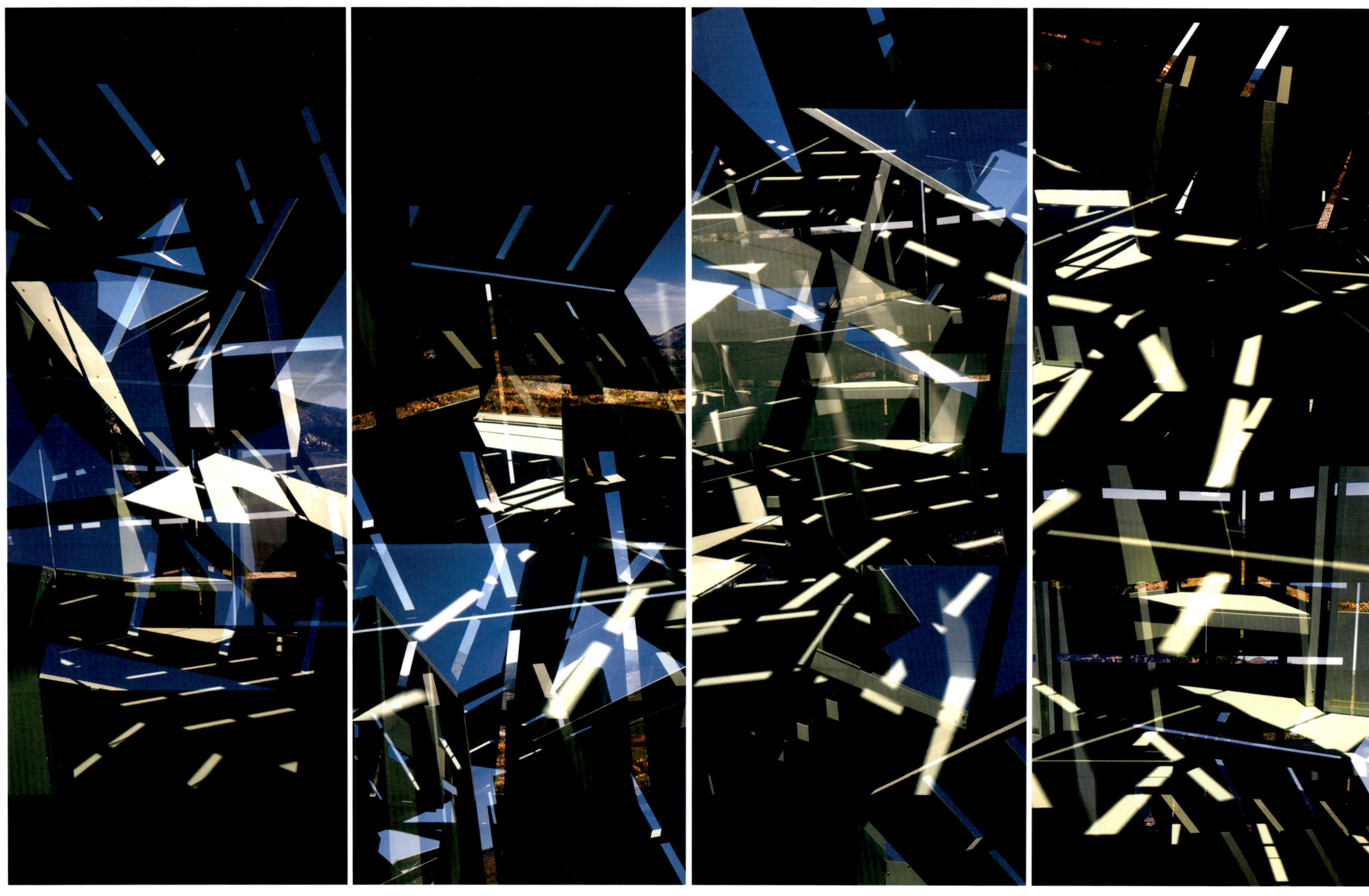

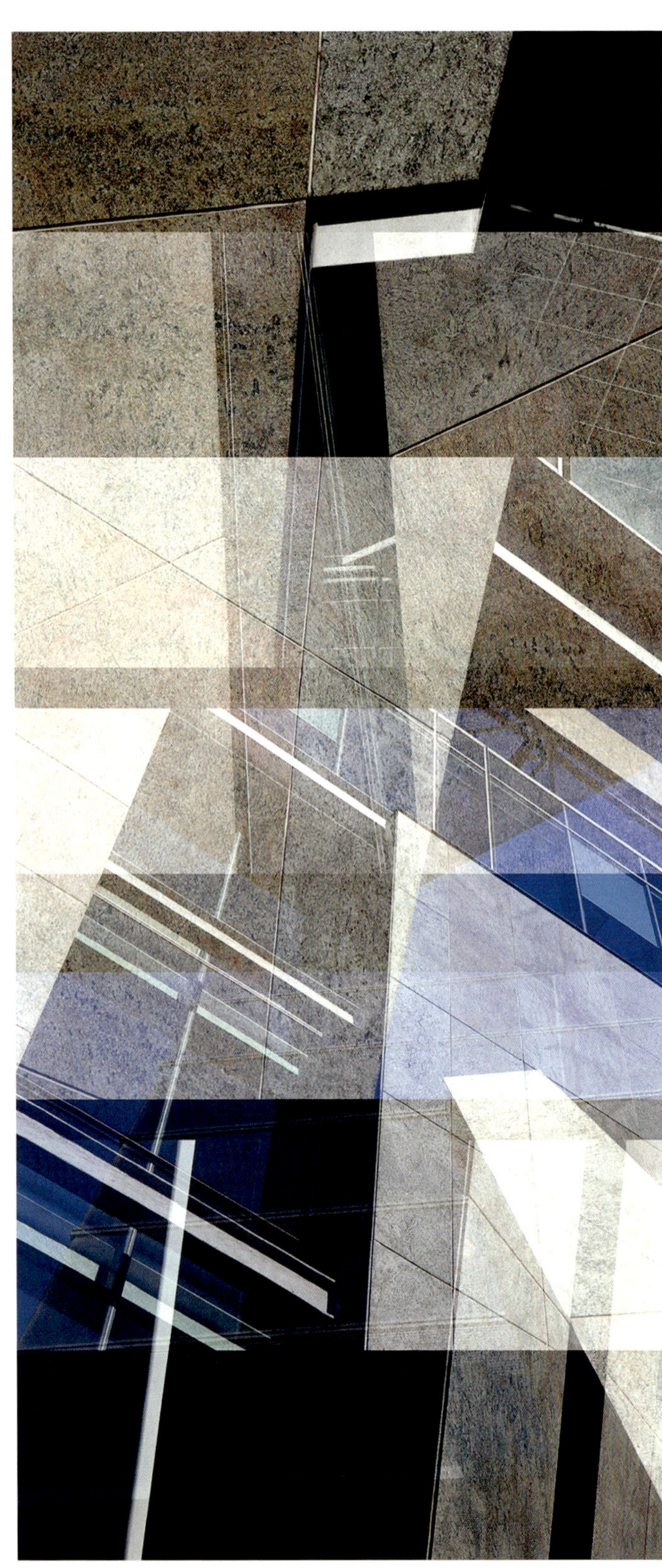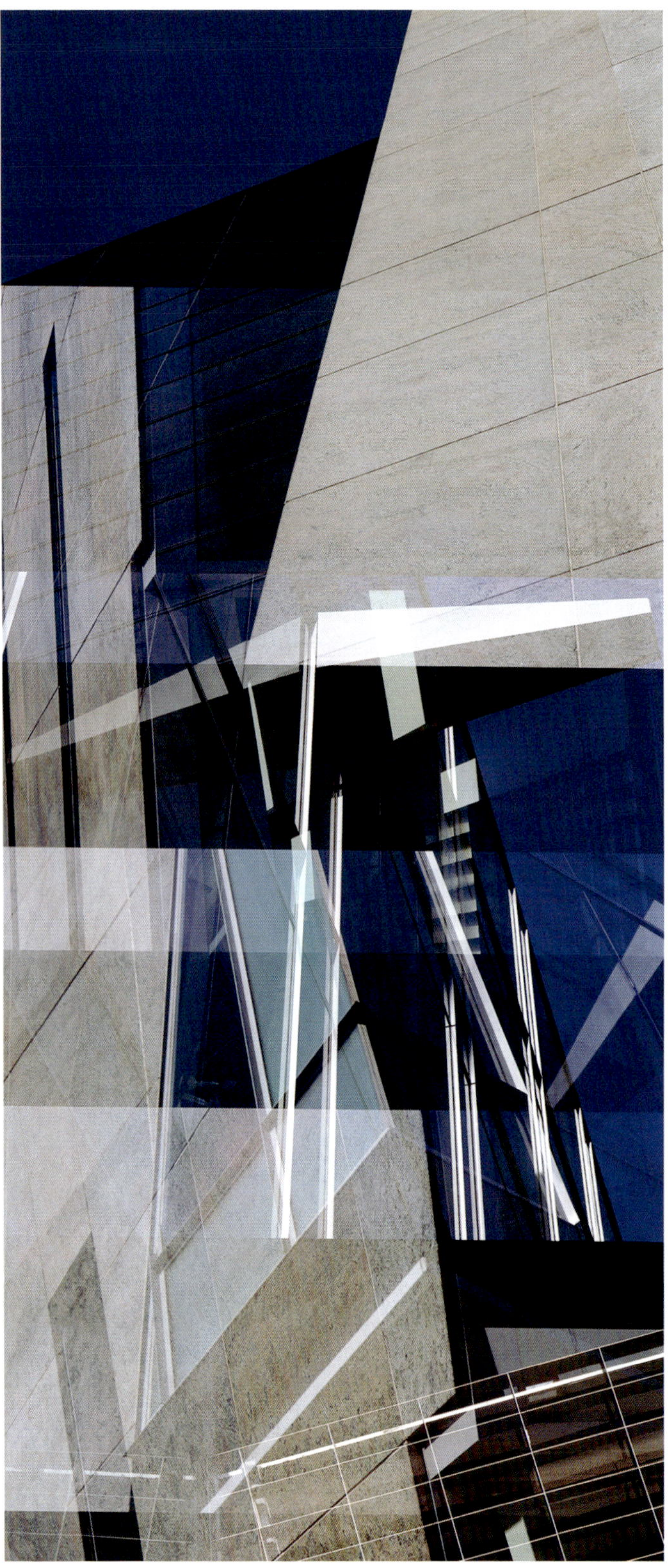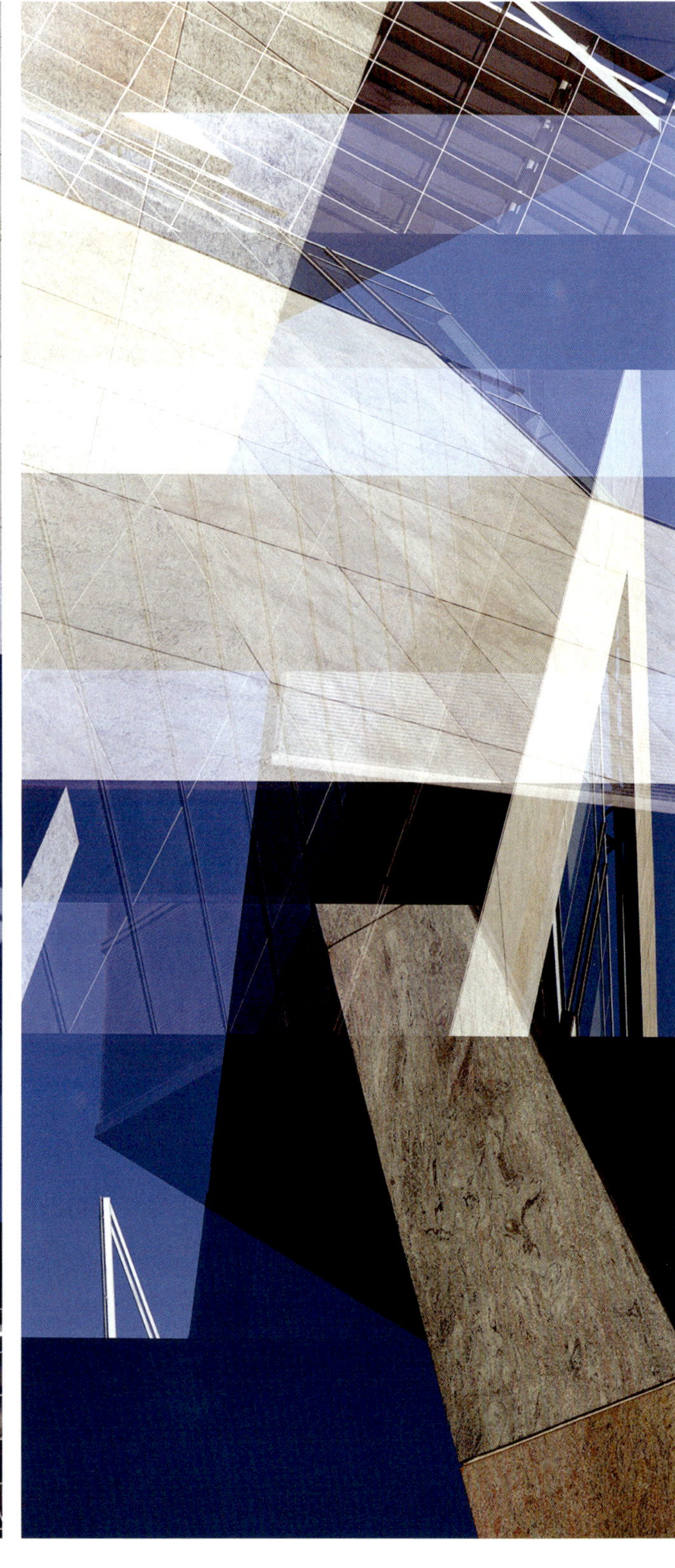

Loyola Triptych   Los Angeles, California, 1988   ARCHITECT: Frank O. Gehry & Associates

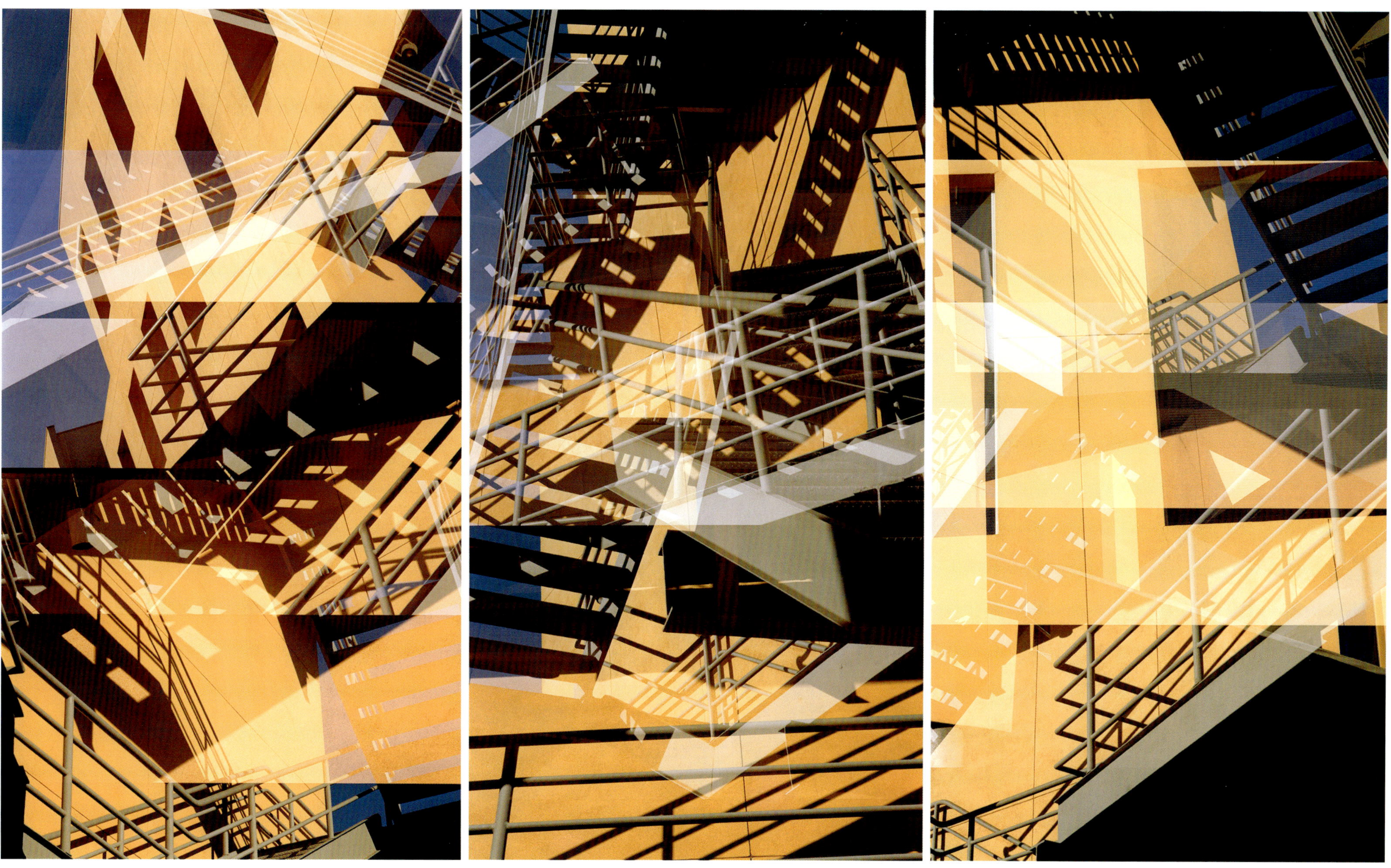

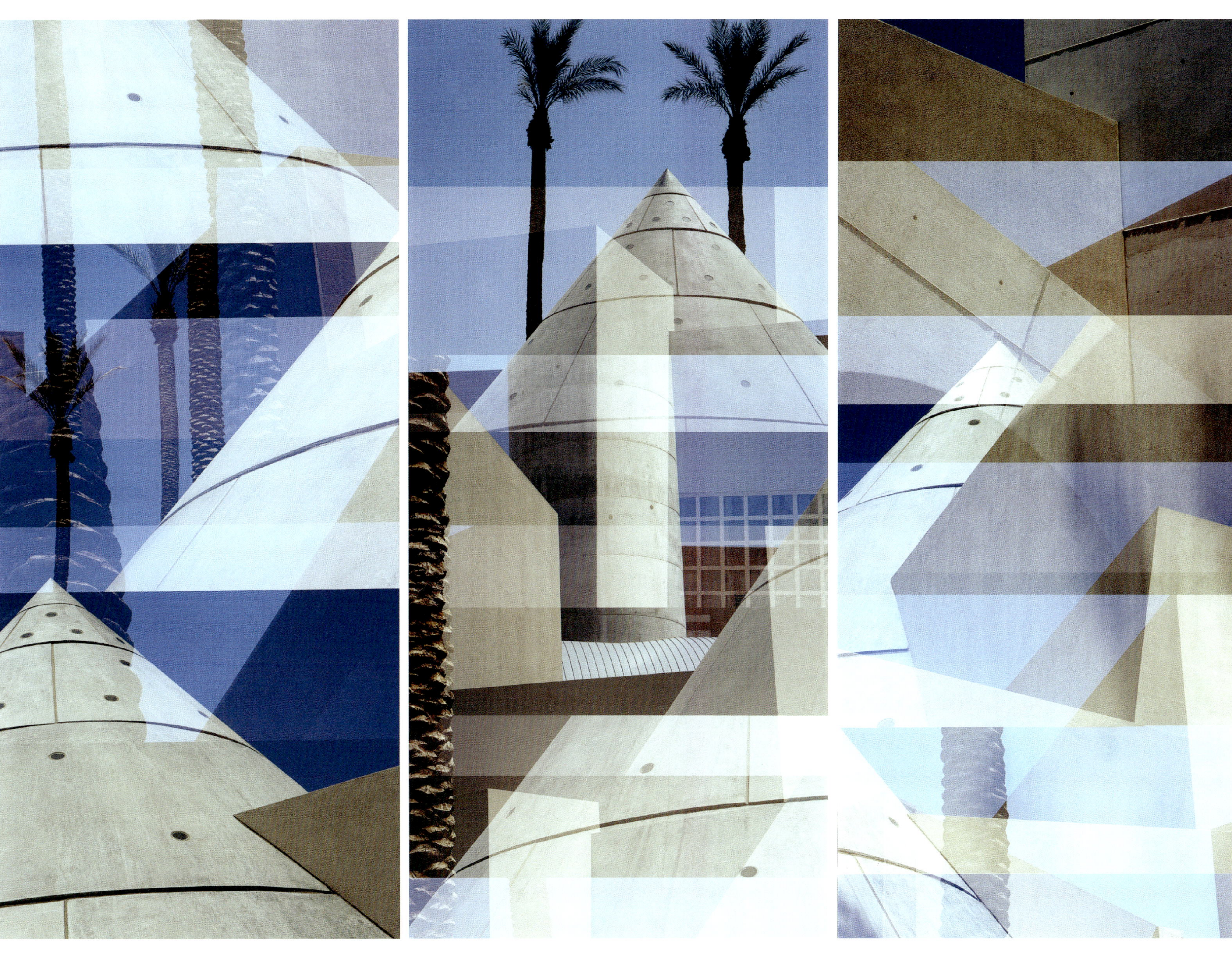

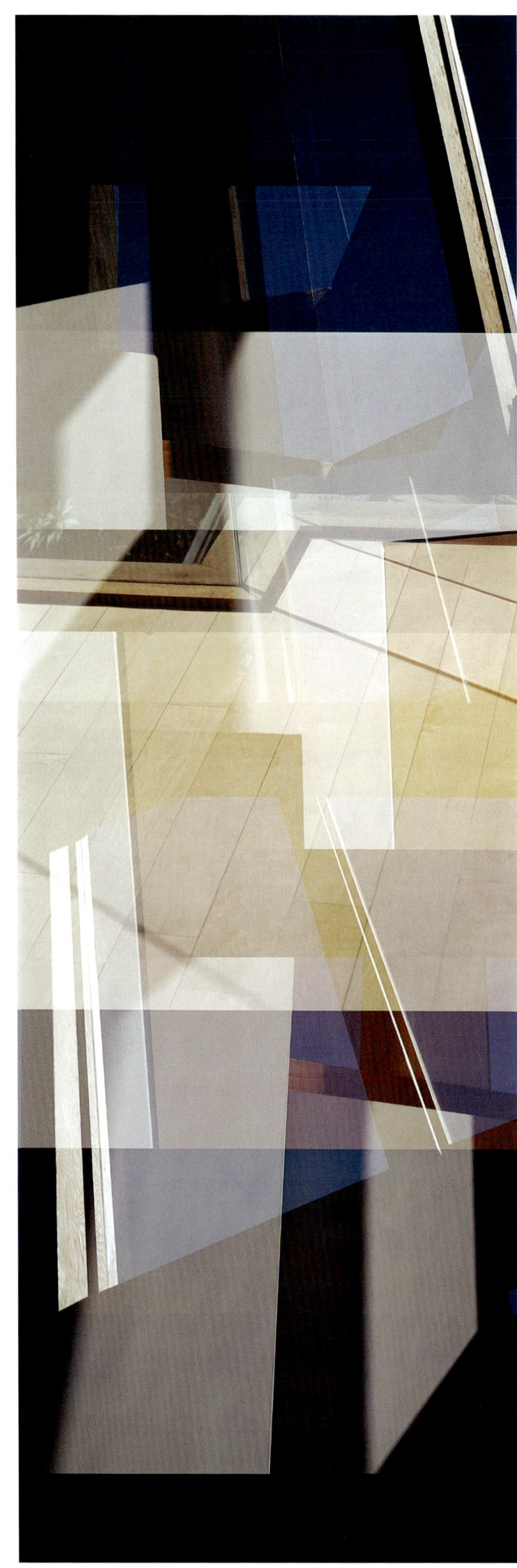
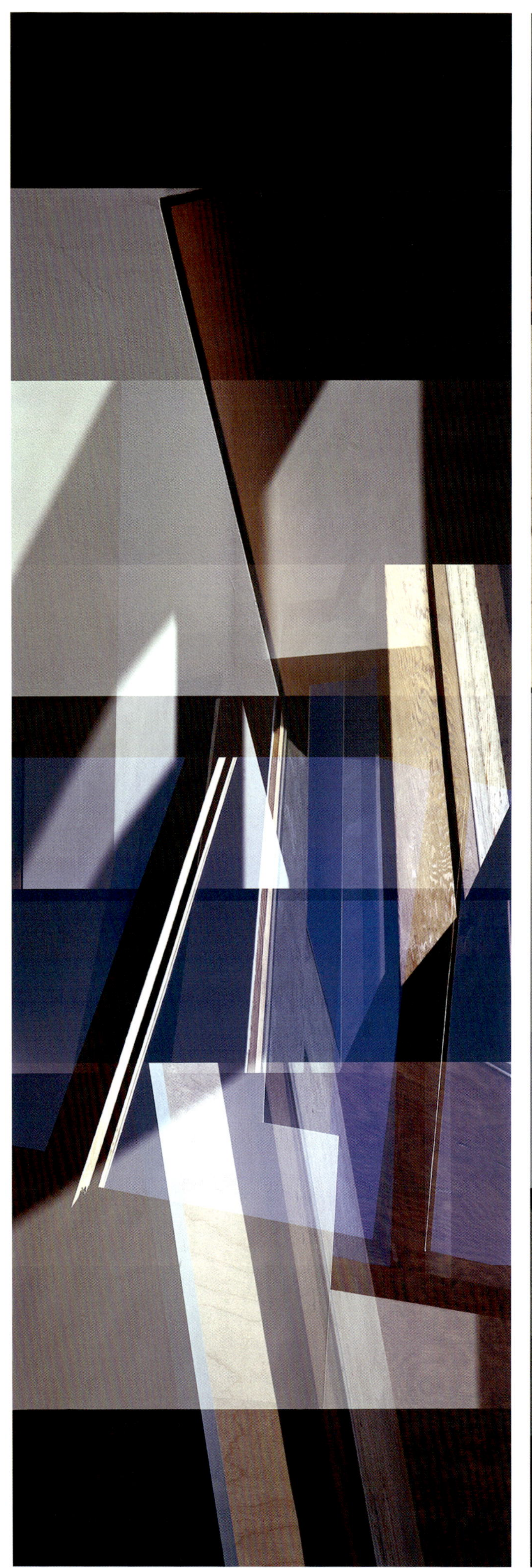
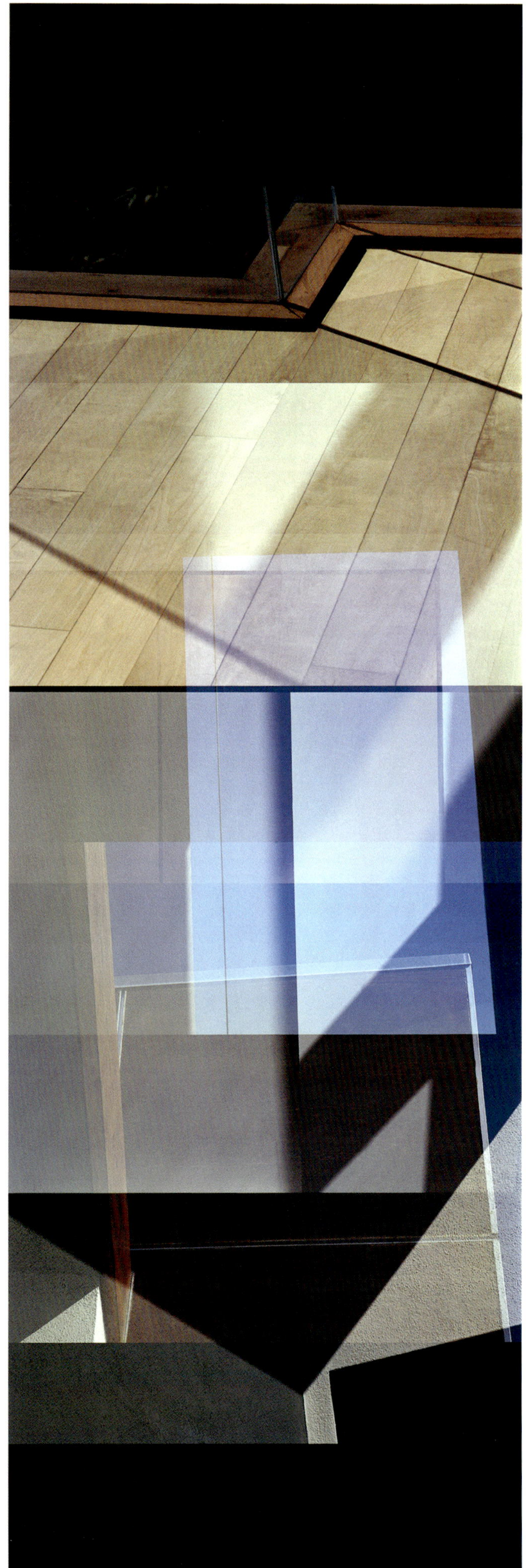

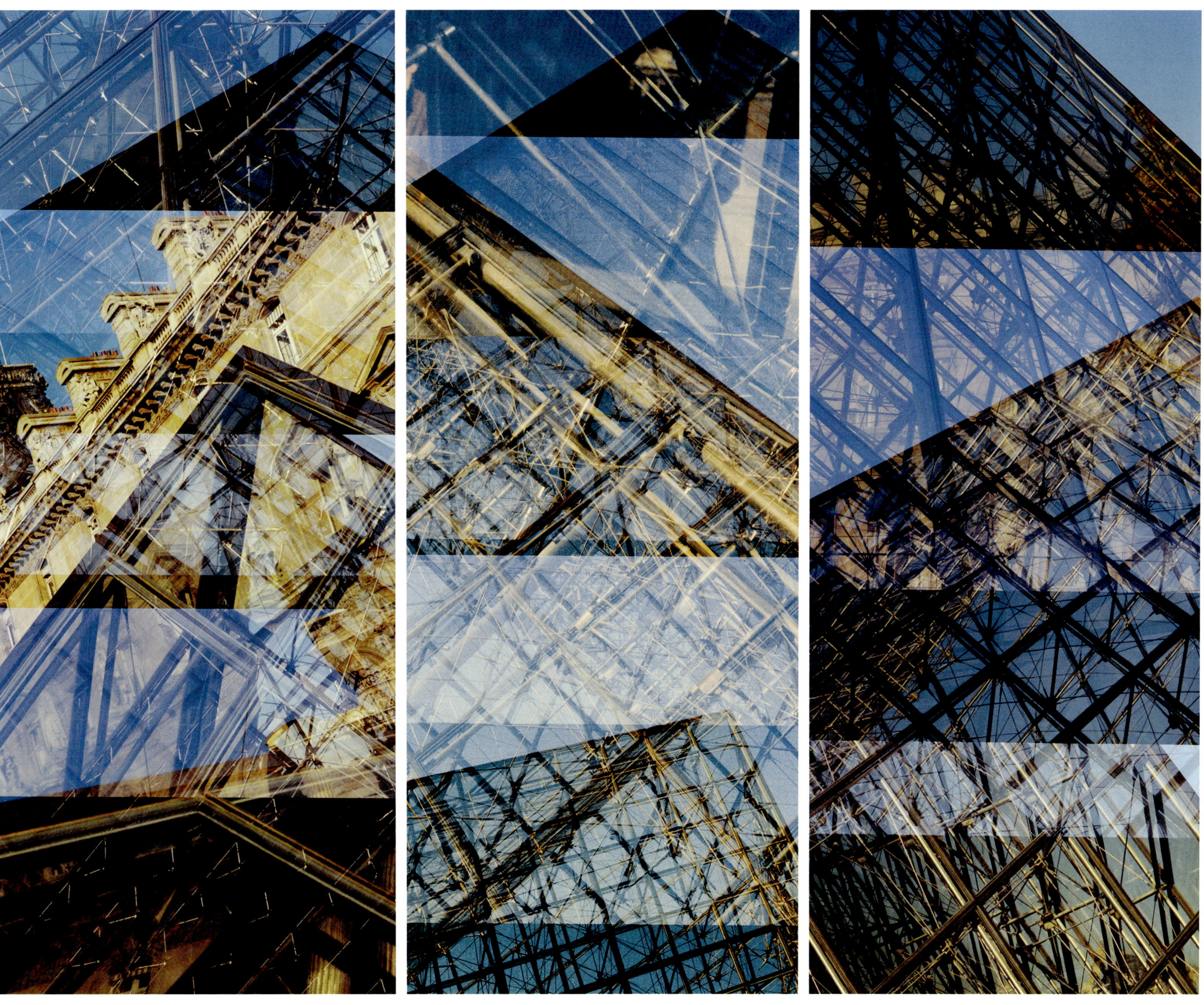

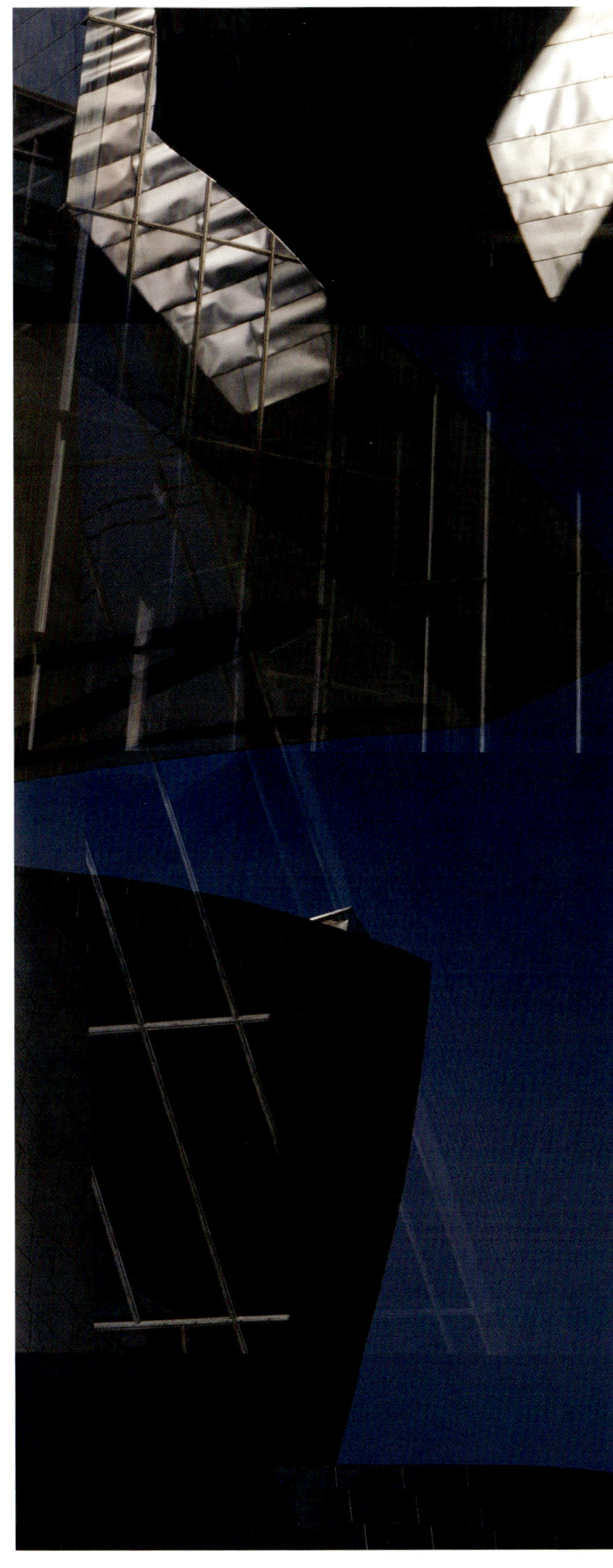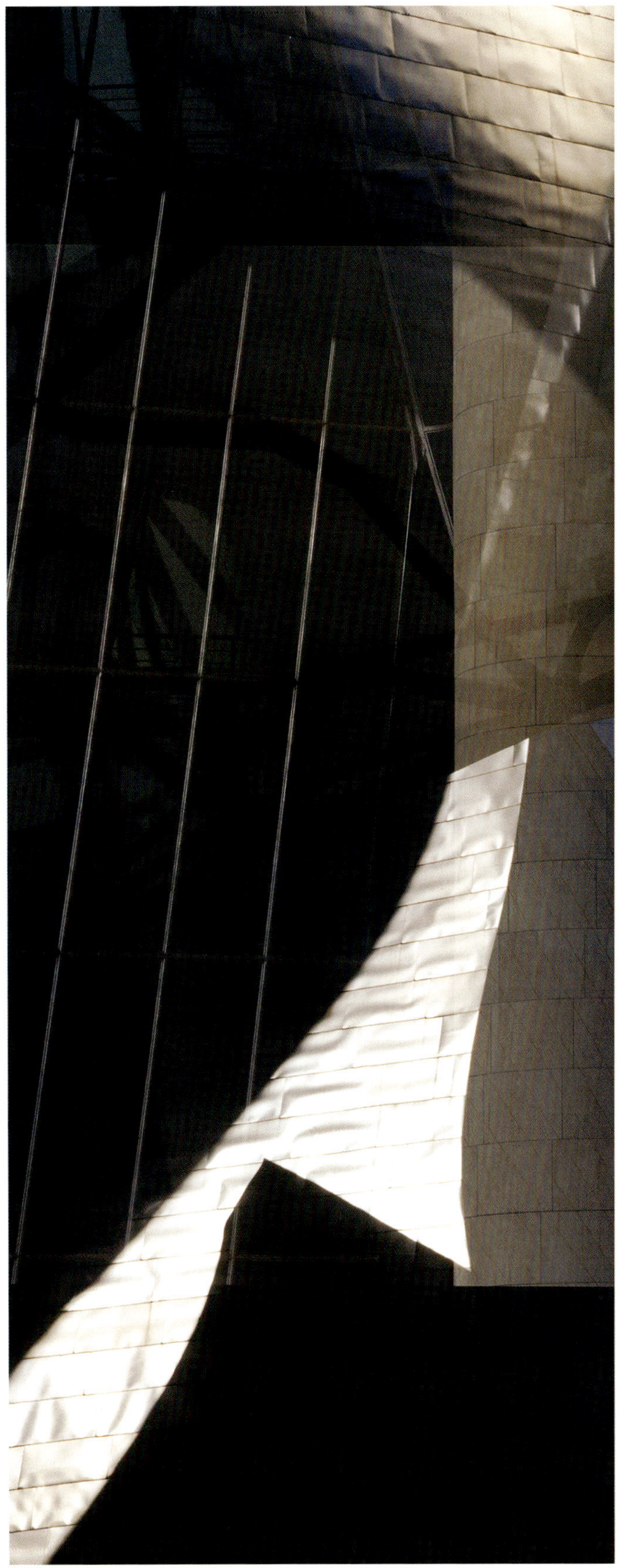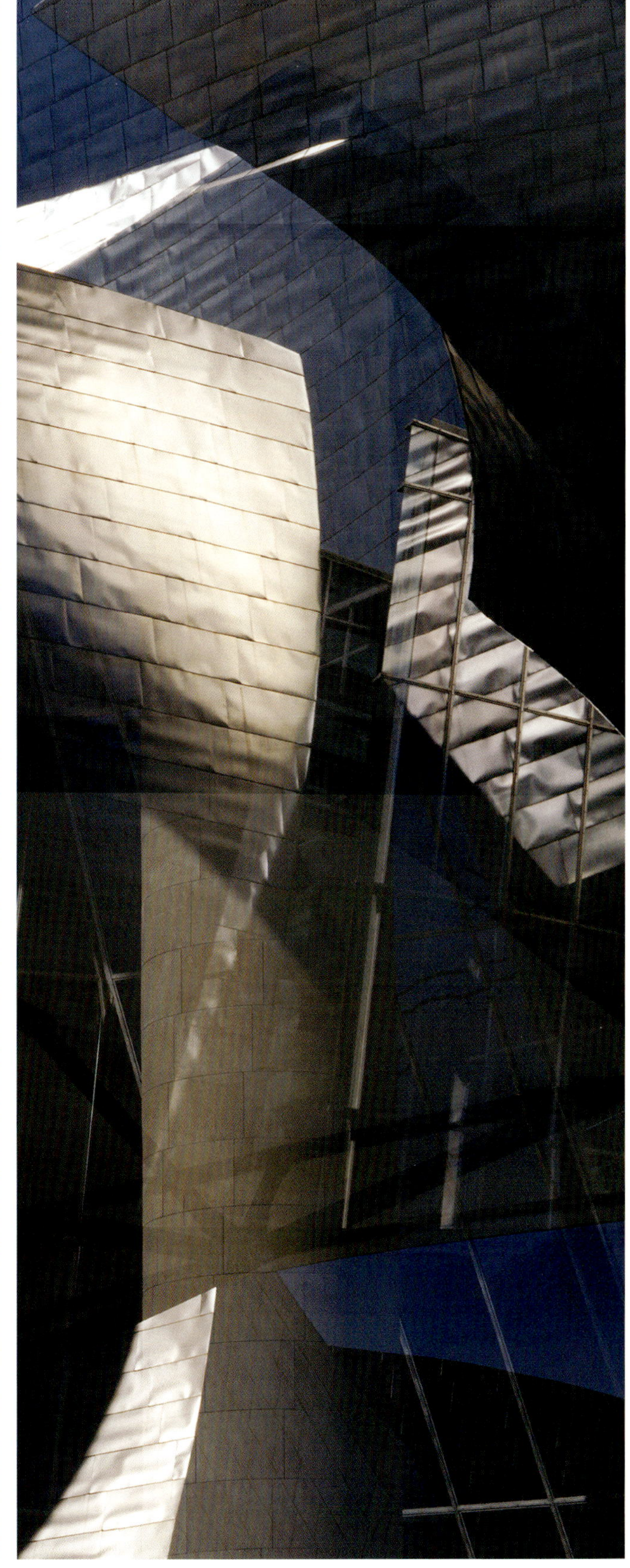

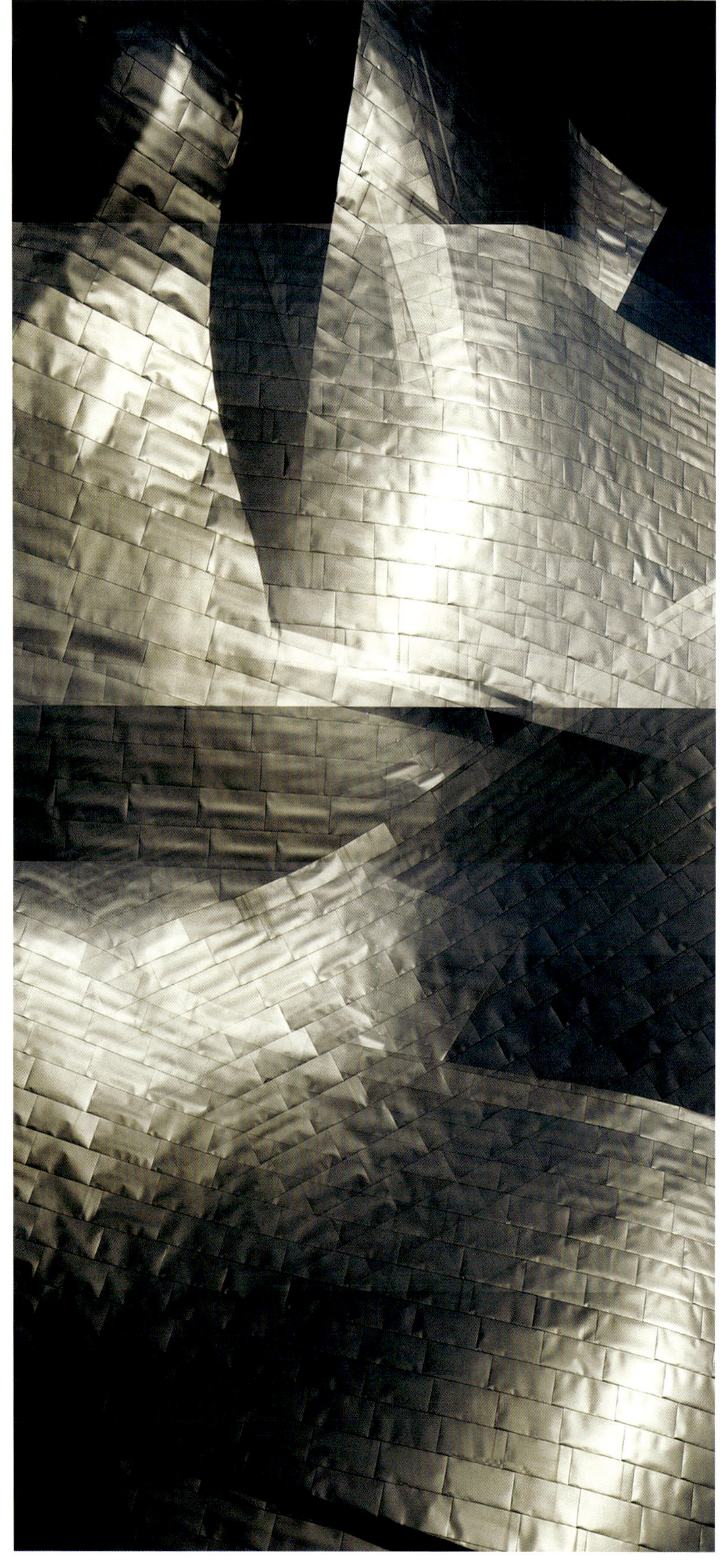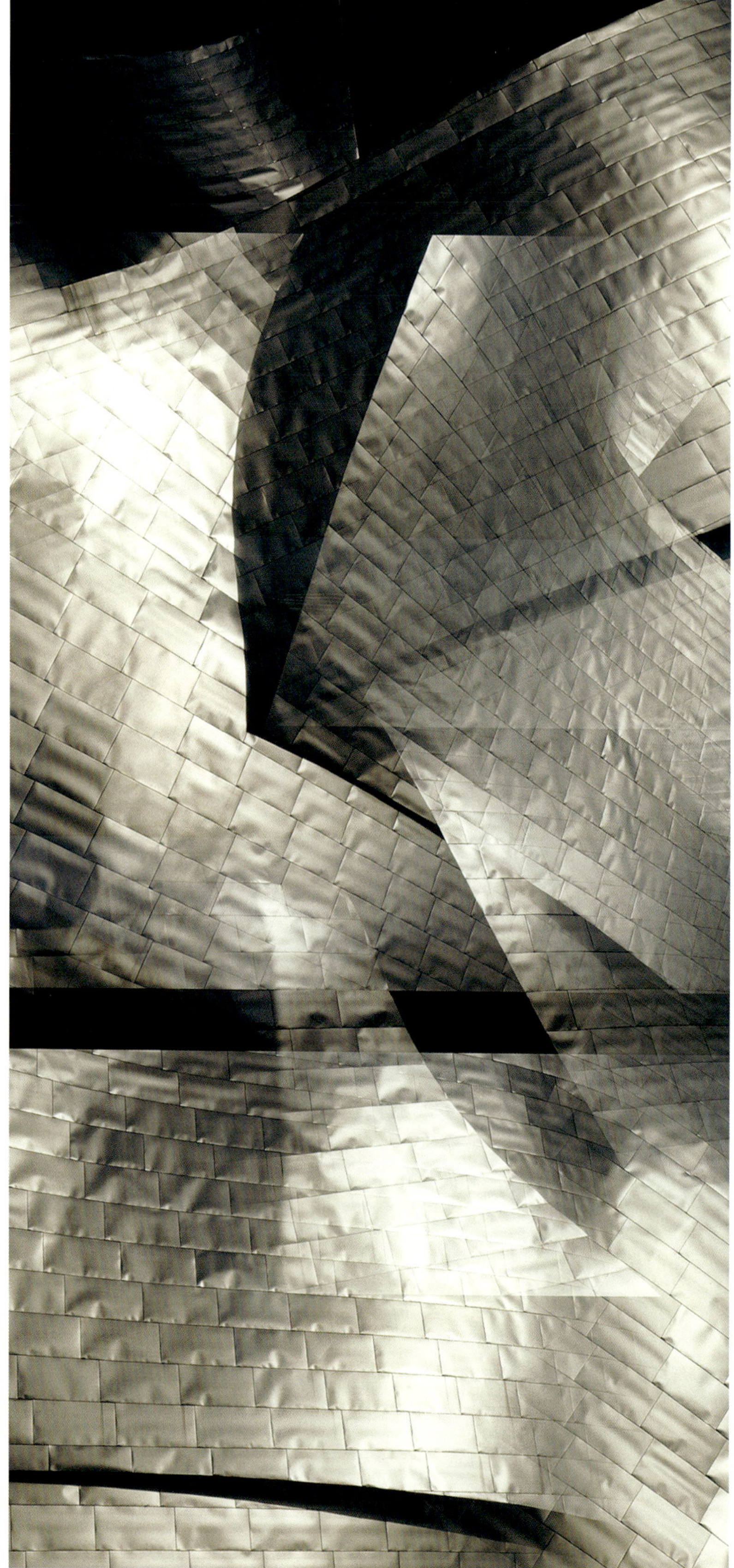

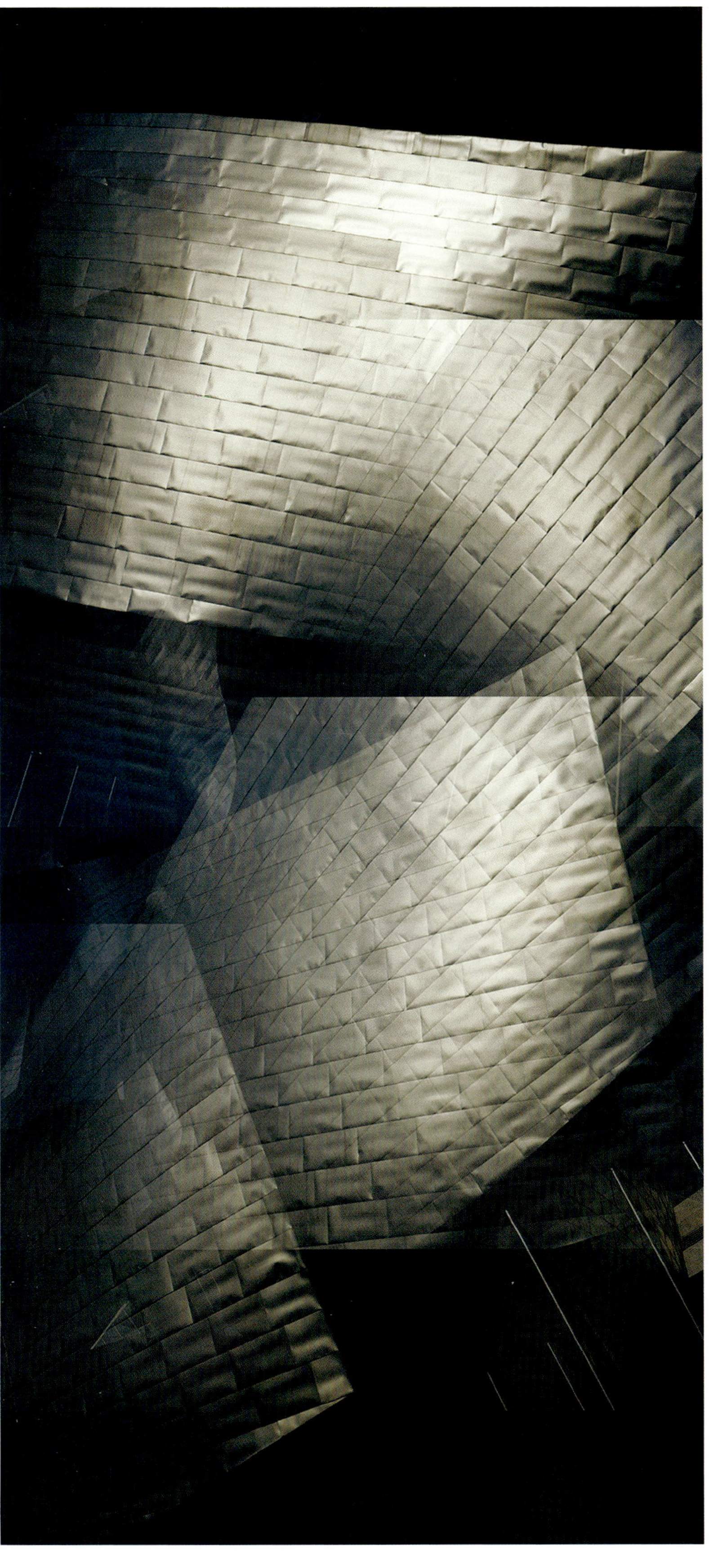

Bilbao Guggenheim Silver Triptych   Bilbao, Spain, 2000   ARCHITECT: Frank O. Gehry & Associates

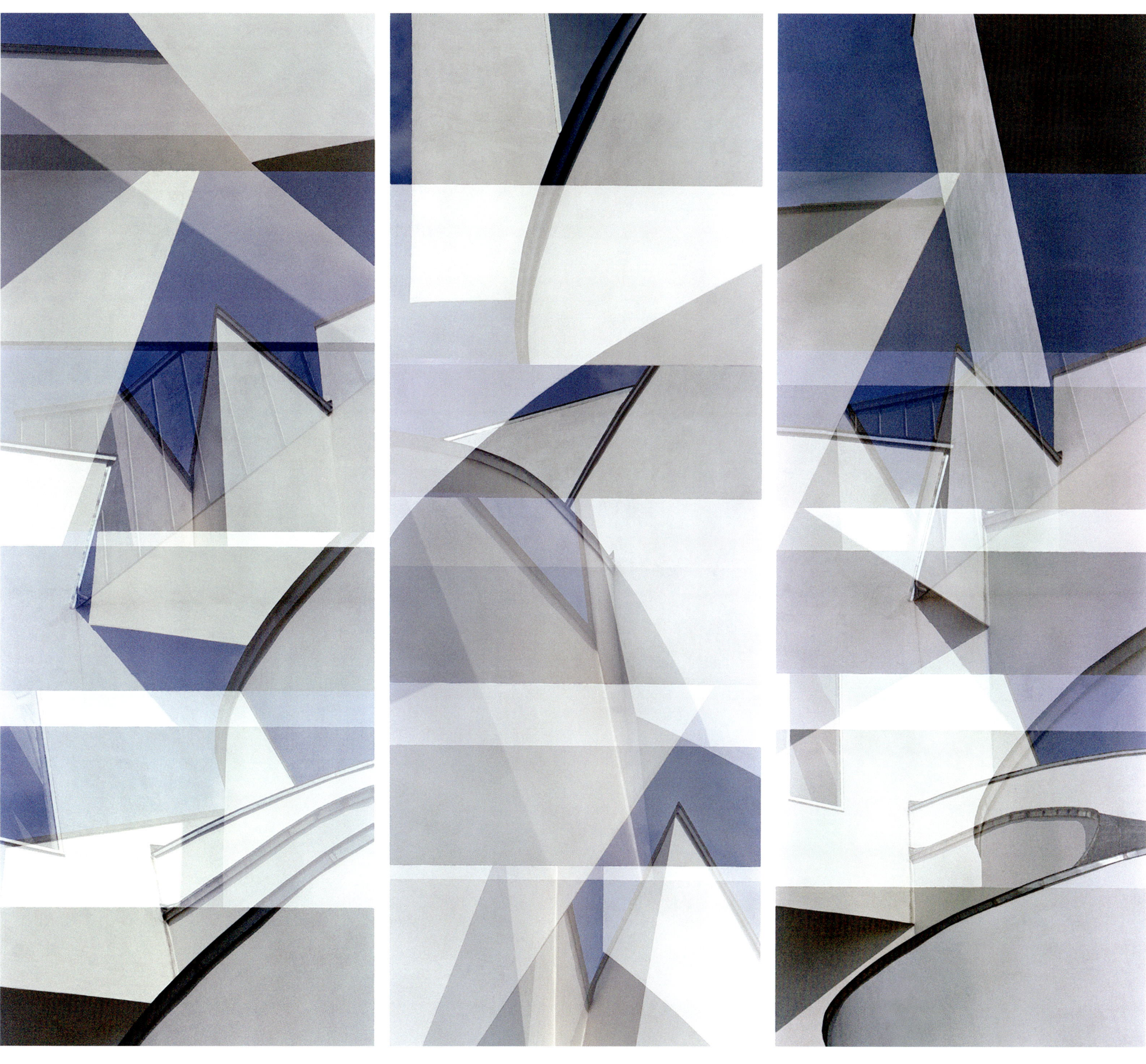

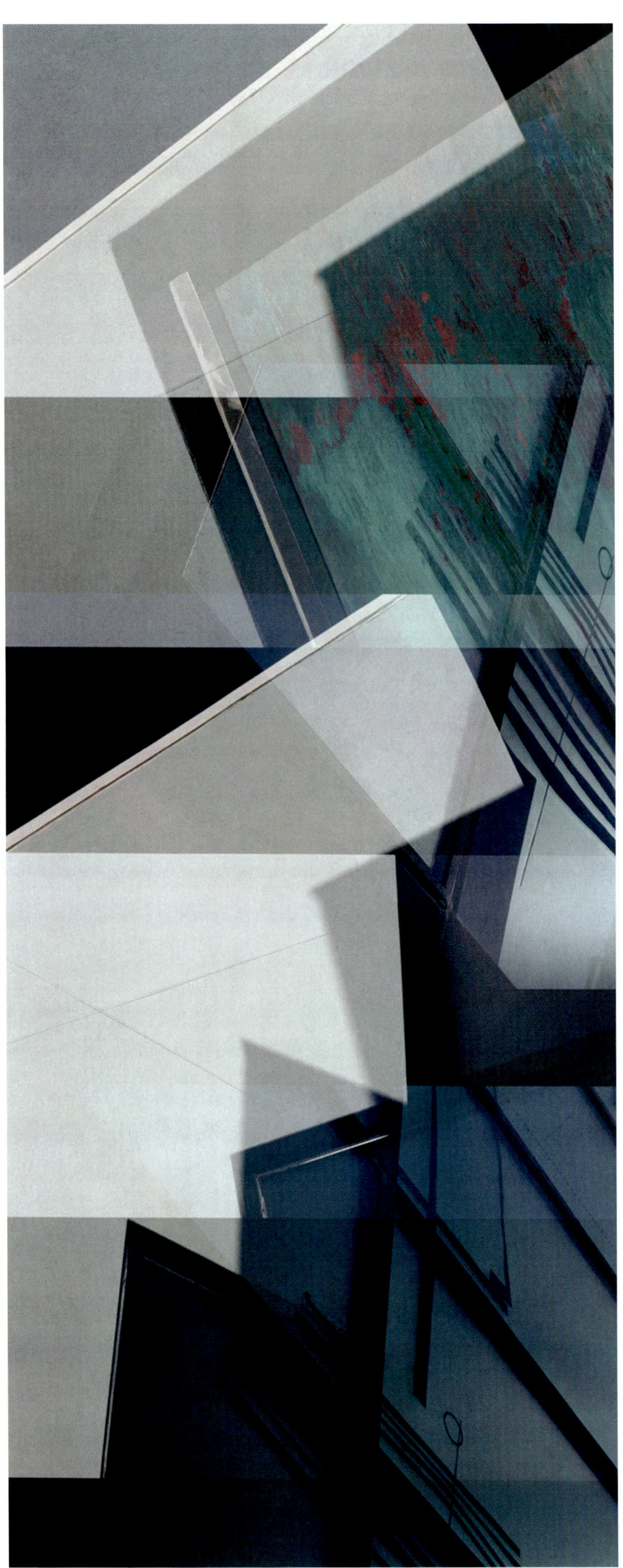

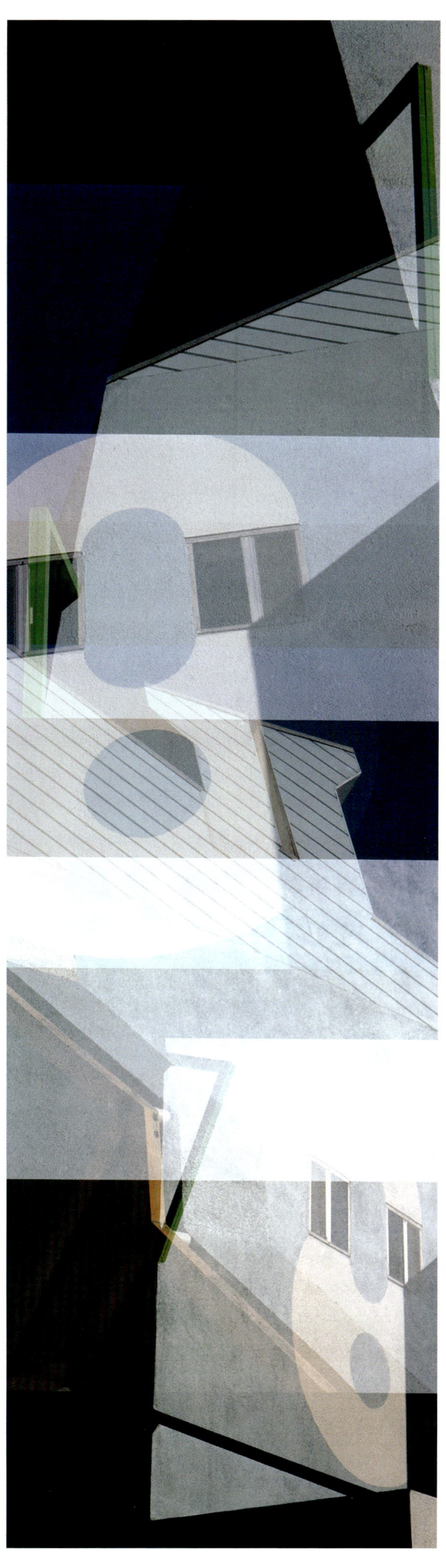

Eric Owen Moss House Los Angeles, California, 1991 ARCHITECT: Eric Owen Moss

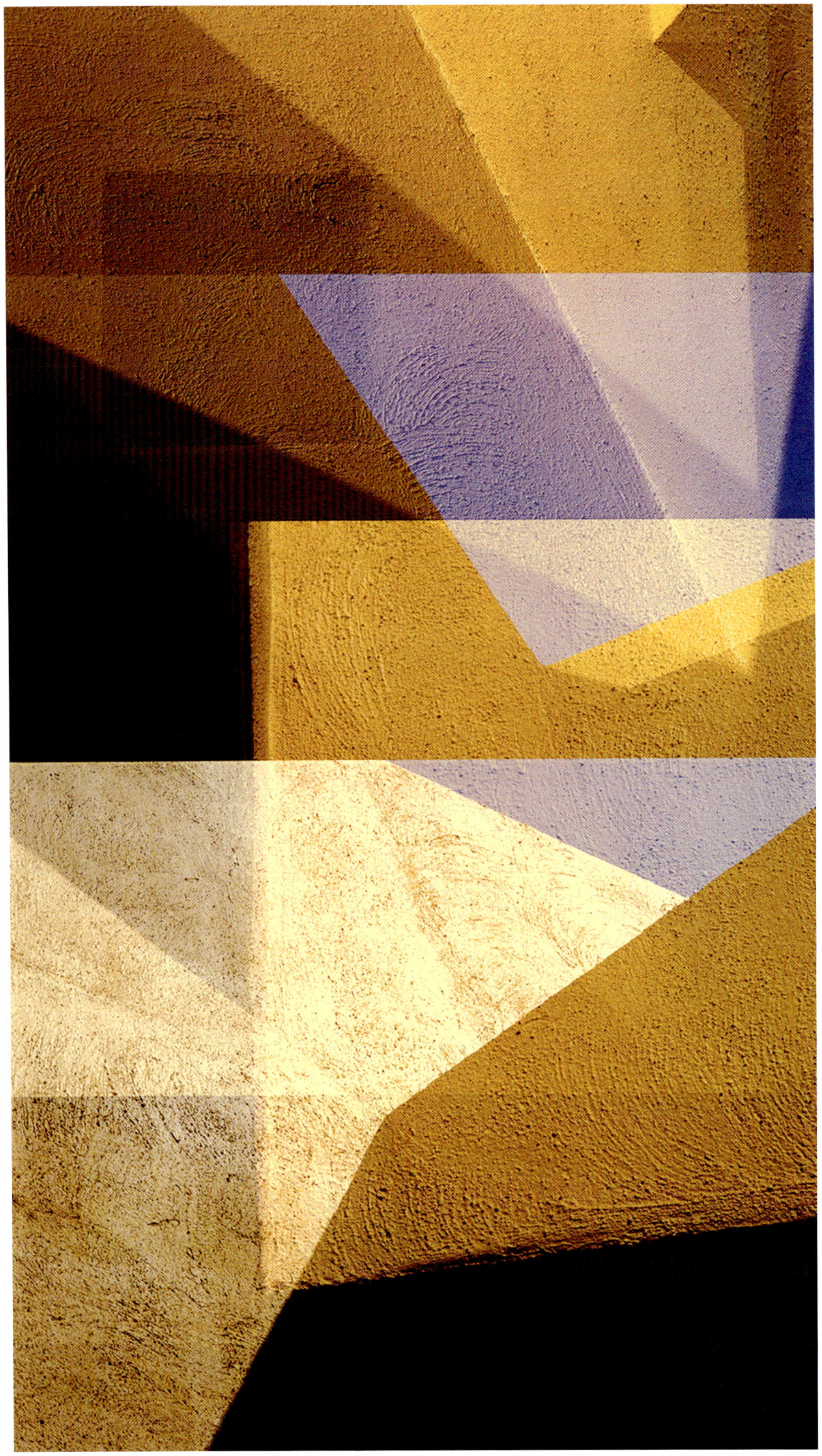

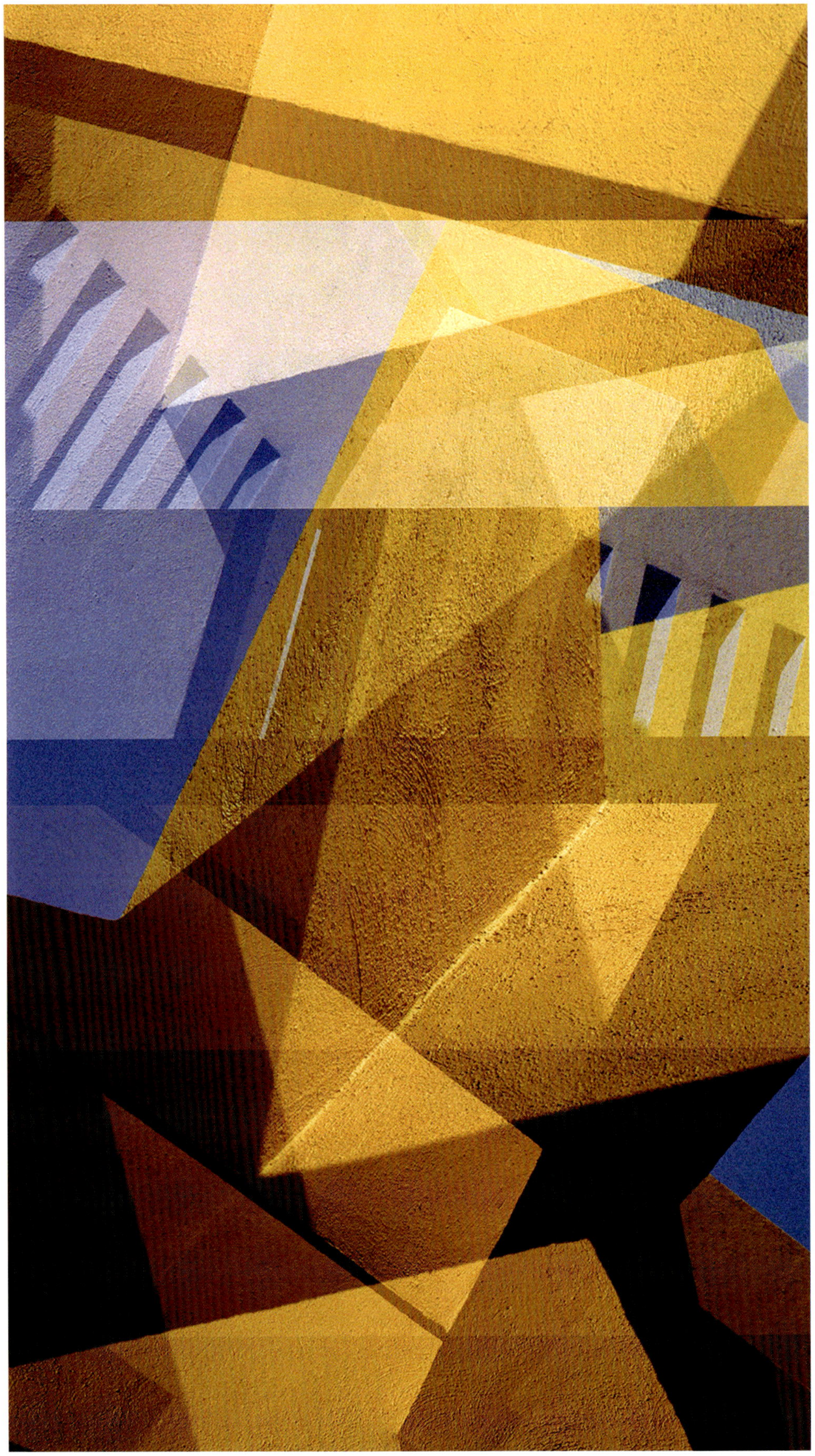

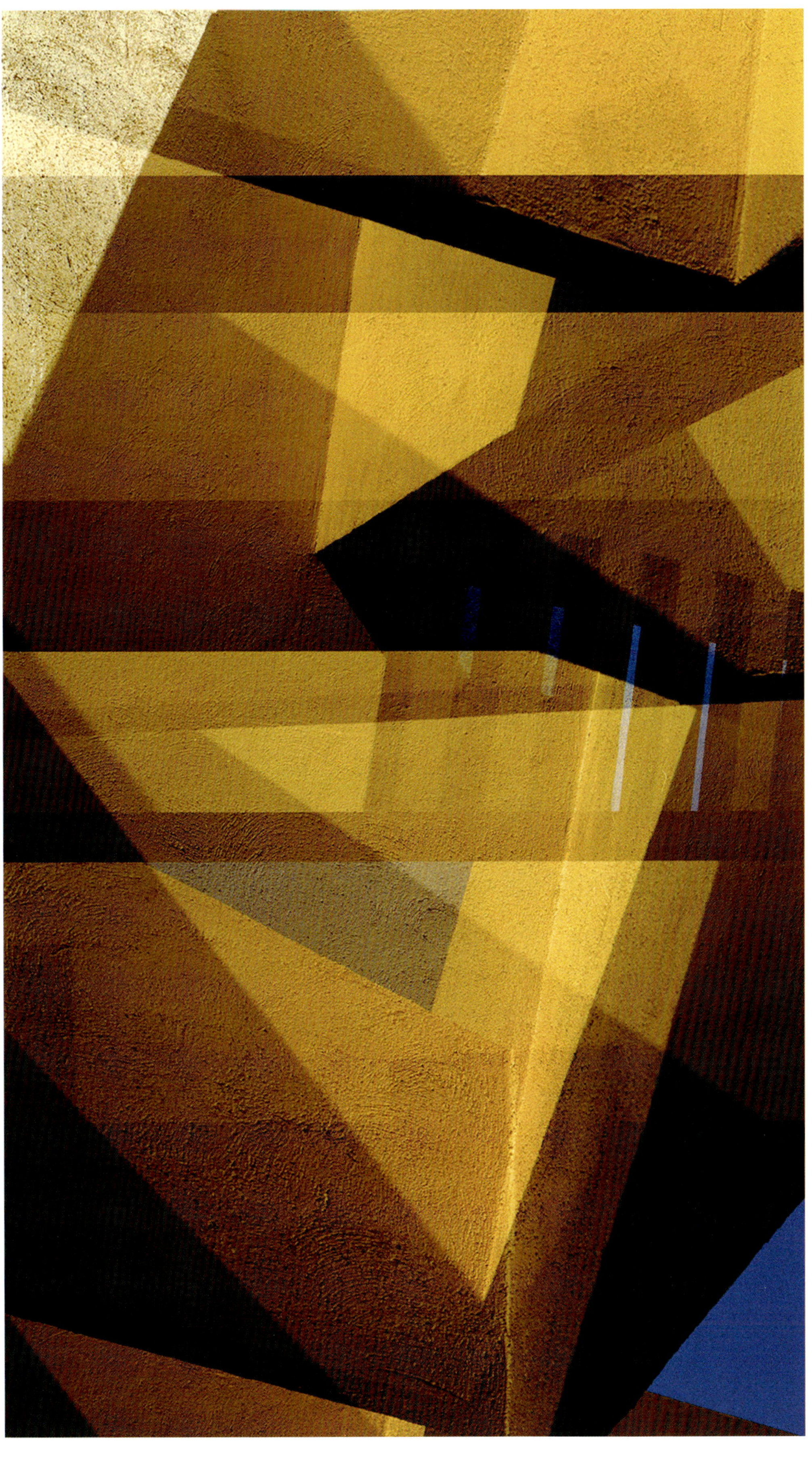

Legoretta Yellow Triptych   Los Angeles, California, 1992   ARCHITECT: Ricardo Legoretta

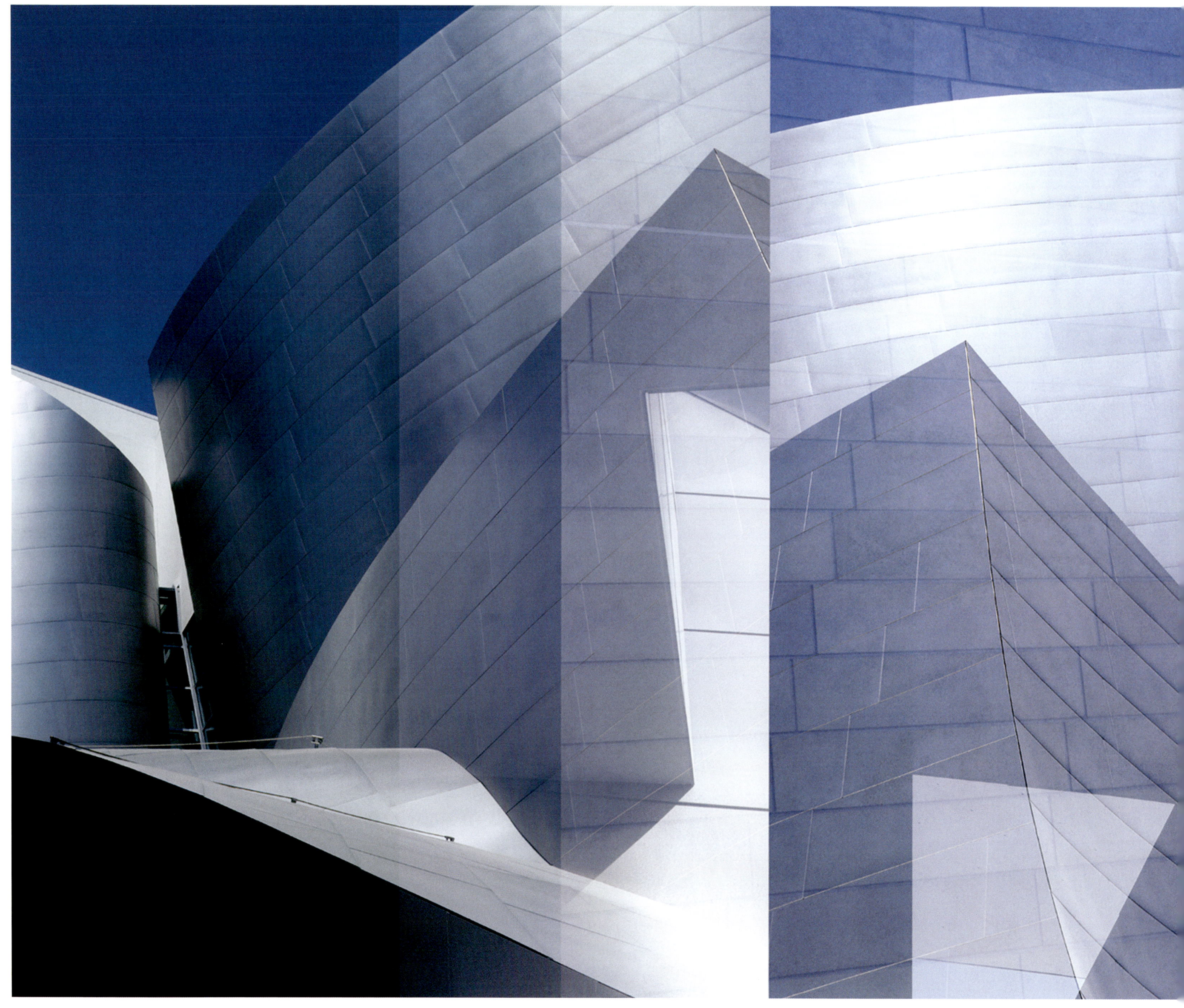

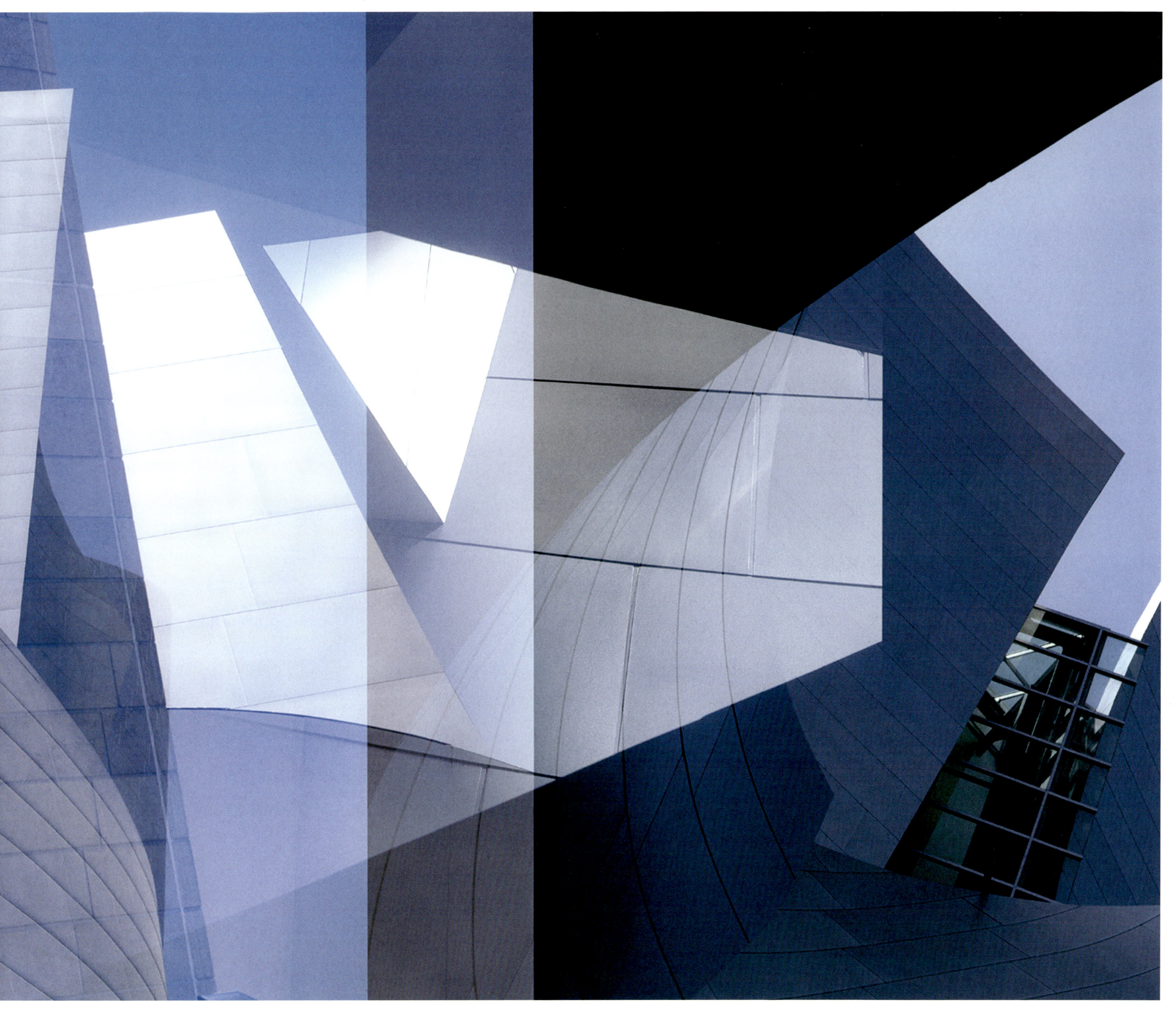

Disney Hall I   Los Angeles, California, 2003   ARCHITECT: Frank O. Gehry & Associates

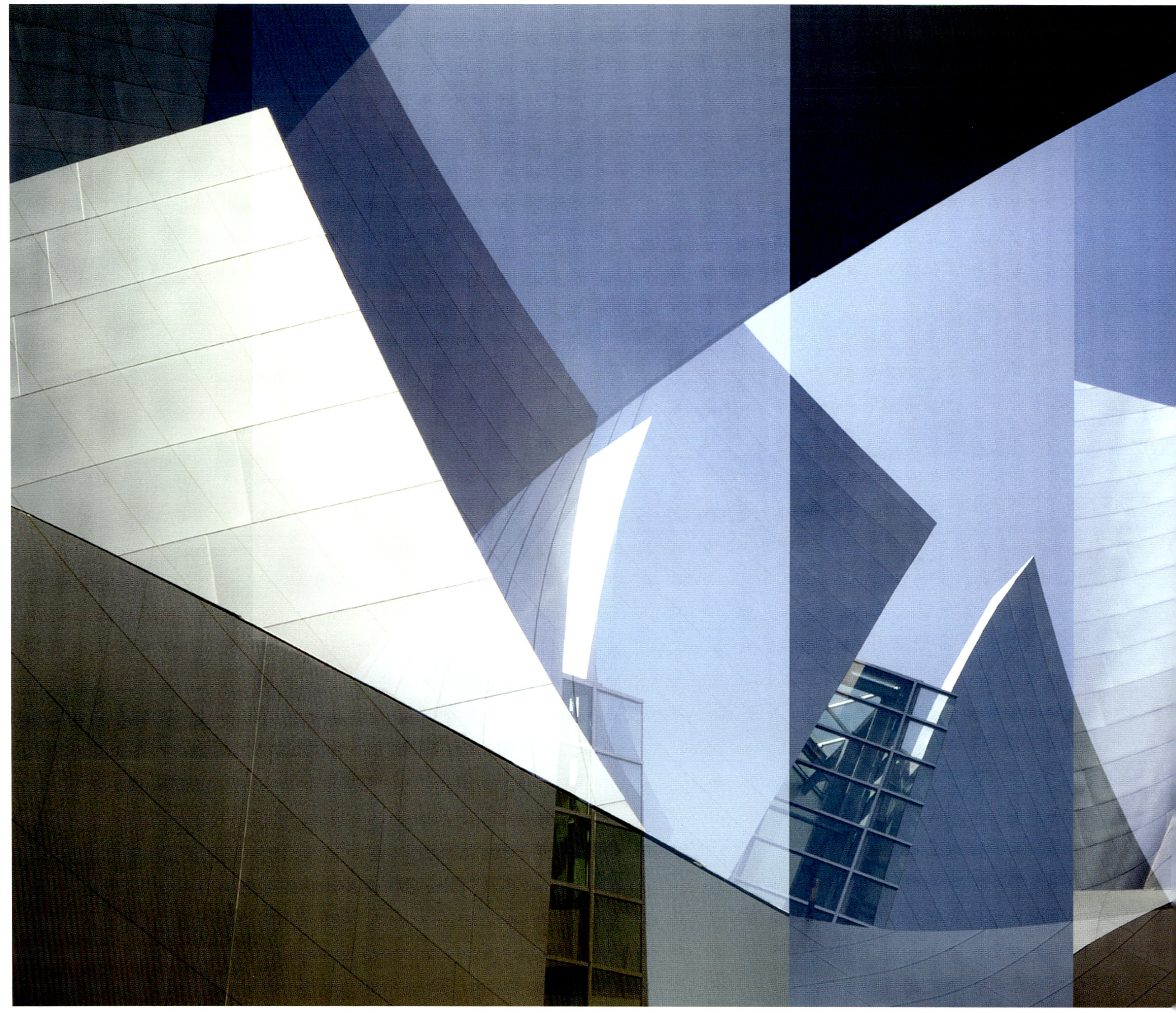

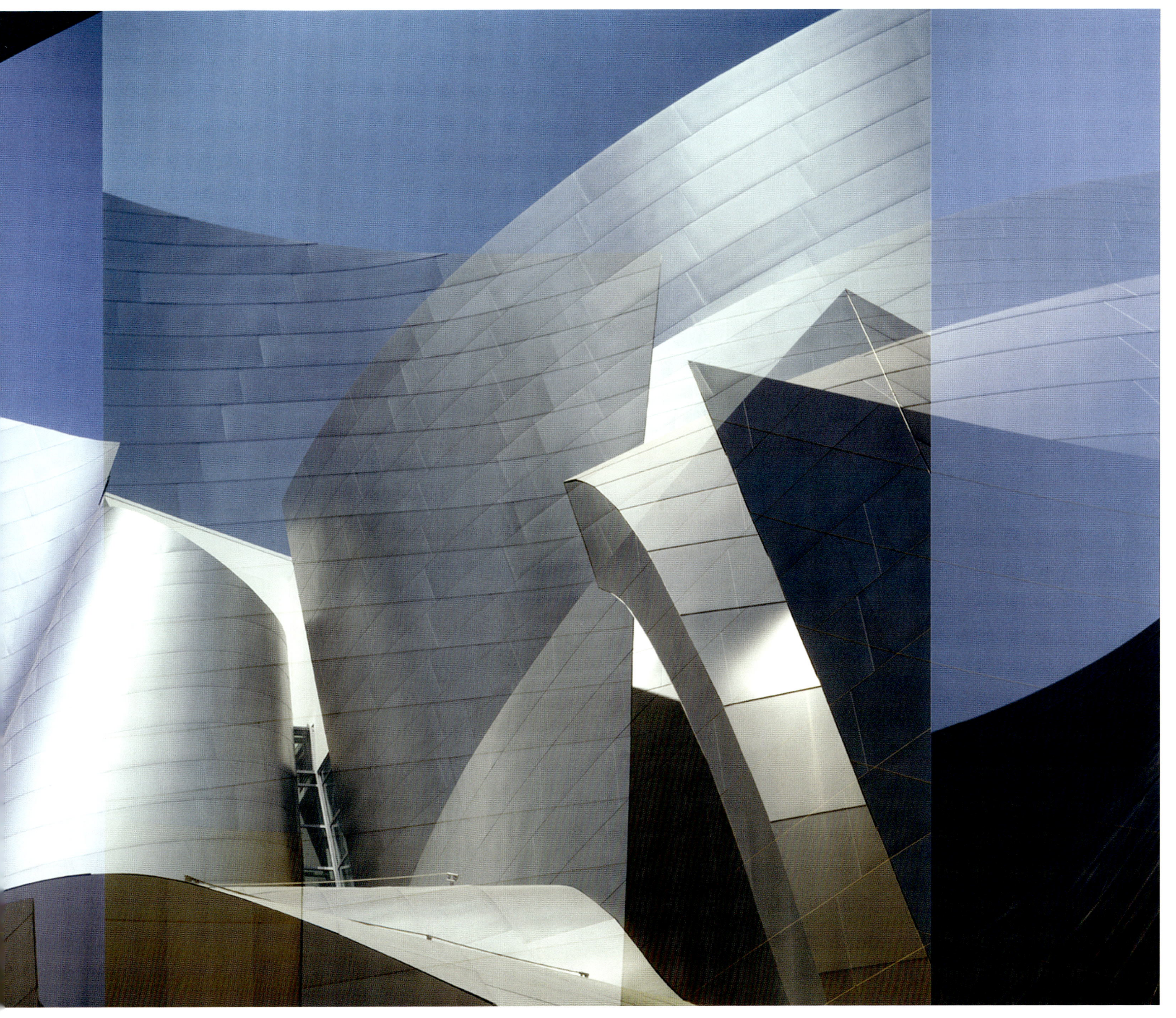

Disney Hall II   Los Angeles, California, 2003   ARCHITECT: Frank O. Gehry & Associates

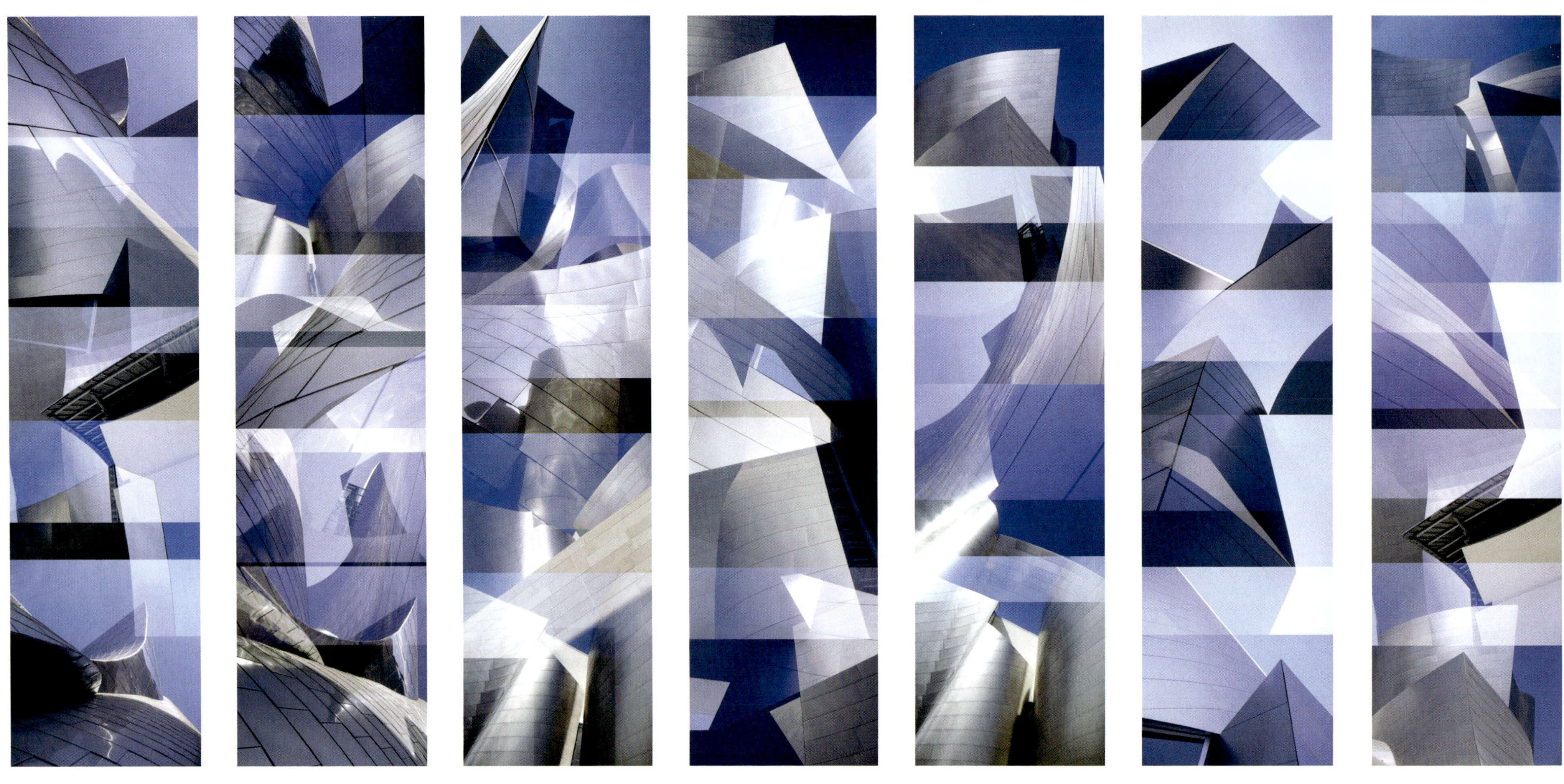

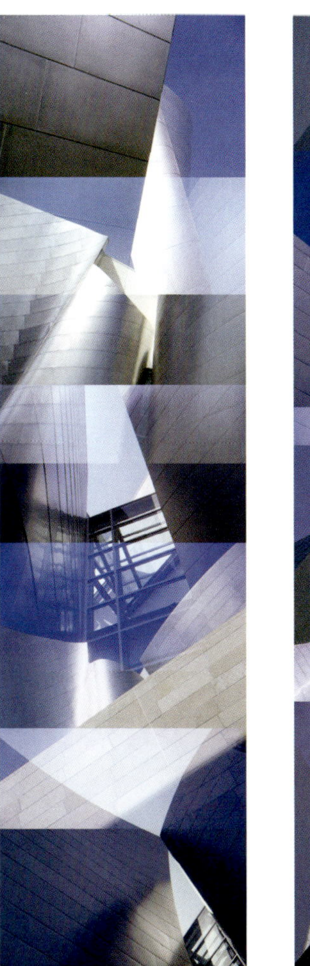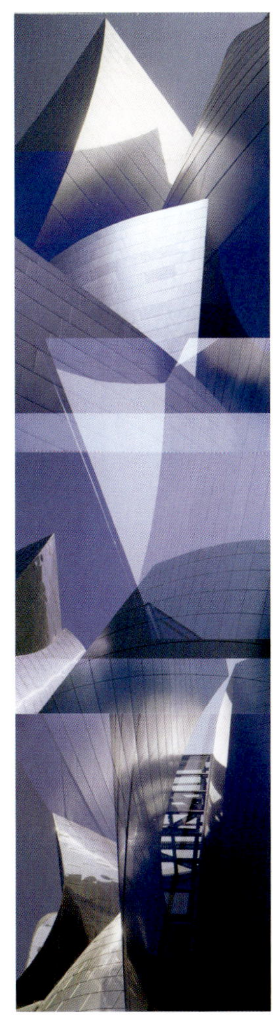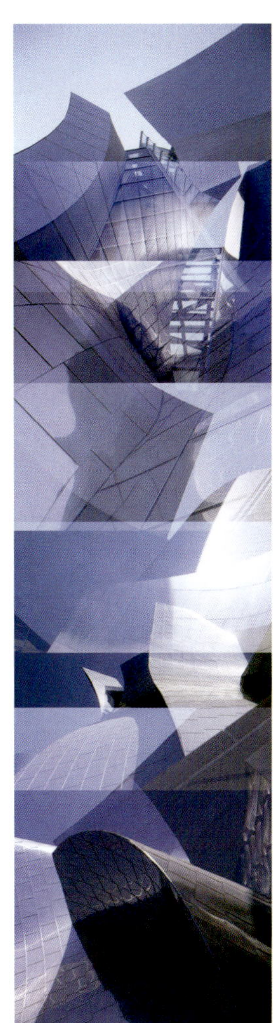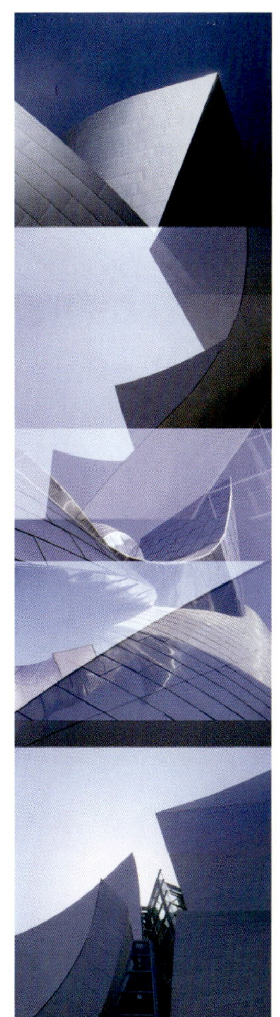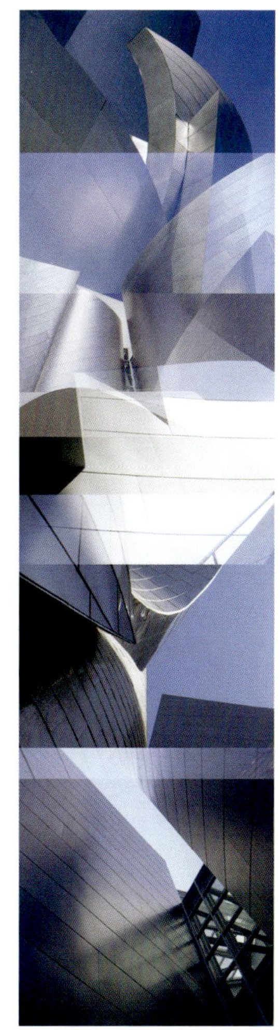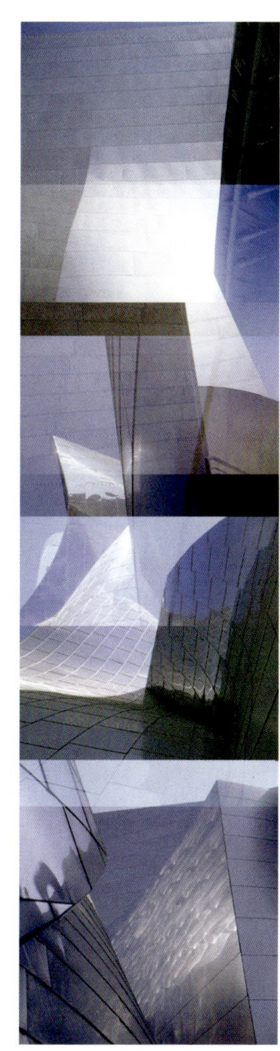

Disney Hall Thirteen Panels Los Angeles, California, 2003 ARCHITECT: Frank O. Gehry & Associates

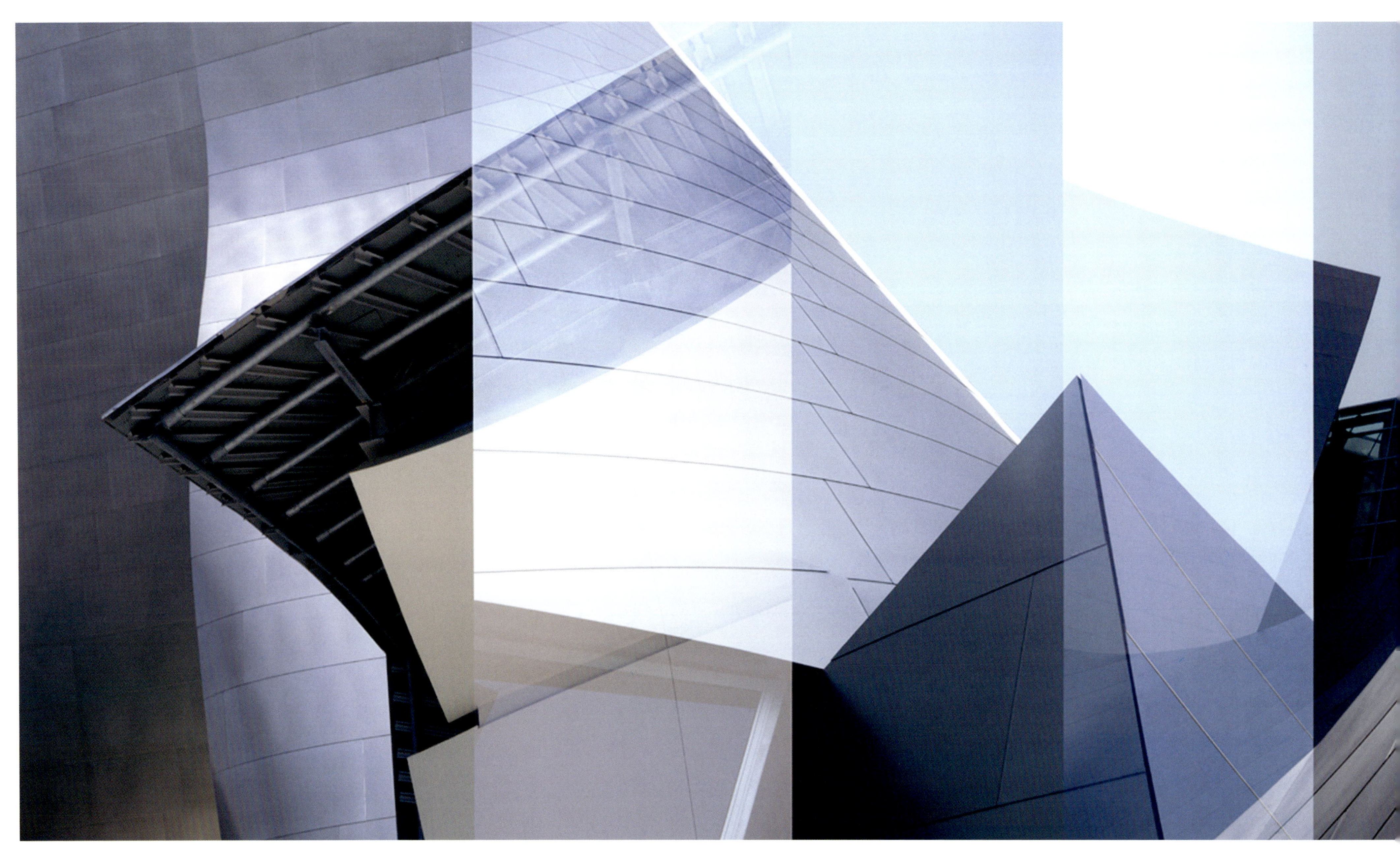

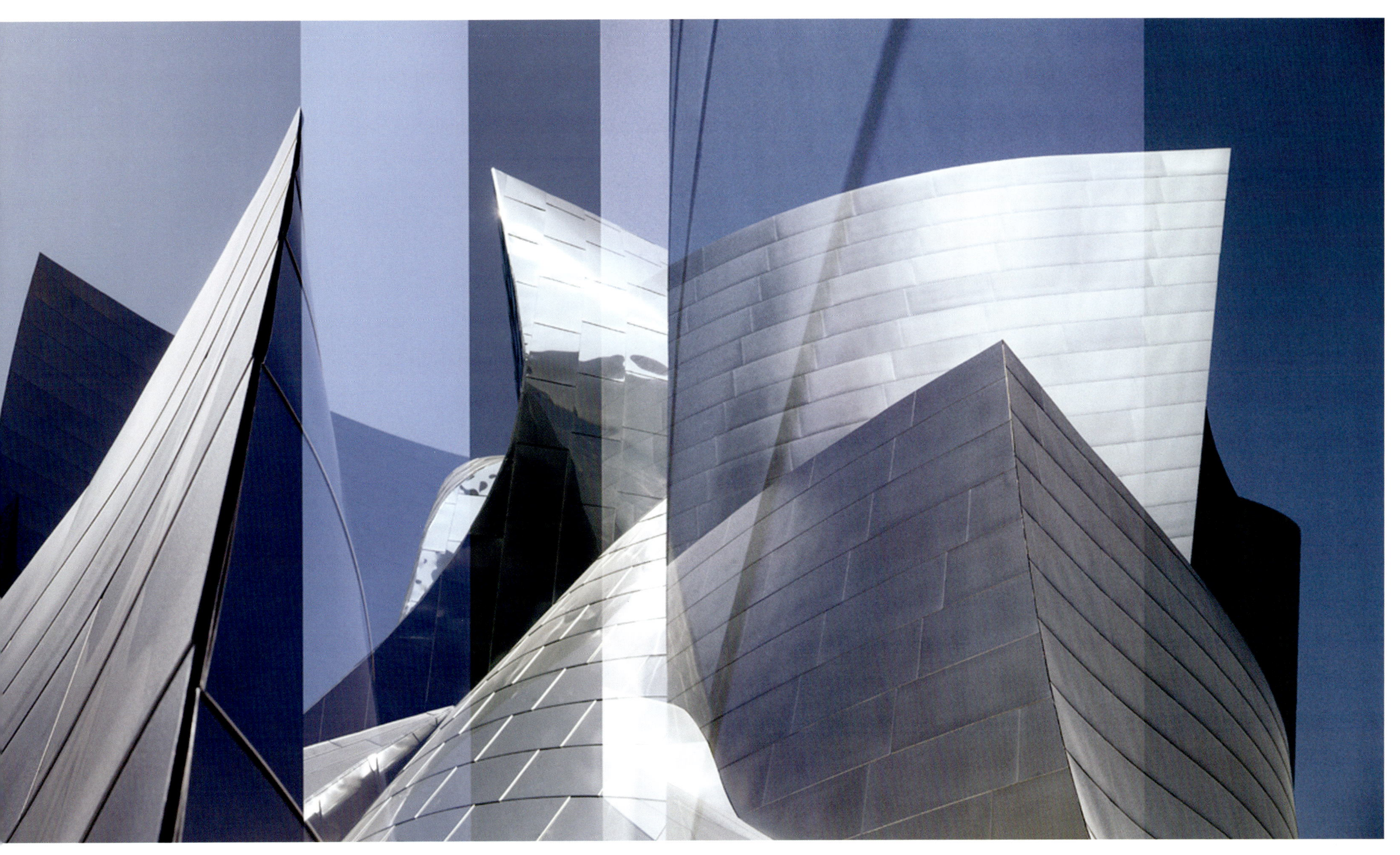

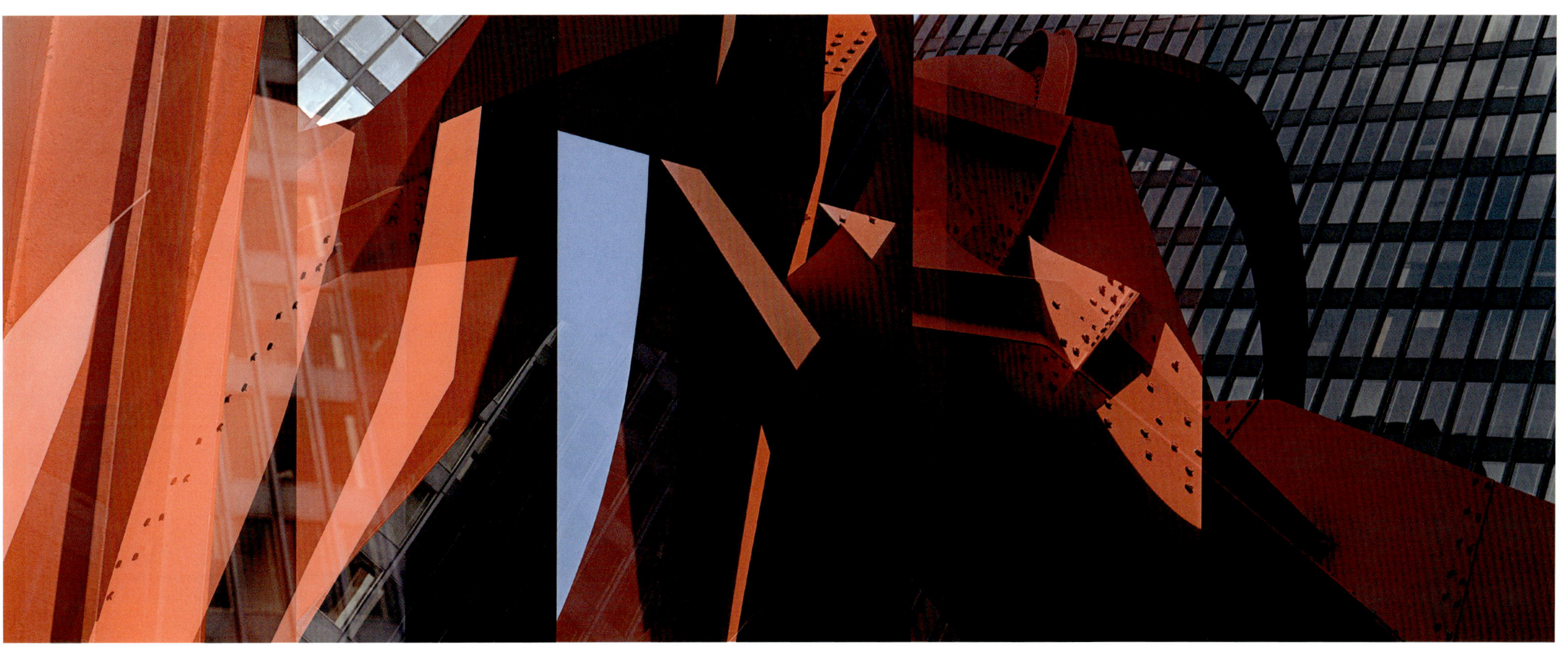

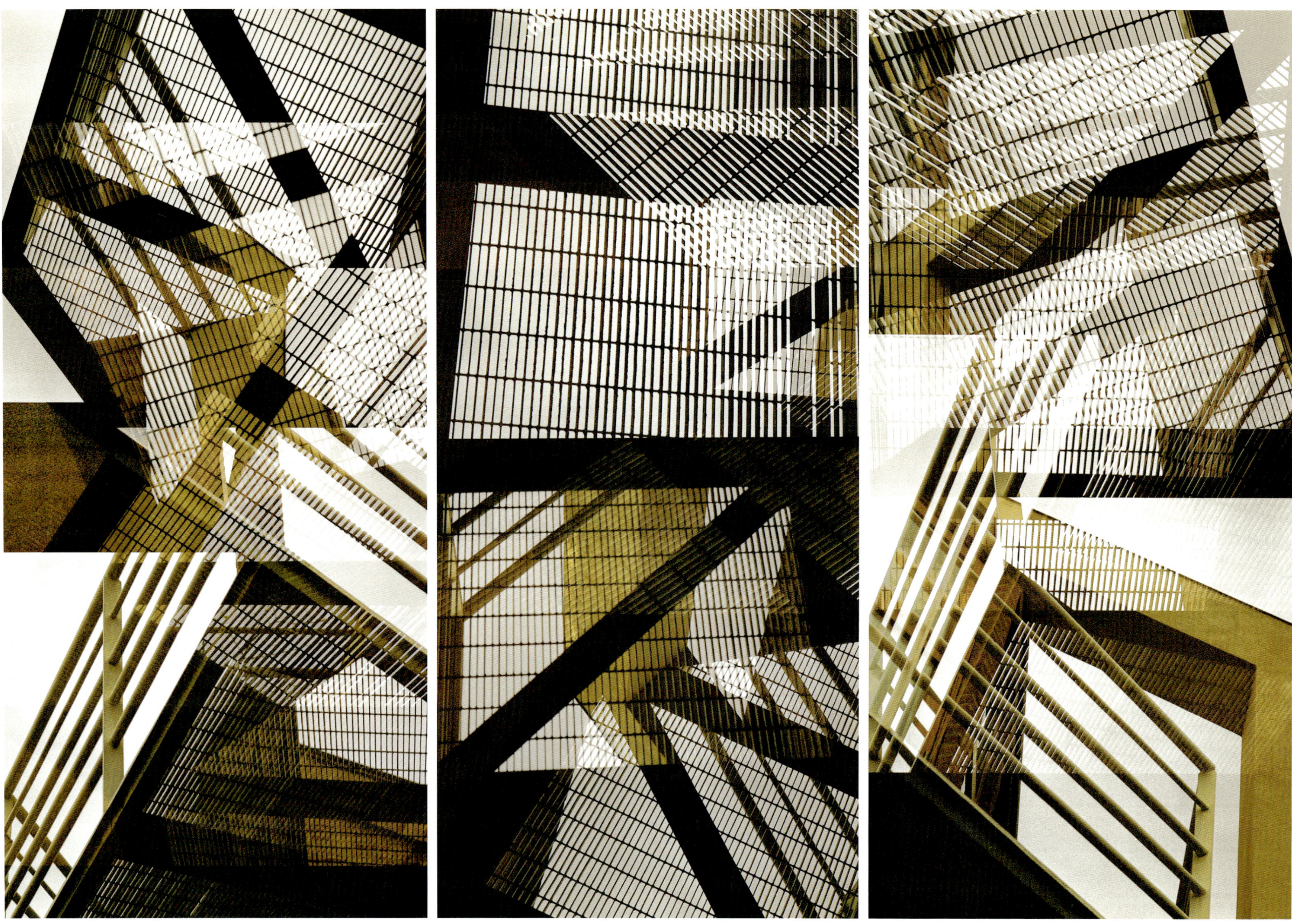

Semerano Overhang Triptych   Padua, Italy, 1999   ARCHITECT: Toti Semerano

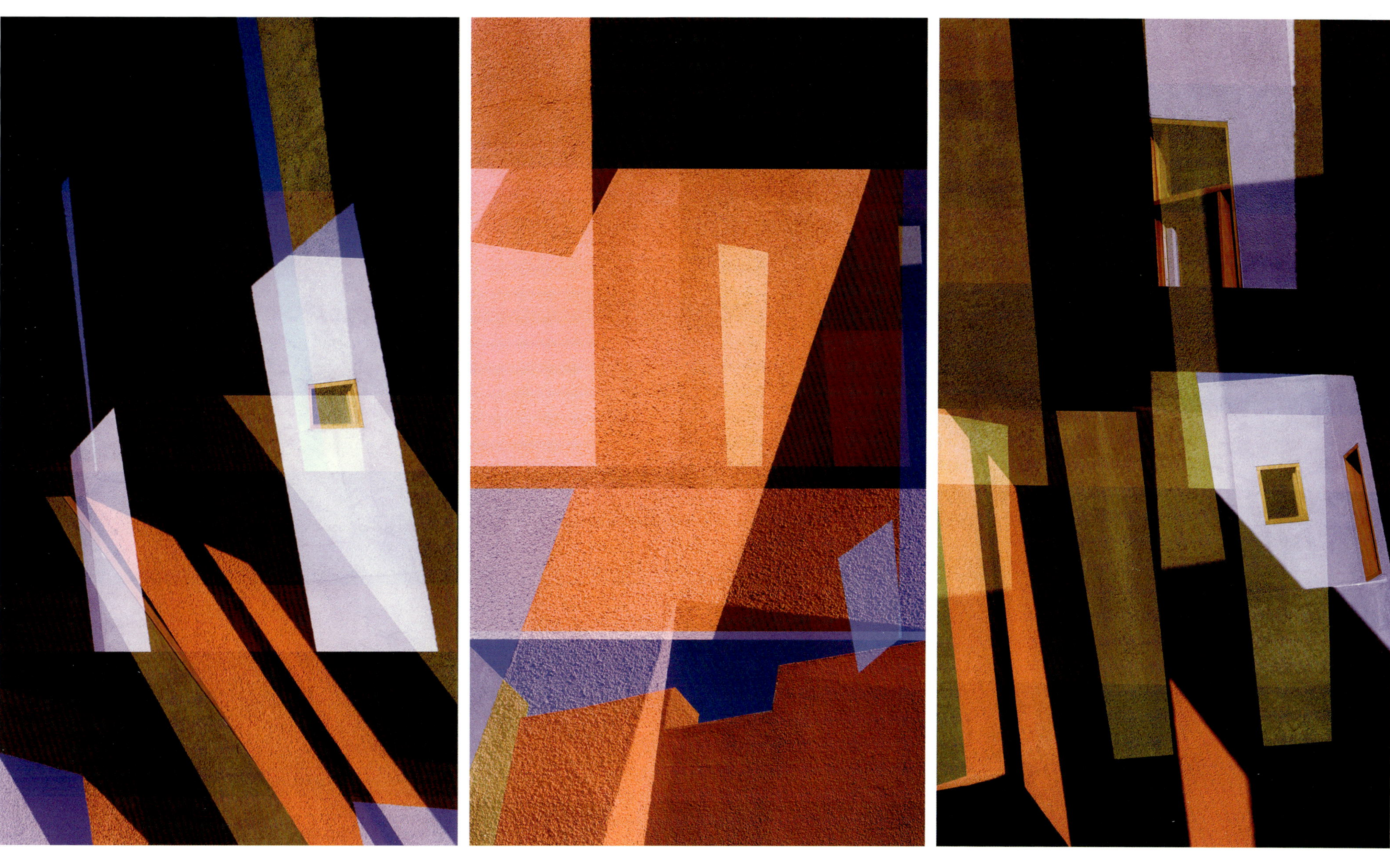

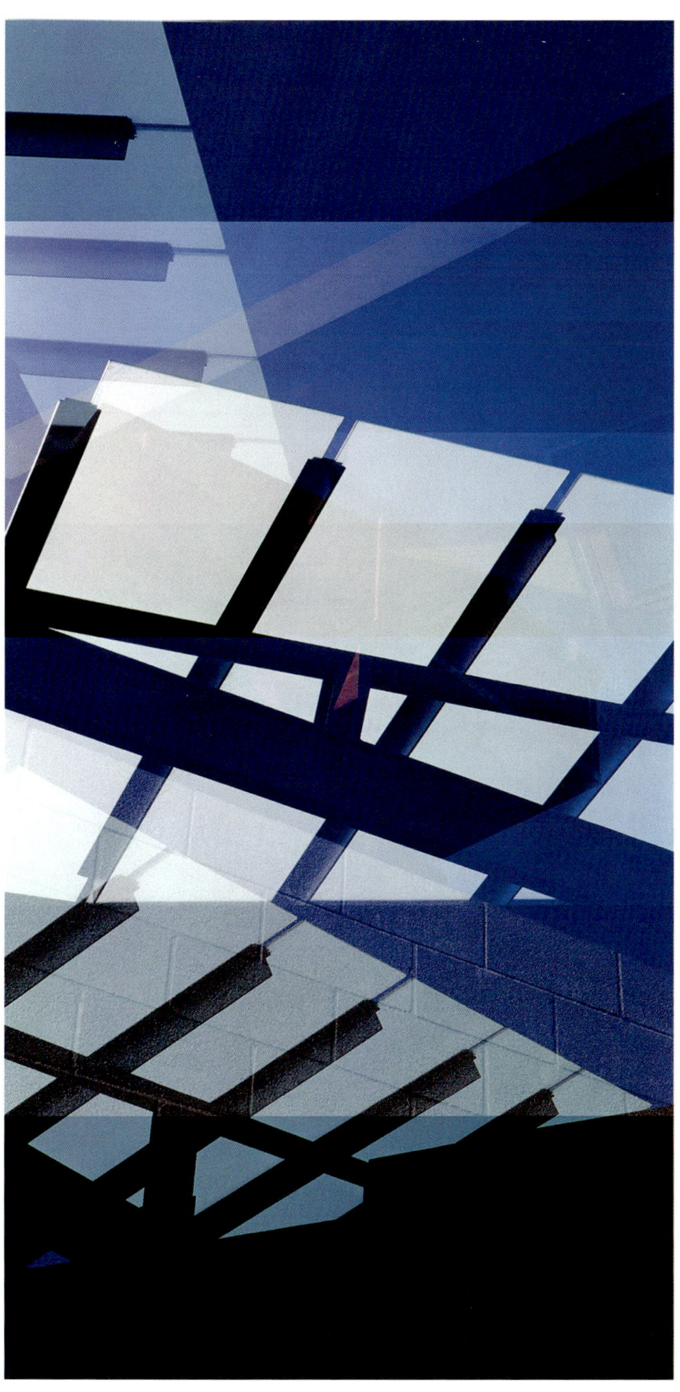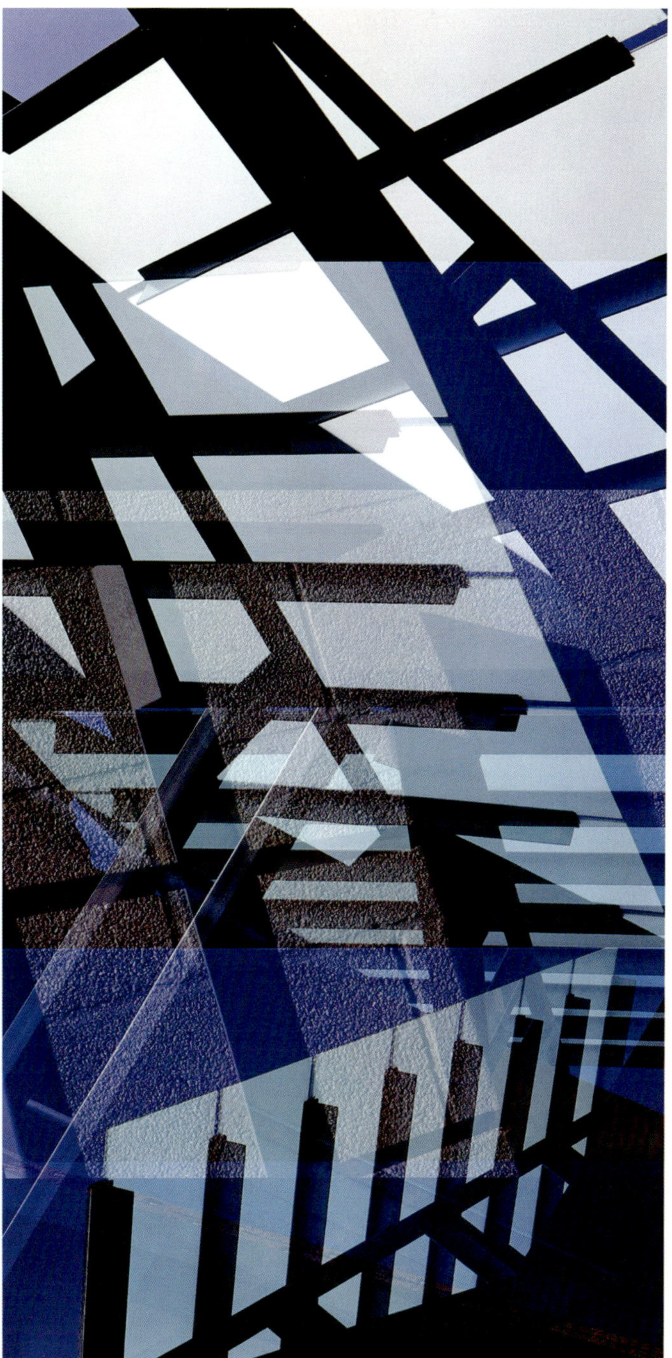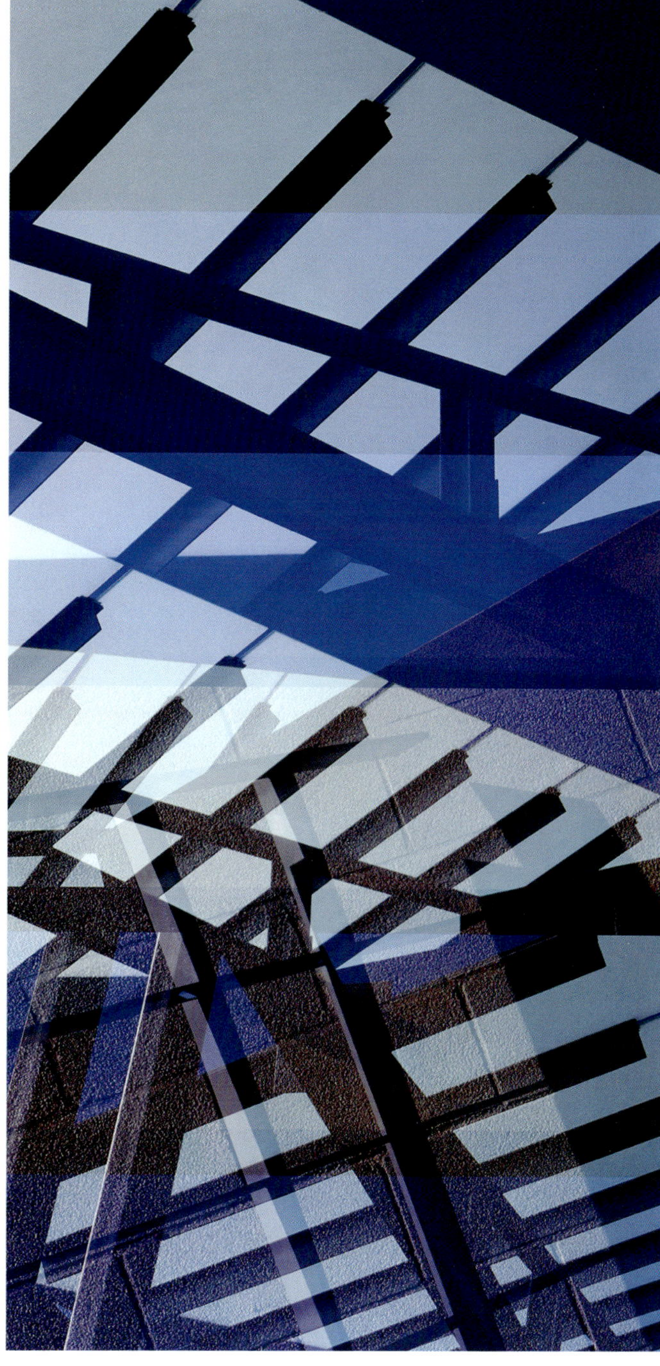

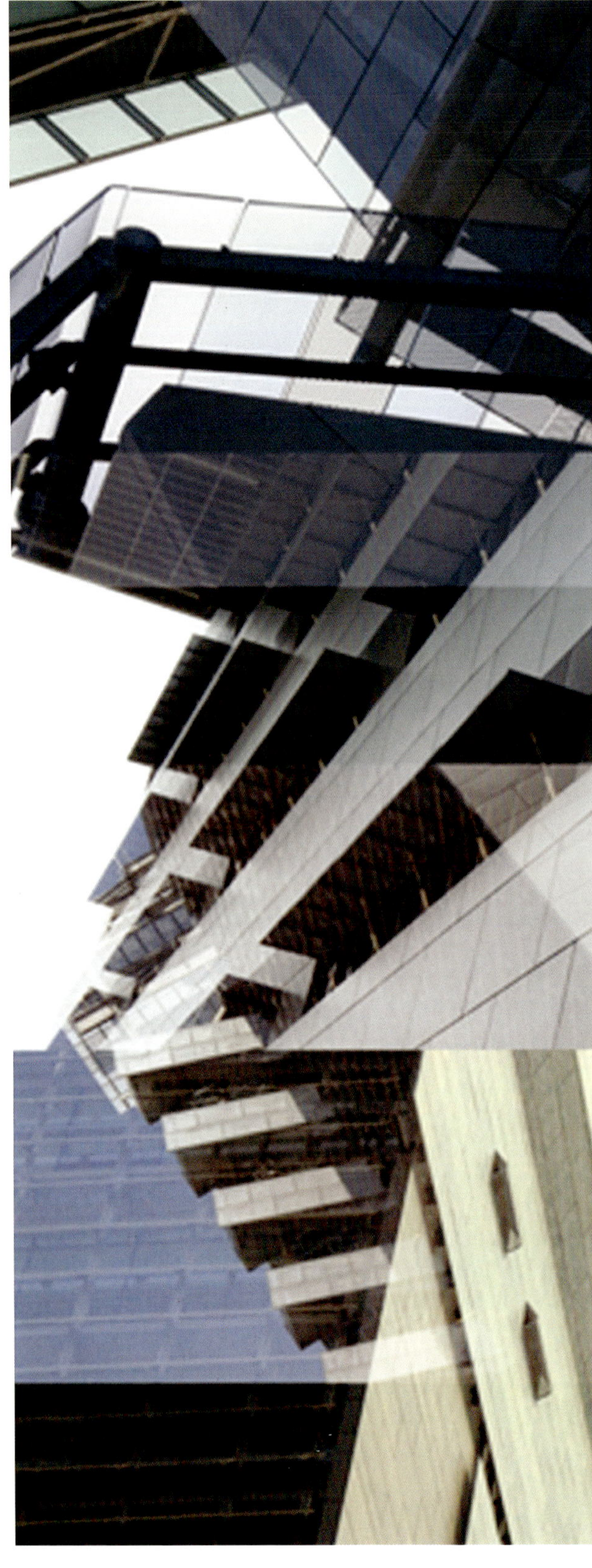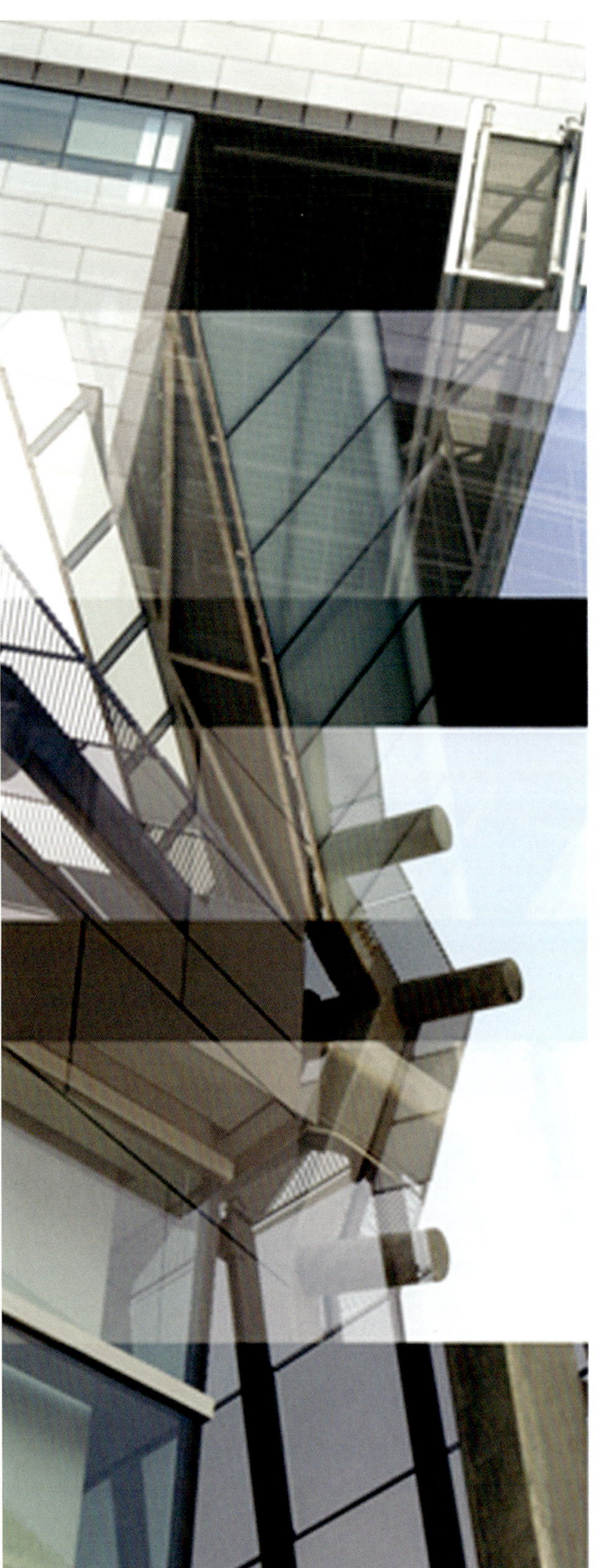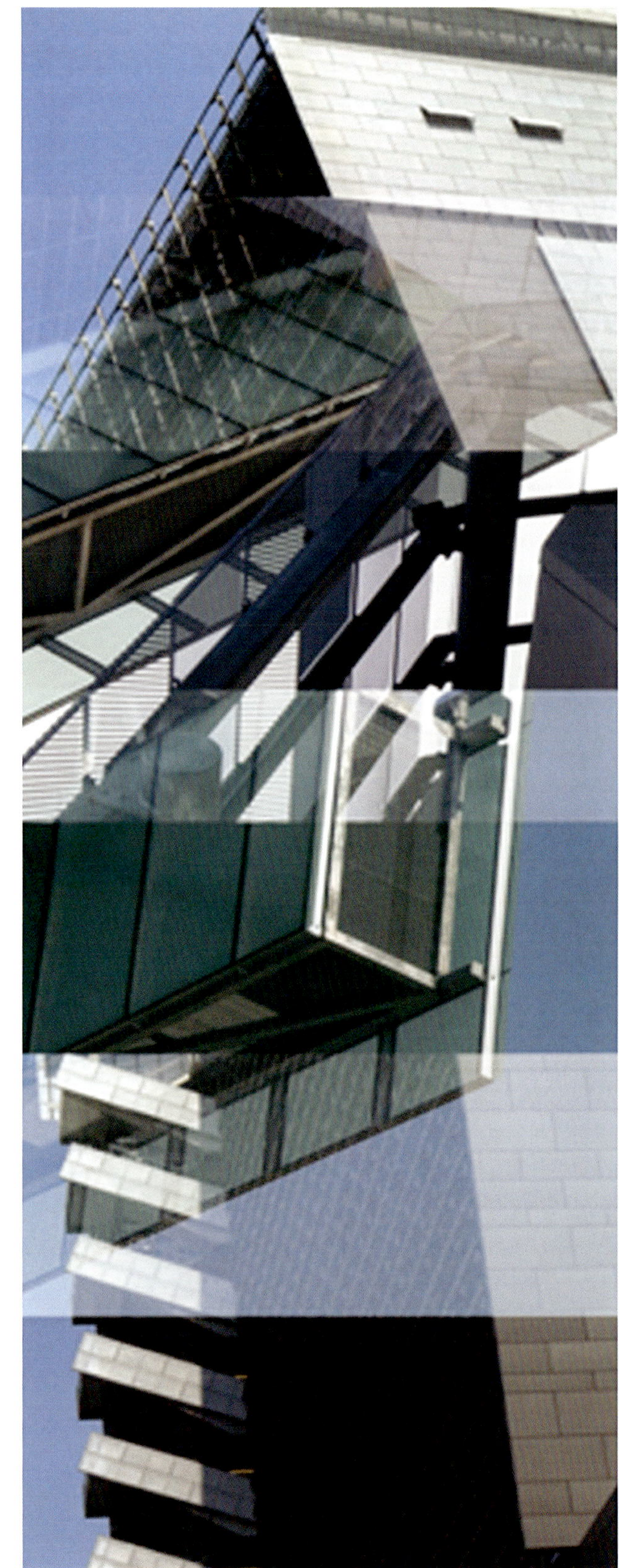

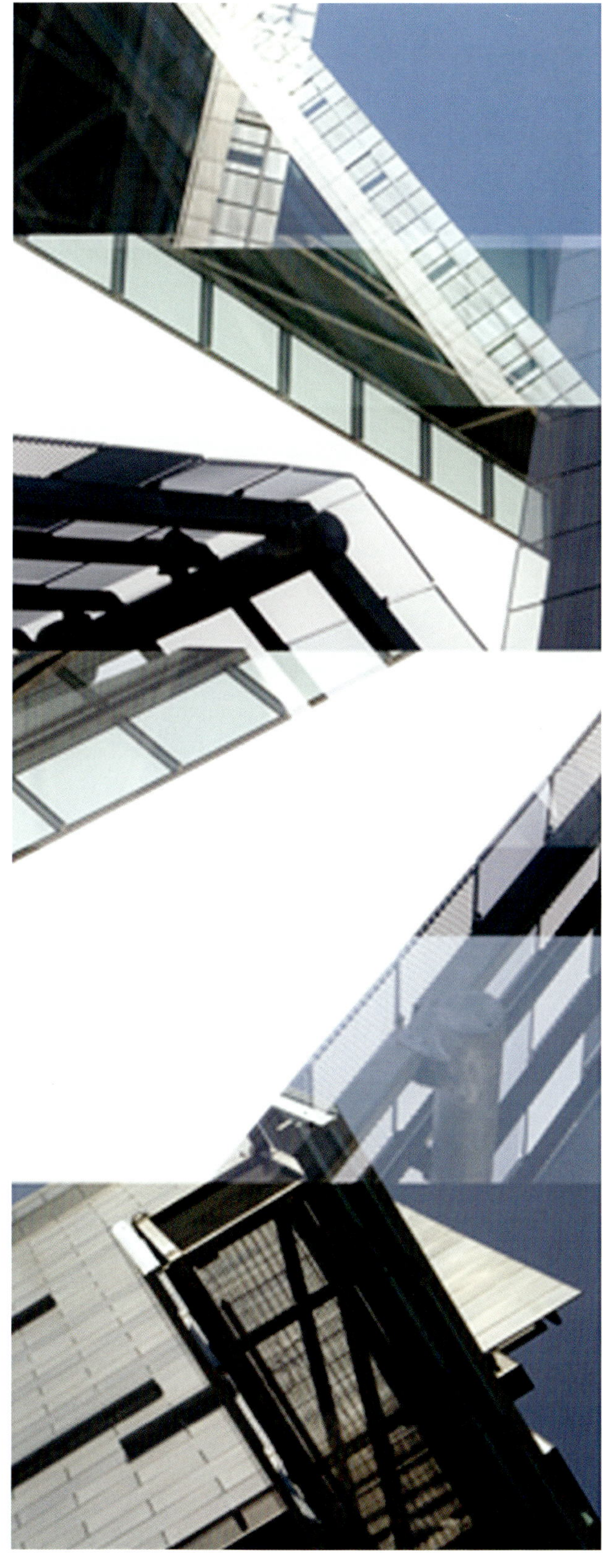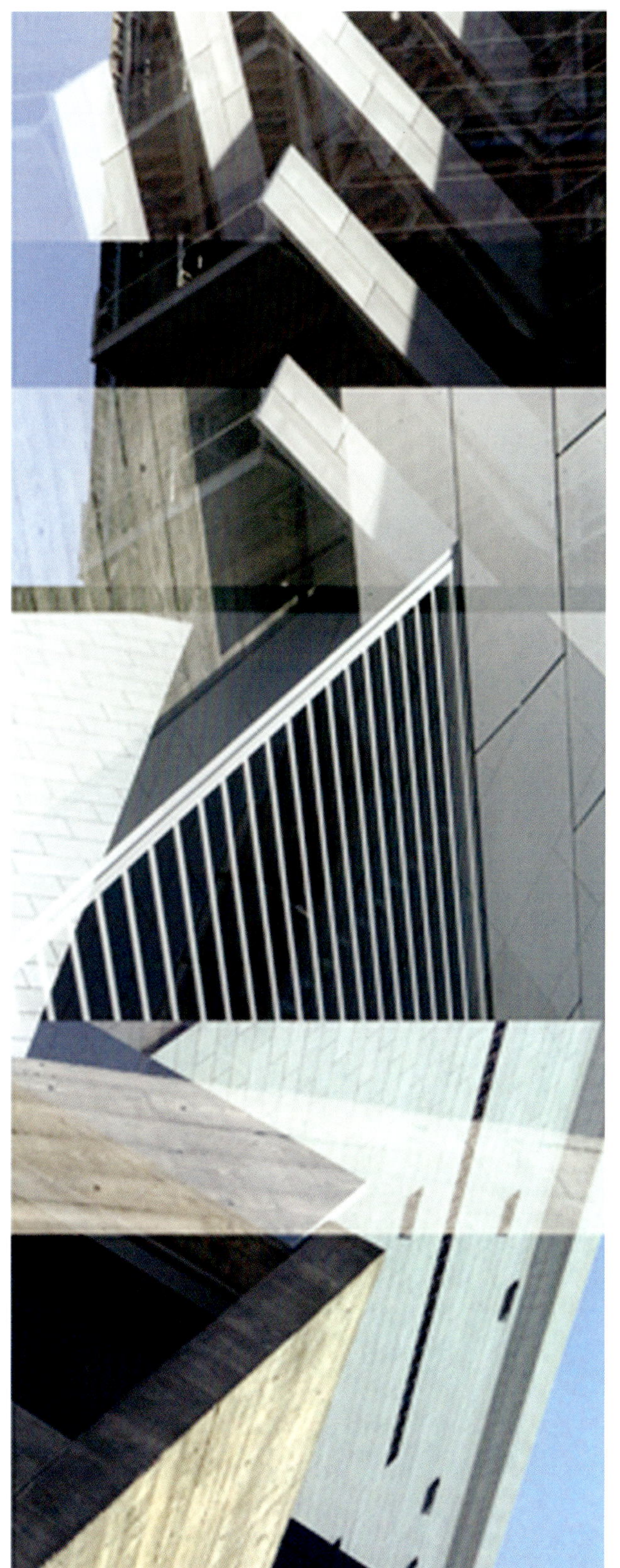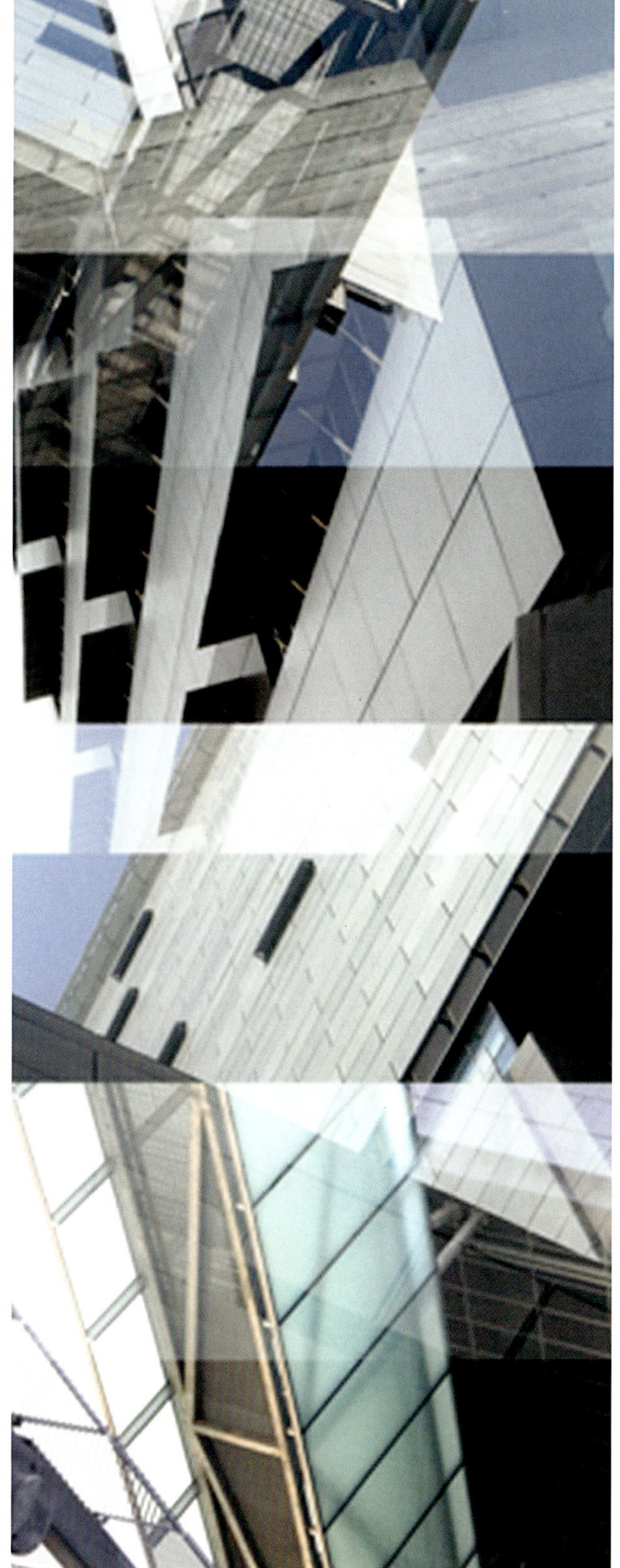

Caltrans Six Panels Los Angeles, California, 2005 ARCHITECT: Morphosis

ACKNOWLEDGMENTS

My grateful thanks to the architecture community, in particular to those who contributed directly to this book: critic Michael Webb, who escorted me to many building sites; Rikki Binder, my sounding board and role model for professionalism; art historian Henry Hopkins, who writes with such enthusiasm; Thom Mayne, who has encouraged me for twenty years and delights me with his evolving architecture; Frank Gehry, who designs buildings so full of wondrous detail; Richard Meier, whose spaces I love to be in; and Richard Rogers, who inspires me to explore texture and framework.

Special thanks to my gallery dealer and friend Craig Krull, who always surprises me with the depth of his perceptions, and to my "three musketeers"—R. Mac Holbert and Graham Nash of Nash Editions, and Five Ties publisher Garrett White: Mac for his printing insights, Graham for his tireless support of his fellow artists, and Garrett for his crusading zeal for books.

Thanks also to Peter Palumbo, for kick-starting a major love of architecture; Janice and David Blackburn, for being the king and queen of commissioning patrons; John Walsh, for convincing the Getty Museum to commission my work and for introducing me to Los Angeles architecture; G. Ray Hawkins, for pooling me with many great photographers in his gallery; Virginia Zabriskie, who recognized the painter in the photographer; Claudia Carr, who tirelessly pushes for excellence; Sandy Nairne, who gave me my first big exhibition; Bridget Brown and Laura Schlesinger, who placed my work in many corporate collections; and Ruth Rosenthal, who helped me get a start in London and directed my BBC debut.

I would also like to acknowledge these artists of the past whose work always amazes me: Man Ray, for not being afraid of new ideas; Fritz Lang, for making emotions epic; Charles Sheeler, for making architecture intimate; Juan Gris, for rearranging my mind; Henri Rousseau, for paring down the elements; and Henri Matisse, for reinventing drawing.

Finally, I want to thank the friends and family who have aided and abetted me over the years, in particular Professor Richard Bender, who alerts me to exciting new projects around the world; my parents, Milton and Rosemary Okun, for their encouragement and enthusiasm; Will Okun and Angeles Ortega Gonzales, my much appreciated studio assistants, who never bat an eyelash at the tasks I ask them to perform, no matter how odd; artist Barbara Strasen, who has traveled with me to many building sites and makes my life festive . . . and last, but by no means least, the two most important people in my life, who have the patience of saints except when they don't: my husband Richard Sparks, who can change a tire as fast as I can photograph a building, and my daughter Lizzi, whose opinions are always so considered and insightful.

Jenny Okun

Five Ties Publishing, Inc., New York
www.fiveties.com

Produced and edited by Garrett White
Associate Editors: Stephanie Steiker, Amanda Thorpe
Book design by AC Berkheiser and Garrett White
Jacket design by AC Berkheiser
First edition 2007 © Five Ties Publishing, Inc.

Photographs © Jenny Okun 2007 (www.jennyokun.com)
"Jenny Okun: Fragment^{2}" © Thom Mayne 2007
"Jenny Okun" © Henry T. Hopkins 2007
"Reconstructing Reality" © Michael Webb 2007
Printed by Dr. Cantz'sche Druckerei, Ostfildern

Printed in Germany
ISBN: 978-0-9777193-3